Westview Special Studies in
Social, Political, and Economic Development

Energy in the Transition
from Rural Subsistence
edited by Miguel S. Wionczek, Gerald Foley, and Ariane van Buren

For the half of the world's population still dependent on wood
and other traditional fuels for basic cooking and heating needs, a
serious supply crisis is emerging: forests are disappearing and
population pressure on other energy sources is mounting. This book
analyzes the energy problems of those caught in the trap of rural
subsistence and explores the role energy might play in the transition
away from subsistence. It includes eight specially commissioned
studies of different developing countries and a review of the small-
scale energy technologies presently available for rural use.

Miguel S. Wionczek is senior fellow and head of the Long-
Term Energy Research Project at El Colegio de Mexico. He has been
deputy director general of the National Science and Technology Council, Mexico. Gerald Foley is a senior fellow of the International
Institute for Environment and Development (IIED) in London and senior
visiting research fellow of the Beijer Institute of the Royal Swedish
Academy of Sciences. Ariane van Buren is a senior research associate
of IIED.

The symposium on which this book is based,
sponsored by the International Institute
for Environment and Development (IIED)
and El Colegio de Mexico,
was held at El Colegio de Mexico, June 1981

Energy in the Transition from Rural Subsistence

edited by Miguel S. Wionczek,
Gerald Foley, and Ariane van Buren

Westview Press / Boulder, Colorado

Westview Special Studies in Social, Political, and Economic Development

Copyright © 1982 by the International Institute for
                    Environment and Development (IIED)
                    and El Colegio de Mexico

Published in 1982 in the United States of America by
     Westview Press, Inc.
     5500 Central Avenue
     Boulder, Colorado 80301
     Frederick A. Praeger, President and Publisher

Library of Congress Catalog Card Number 82-50802
ISBN 0-86531-385-7

Composition for this book was provided by the editors
Printed and bound in the United States of America

Energy in the Transition
from Rural Subsistence

Also of Interest

*Available in hardcover and paperback.

Contents

COUNTRY CASE-STUDIES

Preface

This book is an attempt to define the problem - or complex of problems - of energy demand and supply in the poorest agricultural sectors of the developing world. Some 2000 million people now depend on wood and animal dung for their cooking and heating needs. The merciless arithmetic of population growth and depleting forests is depriving them of these resources on which their survival depends. The fossil fuels they need to increase production of food and raise their standards of living move even further out of reach as developing country economies crumble in the face of world economic recession.

Up to now most people in the rural areas of the developing world have simply gathered their fuel from the countryside around them in the same way as they have always done. It has been an unnoticed and apparently self-sustaining process. Rural energy has not needed to figure in the plans or calculations of national planners. Only in recent years has there begun the systematic and widespread data-collection which is essential for policy-making.

Efforts to deal with rural energy problems, whether by national governments or international agencies, have so far been sporadic; they have also shown few signs of being adequate to the task. There have been some examples of successful tree-planting on a large scale - Korea is notable; China has shown that it is possible to install biogas digesters at the rate of a million a year - though there are signs that the programme has now run into serious difficulties. Apart from that there is little else to show. Solar pumps, windmills, solar cookers, and so on have failed to make the connection with the people they are meant to benefit. Objects of external experiment, they sit too often irrelevantly apart from the deteriorating conditions about them.

What, then, can usefully be done? There is no lack of good will or technical skills, and there are sub-

stantial resources available. More could certainly be
obtained if promising lines of action could be identified.

This book is the result of an 18 month collaborative effort by the International Institute for Environment and Development (IIED), El Colegio de Mexico, the
Technical Assistance Department of the Netherlands Foreign Ministry, and the Gesellschaft fur Technische
Zusammenarbeit (GTZ) of the Federal German Republic. Its
aim is to begin to sketch the outline of future energy
strategies to cope with rural energy problems.

To provide a starting point, a paper delineating
the area of investigation was prepared and circulated.
It was the basis for a series of meetings between the
organising institutions and the funding agencies. A
formal background paper was then written and sent, with
a request for comments and information, to potential
participants in administrative and academic positions in
developing countries, and to key people in development
agencies with a special interest in energy. Following
this, a brief was prepared and case-studies from eight
developing countries were commissioned. In addition, a
paper describing the present position in small-scale
technology suitable for rural use was included to provide an informed technical background.

Finally, some thirty participants assembled in El
Colegio de Mexico for a four-day discussion of the
background material and a detailed review of each of the
case-studies (28 June - 1 July 1981). Each paper was
presented by its author, analysed by two nominated dis-
cussants, and then opened to the meeting for debate in
English and Spanish, with simultaneous translation. The
participants covered a wide spread of expertise, and
came from developing and industrialised countries, as
well as international agencies concerned with energy and
subsistence agriculture.

The objective of the meeting was to work over the
commissioned and pre-prepared background material. All
the authors were given the opportunity to revise their
papers in the light of the discussions. This book is
not a simple record of the proceedings, though it draws
heavily upon them. It is an attempt to present an
authoritative, broad-based, and up-to-date view of energy in rural development.

The problem of devising effective energy strategies
for subsistence agriculture is complicated and far from
being resolved. Nevertheless, in the papers submitted,
and in the discussions which took place in Mexico, the
outline for a more productive discussion than has hi-
therto taken place began to emerge. The first chapter
is an attempt to abstract a number of key ideas and use
them to create a framework in which the case-studies can
be analysed and the next practical policy steps defined.

Chapter 2 evaluates the small-scale technologies available for rural development. It makes the essential distinction between technologies for survival and technologies for production, one which is often overlooked, but which is fundamental to any effective deployment strategy for these technologies.

The range of countries covered in the case-studies is wide. Mexico and Brazil are both rich countries with immense natural resources and high technical capabilities. Each, for example, can support extremely advanced technology in solar power, nuclear energy, and sophisticated biomass conversion. Yet both have deeply impoverished rural subsistence sectors which remain virtually untouched in their traditional use of fuels, and in the problems they are facing.

Nigeria is also a country with a surplus of energy; a member of OPEC, it contributes to sustaining the economy of the industrial nations, but has made little impact on the problems of its own subsistence farmers. The lack of infrastructure, administrative capacities, and technical capacities in the rural population leaves the rural energy problems of Nigeria very similar to those of Senegal, whose economy is virtually crippled by the burden of paying for relatively minor amounts of oil.

Guatemala has an ample endowment of natural resources, but they are so unevenly distributed that the rural agricultural system is in danger of collapse. In addition to the pressures of population growth and declining resources of traditional fuels, it faces immense social and political problems.

India possesses the full spectrum of natural and human resources and a history of successful development in many sectors of its economy. With its huge population, almost a sixth of the world's total, and a vast number of different approaches, India has in many senses been the development workshop of the world.

Korea has been described as having the combined advantage of Confucian ethics and military dictatorship; whatever the reasons, its achievements in dealing with the problems of rural energy supply are remarkable indeed. It has shown that the obstacles of land shortage, adverse climate, inequitable land tenure systems, difficult terrain, and extreme poverty in the rural areas can, in practice, be substantially overcome within a generation.

Senegal and Jamaica are both small impoverished countries with few natural resources or capacities for immediately effective action. Jamaica's rural subsistence sector is the inheritor of some of the most detrimental aspects of the plantation economy. Senegal's best efforts in the past decades have been absorbed in the appalling struggle for survival in the

face of drought, desertification, and the adverse move-
ments in world prices for its primary agricultural exports. Both cases raise the question of global responsibility for those countries which history and present
circumstances render unable to support their own development without external support.

Despite being commissioned against a detailed and
uniform brief, these papers are all very different.
Even when there are similarities, they are seen differ-
ently by the authors, and the possibilities for action
are ungeneralisable. The papers are significant for
what they contain, for the aspirations they portray,
some of which from an external viewpoint may appear
optimistic or ill-founded, but also for what they omit.
They are a unique record of highly varied perceptions of
what has sometimes been seen as a uniform problem.

The final chapter is a review of the final Symposium. It attempts to weave together the principal ideas
which emerged from the four days of discussion. Many of
these are still nebulous, or even contradictory, but
there is a clear sense of movement. Technology may well
be a useful starting point; but it is too often the
sticking-place and progress beyond it fails to occur.
Unless it is recognised that technology is but a mani-
festation of society and executes the tasks it sets for
itself then technological initiatives will almost certainly fail. This means that a technology will "work"
only if it responds to a genuine expression of priorities and reflects the economic and technical capacities
of those employing it. Adopting this broader perspective prevents the question of energy getting out of
proportion. On the evidence of the Symposium, the move
to integrate energy with the whole question of rural
economic development is well under way.

The preparation and organisation of the Symposium
in Mexico City, and of this book, have required a great
deal of work by a large number of people. We owe a debt
of gratitude to the members of the Planning Board,
Professor Gordon Goodman, Dr Willem Floor, Dr H.W. von
Haugwitz, Dr Jorge Hardoy, and David Runnalls for their
guidance and suggestions. The paper writers and participants gave generously of their time and enthusiasm. A
special word of thanks is due to Mr Marc de Montalembert
for undertaking the task of presenting a synthesis of
the ideas expressed at the symposium on its final day -
both the initial and final chapters are indebted to the
forcefulness and clarity of his summary.

El Colegio de Mexico played host to the Symposium
and generously covered the costs of accommodation, food,
and transport in Mexico. We are grateful to the President of El Colegio de Mexico, Dr Victor L. Urquidi, for
this hospitality, and for his chairmanship of the
meeting on its opening day. In addition to preparing

papers and background material, Marcela Serrato and
Oscar Guzman handled the organisational arrangements at
El Colegio with a reassuringly calm efficiency. Support
during the preparatory period at IIED was given by Ann
Petrie; Jane Bicknell was in charge of the production of
this book from typing, formatting, and organising the
initial manuscripts, through to the final camera-ready
copy.

Funding for the travel, commissioning fees, and
staff costs of IIED was provided by the Governments of
the Netherlands and the Federal German Republic;
without this the whole exercise would not have taken
place.

M. W.
G. F.
A.v.B.

1
Energy in the Transition from Rural Agriculture

Gerald Foley
Ariane van Buren

The total energy consumed by a subsistence household may be quite high, even by the standards of industrial society. Statistics, where they exist, are unreliable and consumption varies widely in accordance with climate, custom, and the availability of fuel; but an average consumption of 1 cu.m. of wood per head per year is quite common in many parts of the world, even where heating needs are small or non-existent. For a family of six this amounts to around 3.6 tonnes of wood per year or about 10 kg per day. The energy equivalent of this is about 14 000 kWh per year - which is about 12 times more than the average household energy consumption for cooking in the UK (1). Domestic energy consumption in subsistence has the distinguishing features of being both very high and extremely inefficient.

In contrast, the amount of energy used for productive purposes is extremely low. The average output of work of a farmer during a whole day is just a quarter of a kilowatt hour, about the amount of energy contained in 1/16 kg of wood or a couple of spoonfuls of diesel oil. Even when animals are used, the amount of work they can perform is small. A bullock, in a working day, has an output of little more than 4 kWh, less than the amount of energy contained in a half litre of diesel oil. This low energy use is a major factor in the poor productivity and output of subsistence farming. Unlike the case of domestic energy consumption, improvements in subsistence production will almost inevitably require substantial increases in the amounts of energy used.

The Indian case-study clearly illustrates the difference between domestic and productive energy requirements. In the examples given, household activities account for 83 percent of all the energy used, while crop cultivation consumes only 12 percent. Rural industry, which uses fuelwood and organic residue, and transport, which relies mostly on animal power and some oil, together consume the remaining 5 percent.

1

This distinction between domestic and productive uses is not made simply for analytic convenience. It is extremely practical, with important consequences for policy. It enables technologies to be assigned to their appropriate tasks in the rural economy. Sustaining subsistence patterns of energy consumption, by providing fuelwood plantations, for example, or more efficient stoves to reduce the demand for firewood, will not directly increase productive capabilities. Neither will it raise cash income. The fundamental problem of subsistence is its poverty, and development depends on increasing remunerative production. Energy strategies, therefore, if they are to be relevant, have to be directed towards increasing the energy used for productive purposes, while at the same time ensuring that domestic needs continue to be met. The technical review in Chapter 2 makes a similar distinction between what it describes as energy for survival and energy for development.

CONSTRAINTS ON SUBSISTENCE ENERGY USE

The principal source of fuel for domestic needs for an estimated 1 500 million people - three quarters of the population of the developing world - is wood (2). Dependence is highest in Africa, where wood furnishes an average of 60 percent of the total fuel consumed in all forms, and over 90 percent in some countries such as Tanzania. In Latin America and Asia, the amount of wood used is a smaller proportion of the total energy consumption, but in many rural areas it is still the predominant source of subsistence fuel.

Severe shortages of fuelwood already afflict many areas. In the arid and semi-arid areas of Africa, the Indian subcontinent, and the arid and mountainous areas of Latin America, the available wood supplies are not sufficient for present needs. People are, therefore, having to rely on inferior substitutes such as dung and whatever other vegetable matter is obtainable. Nutritional deficiencies as a result of shortages of cooking fuels have been noticed in some areas. Agricultural productivity is adversely affected by the burning of dung and organic matter which would otherwise serve as fertiliser. The continued depletion of the remaining wood resources and the increasing demand for fuel, as a consequence of population growth, combine to aggravate the already serious shortage of energy and all other resources in these areas.

Even where wood supplies are sufficient to meet current requirements, the future is by no means secure. Rarely does the natural rate of regeneration match the rate at which wood resources are being consumed. Forest area is diminishing as population grows: more land is being used for farming and grazing and at the same time, more wood is being used for timber and fuel. Serious deficits in the fuelwood supply are therefore inevitable in the near and medium-term future in many areas.

A recent FAO study (3) has attempted to quantify the present fuelwood position on a regional basis and examine the consequences of present trends continuing to the end of the century. The results show that already some 90 million people in rural areas are suffering from acute fuelwood shortages. In addition, some 800 million people are consuming their fuelwood resources more quickly than they are being regenerated naturally, or replenished by planting. These figures are projected to rise to 140 million people in acute scarcity and 2 200 million consuming above the rate of replacement by the year 2000.

Depletion of wood resources on this scale has many costs beyond the simple deprivation of fuel. Most wood-fuel scarcity occurs in areas that are already environmentally fragile. The ecological effects of loss of tree cover are well-known and documented. Trees contribute to watershed control, prevention of soil erosion, and the mitigation of adverse climatic conditions. It is noteworthy that the national tree-planting programme described in the Korean case-study arose primarily from these considerations rather than to provide fuel for rural use.

Trees and organic residues usually meet a variety of other needs in addition to their use as fuel in the subsistence economy. Trees provide shade for crops and animals; they can furnish fodder or fruit, fertiliser from deciduous leaves, and poles for building material; in many places they are left to grow between fields to act as fencing. When woodfuel is no longer available and dung is substituted, it cannot be used as a fertiliser nor as a binder in mud for plastering walls and floors. Burning straw as fuel cuts into its other uses for fodder, basketry, and thatch. Fuelwood depletion is thus part of a complex process of rural deprivation. The extra time spent searching for fuel is but one of the most visible aspects of this.

The costs of wood removal are thus very evident, not just to outside observers, but to those suffering from them. Yet depletion appears to continue inexorably as though no one noticed. The reasons, in fact, are rooted in the nature of the subsistence fuel economy. The problem has been described as "the tragedy of the commons" (4): it is the nature of common resources to become depleted since there is no economic or social mechanism which ensures their replacement. When wood is gathered as a free good from common land, no individual has the incentive or responsibility to replace the trees. Once consumption exceeds the rate of natural replenishment, depletion is inevitable.

This is most clearly seen in areas where obtaining domestic fuel is the responsibility of women and no money is expended upon it - as is the case in much of Africa. When woodfuel becomes scarce, women use the only means at their disposal to deal with the problem. They walk further, they cook less, or they use substitute fuels which they can obtain as free goods. They do not replant trees. As long as they are excluded from money transactions, they have no access to commercial substitutes for woodfuels.

In these conditions, the domestic fuel sector is almost totally impervious to outside intervention. Even though improved stoves are capable of burning fuel much more efficiently than the traditional open fire their introduction can be extremely difficult. Anything which requires a cash outlay, no matter how small, is almost impossible to introduce into a cashless sector of the economy. Thus the reduction in energy demand by improved efficiency in end-use remains barred not, as is commonly supposed, by the technical and social problems of stove design and dissemination, but by the nature of the subsistence economy itself. It is also worth noting that improved efficiency in use, although it may reduce consumption, does nothing to attack the problem of replenishment; it simply postpones the date of final depletion.

On the productive side of the subsistence economy, similar problems of transferring resources effectively into it are encountered. The rate at which even well-proven technologies like small-scale hydro, or just more efficient and durable manual tools, are penetrating productive activity is minute in comparison with the magnitude of the need. Where there is scarcely any capital to invest, tools remain rudimentary, machinery is virtually non-existent, and there are few ways of getting more energy into production. Any available cash is spent on critical items such as transport, fertilisers, and pesticides, all of which are only obtainable commercially. The revenue from subsistence cultivation is thus being continually transferred to the industrial and commercial sectors rather than being reinvested. Productivity is often additionally constrained by the small size of land-holdings which cannot even absorb the available family labour.

It is becoming clear that, within the constraints imposed by subsistence, the major part of the energy problems now being experienced, or approaching in the future, cannot be resolved. New and renewable energy projects have enjoyed a brief, but mainly futile, vogue over the past five years; the true extent of their failure is just being realised. Community forestry was seen as a saviour, but is proving too demanding in

organisation and expense to play a major role within a
largely unmonetised system of energy use.

Attempts to improve energy use are thus far running
into a barrier caused by the lack of economic and political power in the subsistence sector. Few people with
a reasonable income in developing countries suffer from
any serious shortage of domestic fuel. Many ways of
supplying energy can be imagined; but if they require
anything beyond a miniscule level of investment they are
too costly for the rural poor. Answers must, therefore,
be sought in ways of breaking out of the trap of subsistence.

THE TRANSITION FROM SUBSISTENCE FUELS

Examination of societies which have made the transition from free-good subsistence fuels shows that this
occurs as part of a general economic progression in
which fuel supply becomes commercialised. This can
bring severe hardship when limited cash resources have
to be expended upon goods which were previously available for labour alone, but it appears to be a crucial
step in liberating people from dependence upon inevitably depleting traditional resources. The commercialisation of fuel cannot be entirely separated, of course,
from the general transition from a subsistence to a cash
economy, but some useful insights for energy policy may
be gained from looking specifically at what happens in
the case of fuels.

The traditional method of using woodfuel is in the
open fire; frequently this consists of just three
stones laid on the ground. Although the thermal efficiency may be extremely low, as a method of using the
available resources to their maximum effectiveness it
has much to be said for it. It is extremely versatile
in the type of fuel it can burn. It requires no investment of labour or capital. It does not even require
that wood be cut before use, since large logs can be
simply pushed into the fire when required and withdrawn
when cooking is finished. This is a crucial consideration in societies where axes and machetes are not readily available.

The open fire can therefore be regarded as a technique admirably suited to the subsistence way of life.
But it has many disadvantages. Out of doors it is at
the mercy of the weather, and cooking must be done in
wind, heat or rain. Indoors it creates smoke, dirt, and
fire hazards. Either way, it wastes most of the heat-
energy in the fuel.

There are, therefore, good reasons to abandon the
open fire and, with growing prosperity, this is what
happens. It occurred in the long European transition
into the industrial revolution and is evident today all

over the developing world.   As people acquire some   financial resources,   they invest to improve their living
conditions and upgrade the standards of their dwellings,
in accordance with their priorities.   Methods using
energy become more diverse and   sophisticated.   Stoves,
ovens, and cookers of various kinds are bought or built.
Fuel needs become more precise and people no longer rely
on random   logs and branches gathered from the   hinterland.   Bundles of cut fuelwood come on sale;   charcoal
comes into use;   as does kerosene, when income permits.
     Economic growth thus changes the nature of the
fuelwood problem.   If local supplies become   scarce   a
wide   range   of commercial alternatives   is   accessible.
Marketed   wood and charcoal can be transported over long
distances,   or even imported;   kerosene, bottled gas,
coal, or electricity can be chosen on the basis of their
price   and convenience.   Investments can be made in new
types   of stoves and cookers to improve   efficiency   and
economy of fuel-use.
     The example of Korea shows this clearly.   Fuelwood,
which was becoming extremely scarce,   has been variously
substituted by kerosene,   anthracite, and electricity in
the rural areas.   These substitutions were made possible
by   the   rapid growth in the national   economy   and   the
determination of the Government to bring about effective
fuel   substitution   on   a national scale.   It   is   also
significant that in Guatemala and Nicaragua,   where   the
Lorena   stove programmes are showing impressive results,
people buy their fuelwood, often have electricity available,   and are willing to invest $15-40 in a stove which
uses   half   the amount of fuel   and   brings   substantial
improvements in domestic living conditions.
     With   economic   growth   there also   comes   a   major
change in the use of energy for agricultural production.
Muscle   power alone is extremely limited in what it   can
achieve, although human ingenuity, particularly in Asia,
is   adept   in making the best use of what   is   naturally
available.   Gravity-fed   irrigation systems are perhaps
the   best example of what can be achieved   with   minimum
expenditures of energy.   Commercial energy sources cannot be avoided,   however,   if subsistence agriculture is
to   be   transformed.   They are essential for   achieving
higher   levels of production,   transporting inputs   and
outputs, and operating marketing systems.
     The   output   of a small   diesel engine,   say 40 kW,
which is about the size used in a small   automobile,   is
equivalent   to that of 1 300 people or 80 bullocks in   a
working day.   The transformation in productive capacity
is   enormous but it can also bring grave problems if   it
is   not   properly   integrated into the totality   of   the
rural economy.   The subsistence agricultural system is,
of   necessity,   geared to a parity of power   inputs   all
along the production sequence.   What the farmer sows he

must be able to harvest, transport, store and consume; if there is a surplus he must be able to get it to an adequate market. Introduction of mechanisation anywhere along the chain without an enlargement of capacities elsewhere in the system can be disruptive or even counter-productive. The most certain consequence of the transition from subsistence to higher levels of agricultural production is the displacement of manual labour.

A further concomitant of economic growth is rural industry. Crop processing, brick-making, vehicle repair and maintenance, forges, bakeries, and other concentrated energy uses come into existence. Each makes its own particular demands upon fuel supplies and contributes to the economic diversification of the rural energy supply. The effects of such changes can be complicated, however. In the Senegalese case-study it was found that the introduction of small oil-driven machines for agricultural production has, in some instances, had the surprising result of causing an increase in the demand for charcoal - to operate forges for machine repair. The energy transitions may also be reversible. In certain places industries, such as brick-firing, which had moved to oil use are now switching back to charcoal as oil prices rise.

Aspects of a transition from the subsistence fuel economy - or the consequences of having failed to achieve it - will be noticed in all of the case-studies. Energy, however, is not the sole determinant of what happens economically and it is doubtful whether it should be allocated a leading role even in projects where shortage of energy appears to be the dominant factor in rural deprivation. This is not to downgrade the importance of energy, which is clearly an essential requirement of development, but rather to locate it in context before attempting to take action.

The level of energy use, the kind of fuels and appliances, the nature of the supply system, are all characteristic of a particular level of development. They are, perhaps, best seen as indicators of that stage of development rather than causal factors of the deprivation and problems inherent in it. If this is so, then providing an additional energy supply will not necessarily bring any benefits. It is essential also to create an effective energy demand. Before any policy initiative on energy supply is taken it is therefore necessary to examine the constraints on effective demand imposed both by the context and by the energy technology itself.

THE CONTEXT FOR POLICY

The oil price increases of the 1970s are undoubtedly a major factor in the present economic plight of many developing countries. Oil is a major

8

component in the adverse trade balances from which many are now suffering; it is 60 percent in the case of Senegal and Jamaica, for example. This has led to shortages of diesel oil, electricity, and imported equipment, with consequent blockages in the collection and transport of food crops to markets and export ports.

Table 1. Commodity price index, March 1981 and quantity of oil bought by 1 tonne of each commodity in 1975 and 1981 (1975 = 100)

Commodity	Price indices (1975 = 100)			Barrels of oil purchased by 1 tonne of each commodity	
	US$	Sw.Fr.	Yen	1975	1981 (March)
Copper	146.78	109.29	103.13	115.4	56.7
Lead	175.71	130.85	123.45	38.5	22.7
Tin	198.01	147.45	139.13	640.9	425.2
Zinc	101.08	75.27	71.03	69.6	23.6
Aluminium	166.64	124.09	117.09	73.0	45.2
Cocoa	116.60	86.82	81.93	147.7	60.2
Coffee	166.65	124.10	117.10	147.5	82.4
Tea	160.02	119.16	112.44	129.0	69.3
Sugar	107.36	79.95	75.48	41.9	15.1
Cotton	140.36	104.52	98.62	119.0	56.1
Jute	82.92	61.75	58.27	35.0	9.6
Rubber	229.00	170.52	160.90	62.0	40.9
Soya beans	138.08	101.33	95.67	19.0	8.5
Maize	119.99	89.33	84.31	10.6	4.3

Note: Figures have not been deflated. Indices in Sw.Fr. and Yen, however, give an indication of real price performance.
Source: South Magazine, April-May 1981.

These facts, and the prospects of future price increases, have led to an exaggerated attempt to find new energy sources as alternatives to oil. This was, in fact, the rationale for the UN Energy Conference in Nairobi in August 1981. A closer examination of the position of developing countries in the world economy reveals that their predicament is considerably more complicated than might be inferred from looking solely at the problem of oil supply.   Table 1 gives a comparison between commodity prices over the period 1975-1980 and oil prices during the same time.   It shows that while the price of oil was rising, approximately doubling in the period, that of most agricultural products fell. Moreover, in most developing countries there were declines in the per capita food production, and food has become a major item in the import bill of some.

The fact that the developing countries have fared so poorly in recent years is thus a result of poor commodity prices, agricultural stagnation, the impact of drought and natural disasters, recessionary tendencies in the world economy, trade protectionism in the industrial countries, rising interest rates and debt servicing requirements, and the perennial severe shortage in skilled planning and managerial resources. The so-called oil crisis and its effect upon developing countries is not, therefore, primarily an energy crisis. It is not, in consequence, resolvable by energy measures.

Oil remains the world's most versatile and convenient energy source and the mainstay of energy supply for industrial society.   Large-scale substitution for it by other energy sources remains a distant prospect in the majority of applications. For most rural energy uses in developing countries, even at today's prices, oil is still the cheapest source of energy after woodfuel, as can be seen in the review of technologies in the next chapter. Moving to abandon the use of oil in developing countries is therefore likely to be technically and economically retrogressive at this stage. The reason developing countries are encountering greater problems than industrial countries in acquiring the oil they need is that their economies are insufficiently productive; there is also evidence that their use of oil is considerably less efficient than in industrial countries. Attempting to replace oil by more expensive, less versatile, or less efficient energy sources within the present patterns of consumption is likely to make matters worse. The developing countries consume a small portion of the world's oil. Instead of trying to abandon its use they need to deploy it as productively and efficiently as possible.

This carries the discussion beyond the realm of rural subsistence and into that of national energy and economic planning. Nevertheless, it is necessary to place rural energy planning within this wider context in order to dismiss the notion that the rural subsistence sector – or from a global perspective, the developing countries – constitute separable entities susceptible to esoteric energy solutions or uniquely suitable for the implantation of special new technologies.

Consider, for example, the problem of substituting woodfuel for cooking. The next cheapest source of energy is usually kerosene. Here, the impediment is not an absolute shortage of resources. If all 250 million families in the poorest rural areas of the world were to switch to cooking by kerosene, and even if they were to use as much energy for cooking as the average UK family (1), the total quantity of kerosene would be a mere 40 million tonnes per year. This is only 1.3 percent of the total production of oil in the world. It represents about a 14 percent saving in the fuel economy of the US car fleet. The energy crisis is not that wood is disappearing but that those who rely upon it cannot afford substitutes.

The greatest constraint upon rural energy policy in developing countries is the poverty and economic stagnation of the rural areas. Independent energy initiatives were not necessary in the past when economic growth almost automatically brought with it the transition to a diversified system of commercial fuel supply. Now, it is being found that such initiatives are rarely successful where economic growth is not occurring. It also needs to be recognised that there are no energy solutions to many of the problems of energy deprivation that now manifest themselves. The case of Jamaica gives vivid examples. No technical devices will meet the energy needs of the dispossessed and marginalised rural poor and it is idle to pretend otherwise.

Nevertheless, and in spite of these constraints, many opportunities for useful action undoubtedly remain. It is possible to improve the efficiency of domestic energy use, to channel more energy into productive applications, to encourage the commercialisation and diversification of energy forms, and to bring new sources of supply into the local pattern of consumption. But identifying these possibilities needs care. There is a superficial attraction to enumerating the tasks that might be performed if a new energy supply were available, and then taking this catalogue of possible uses and benefits as the justification for providing energy supply hardware, be it windmills, diesel engines, or small-scale hydro plants. Many failures have occurred as a result of such over-simplified analyses carried out without a proper consideration of the contextual constraints, and the priorities of those supposed to benefit from these energy initiatives.

The distinction has been made between domestic and productive uses of energy both in subsistence and the transition beyond it. This provides a basic taxonomy of problems and a preliminary definition of the conditions under which solutions might be sought for them. Above all, it makes clear that a low level of energy use is not necessarily evidence of a low level of energy supplies. It may well be that the shortage is one of effective demand, and that a lack of financial or credit resources, technical or managerial experience, access to markets, or a variety of other factors - such as the maintenance of a cheap and undervalued labour supply - is preventing people from utilising or mobilising resources which are locally available. The cases of Mexico and Nigeria illustrate this; they are both energy-surplus countries, yet with impoverished rural subsistence sectors. The low level of energy use in these sectors will not be improved by widening the opportunities for supply, but rather by creating the conditions under which an effective demand for the countries' own petroleum resources can occur.

One of the greatest problems facing the developing countries in energy, as elsewhere, is in finding the necessary management resources to deal with the multiplicity of problems they are facing. Because of the wide diversity of energy requirements, and the detailed analysis required in each case, the developing countries are faced with greater - not lesser - managerial problems than the industrial countries in dealing with energy. As much, if not more, effort may be needed to find a solution to an energy problem that is local and particular to a relatively small number of people. The solution, on the other hand, may be greatly restricted by its particularity.

An important consequence of this is that management training in industrialised countries, particularly that concentrating on the conventional technical and economic quantification of projects, can create a simplistic view of what should and can be done in developing countries. The well-proven tools of economic analysis, project evaluation, cost-benefit analysis, resource allocation, and personnel training are based on the validity of abstraction from the particular, and upon a high degree of transferability and interchangeability of different kinds of resources. These are not necessarily valid in the context of the developing countries in which they may be applied. The greatest danger is that they can make the energy problems in rural areas appear a great deal simpler than they really are.

In summary, the constraints acting upon energy policy in the developing world are deeply embedded in the total problem of creating the conditions for economic progress. Energy will rarely be the dominant element in the complex of obstacles to be overcome; but it may, on occasion, have a pivotal role as a discrete factor inhibiting a particular course of action or, more optimistically, it may be capable of creating opportunities for development. It is therefore useful to look briefly at some individual energy technologies - and techniques - and the broad limits and constraints which define their potential roles.

CONSTRAINTS ON ENERGY TECHNOLOGY CHOICES

The economic and technical characteristics of some
small-scale energy technologies such as solar power,
windmills, and small hydro-power are discussed in Chapter 2. Their capabilities are by now well-known; it
remains to find ways of identifying the exact uses for
which they will be technically and economically suitable, in answer to needs that are locally perceived.

It is extremely difficult to transfer any resources
into the subsistence sector either rapidly or effectively. Energy is no exception to this and the problem
is aggravated in the case of these new technologies.
They tend to be generally less versatile, considerably
more costly, and more demanding in repair and maintenance than conventional hardware. Compare the availability of mechanics who are familiar with windmills or
biogas digesters with those who can service diesel engines, for example. The chances of introducing new and
renewable energy technologies as a stimulus for productive development are thus less than those of conventional technologies.

On the other hand, where conventional energy techniques are already in use there may be opportunities for
supplementing or even replacing them with new energy
technology. Windmills may be successful where diesel
or animal-powered pumping for irrigation is taking
place. Small-scale hydro may be competitive with
existing diesel-generation of electricity, or cheaper
than making a connection with a central grid.

Flat-plate solar collectors are a particularly
interesting example. They have already found widespread
application for water-heating in Israel, Japan, and some
parts of the United States, and could well find uses
within similar conditions in developing countries.
Their initial impact would therefore be in urban applications where there are established economic demands
for hot water, and already-existing plumbing and heating
systems. If solar heaters prove themselves there, it is
possible they will be adopted in rural applications; but
the chances of a successful dissemination programme
starting in the rural areas are very much less.

Another group of energy sources presently
attracting considerable attention is that which relies
upon the flow of solar energy through the natural route
beginning with photosynthesis. It includes wood and
crops which can be used directly as fuel; human and
animal muscle power; and techniques for processing
organic material such as ethanol and methanol manufacture, biogas digestion, and gasification by partial
combustion of vegetable matter. All differ widely in
their applications and potential for development, but
they share the common characteristic of being ultimately

limited by the capacity of natural systems to capture
and convert solar energy.

Human and animal muscle power are at the heart of
subsistence farming but their potential for development
is limited. As has been seen, they provide negligible
quantities of energy in comparison with those which can
be delivered by oil-fired machinery. The transition
from subsistence seems to require the deployment of this
kind of machinery, but in the meantime much can be done
to make animal and human labour more efficient and
productive. Implements for digging, cutting, harvesting
and so forth are often primitive and ineffectual; in
parts of Africa, in particular, even machetes and axes
are not available. Similarly, harnesses and carts, and
the large variety of animal-powered devices can be improved, or introduced where they are not in use.

The dominant problem, however, is the depletion of
the wood resources on which so many people depend. The
most obvious substitute for wood is wood; it is for
this reason that an increasing amount of attention is
being given to reforestation and community fuelwood
plantation projects. Korea apart, however, little success has been reported with reforestation for anything
except large-scale commercial wood and pulp industries.
Even the much-publicised successes in the Gujarat commu-
nity-plantation projects in India are beginning to look
suspect, especially when the question of their long-term
maintenance and further dissemination are considered.

One reason for this is undoubtedly that community
forestry is extremely expensive. It is not just a
question of mobilising free community labour and
planting seedlings donated by the forestry service.
Intensive promotion must be followed by the creation of
an infrastructure for the continued supply of advice and
supervision, and a guaranteed supply of seedlings at the
correct time. Figures of $300-650 per hectare are given
as the cost of the India schemes in Gujarat, but the UN
Conference on New and Renewable Energy Sources Technical
Panel on Fuelwood and Charcoal quotes a range from $200-
2 000 per hectare. Furthermore, planting trees may require considerable organisation in order not to impinge
on crop cultivation; the economic incentive must be
sufficient to cover the years before the wood can be
harvested; and complicated questions of ownership and
access have to be resolved before any commitment by the
people concerned can be expected. Nor, indeed, are
trees necessarily seen as entirely beneficial. They can
cause serious problems by harbouring pests such as tsetse fly and crop-eating birds; and when densely planted
they may lower the local water table.

An even more serious question is the actual yield
which can be obtained. Under quite favourable conditions a yield of 10 cu.m. or 6 tonnes per hectare per

year can be expected from plantations in dry areas; certain species in highly productive regions might yield 12 tonnes per year. A family of six with a consumption of 3-5 tonnes per year therefore needs up to half a hectare dedicated solely to wood; spaced 3 metres apart this means 500 trees per family for a self-sustaining wood supply. In any but the most sparsely populated areas, such allocations of land are virtually unthinkable. In the Guatemalan case-study it is pointed out that 80 percent of farming families in the country have an average of only 1.4 ha and the poorest 20 percent only 0.4 ha of land for their entire production of food.

The reason people are still able to draw such amounts of wood from the countryside is because they are consuming the existing stock of trees. This reserve can be very substantial; an untouched temperate forest may contain around 300 tonnes per hectare. Eating into this stock to supplement the wood made available by new growth each year can create a very misleading impression of what is actually the sustainable yield.

As is clearly recognised by FAO (5), no large-scale forestry solutions can be envisaged for most of the present areas of acute fuelwood scarcity. The potential yield is insufficient and the timescale for organising plantations and waiting for trees to mature too great. This is not to say that tree-planting is futile. On the contrary, in many areas it is essential in preserving soil from erosion and hence sustaining agricultural production, even if the wood were never used for fuel.

Trees will also continue to play a vital part in meeting future fuel needs. But the expectations placed upon afforestation must be realistic: alone, it will not be able to sustain present levels of energy consumption. There must be a parallel effort to introduce substitute forms of energy and to increase the efficiency of energy use. In short, tree-planting for future energy needs only makes sense if it is part of a general progression towards the commercialisation and diversification of energy supplies.

Burning wood is the most direct method of using the solar energy captured in photosynthesis; other methods all depend on intermediate processing stages. The techniques for transforming organic material into ethanol and methanol are discussed in detail in the next chapter. Methanol remains a technological dream rather than a realistic possibility for small-scale rural use; the fact that the minimum economically feasible operation would require a plantation area of 55 sq.km. is perhaps a sufficient comment here. Ethanol, on the other hand, using the time-honoured techniques of alcohol brewing and distilling is certainly a more likely prospect for small-scale rural use. It too, however, will be subject to severe restrictions because of the areas of crop-land which must be devoted to growing the feedstock. Possible yields of ethanol per hectare are 2.8 tonnes/year for sugarcane, 1.7 tonnes/year for cassava (6) under optimum conditions; under actual operating conditions yields would be much lower. If mechanical methods of harvesting and transport are used, the net liquid fuel yield will be further reduced. It is probably reasonable to assume a net yield of 1.5 tonnes/year as the reasonable achievable maximum sustainable under developing country conditions. Used in an internal combustion engine at 30 percent efficiency this contributes roughly the same amount of work per year as a pair of bullocks.

Despite the fact that ethanol is a highly versatile energy form, the fundamental reality is that the density of energy flow through the ethanol production system is little different from that through a subsistence farming system. Where population densities are high and land is scarce, the effect of introducing ethanol production into the system will do little to increase its total productive capacity; rather, it may divert land use away from subsistence cultivation and channel its output to the oil-using sectors of the national economy.

A further point is that ethanol, as beer, wine, or any distillation such as rum, whisky or simply grain alcohol, is an integral part of many, if not most, traditional cultures. Assuming that the alcohol from small-scale rural production will be used for fuel thus has a certain improbability about it. That no mention is made of this is perhaps indicative of a certain degree of academic detachment in most studies of ethanol production for rural use.

Biogas production has made spectacular progress in China and the example has inspired numerous programmes in other developing countries. Biogas, in fact, appears to have become a beacon of hope for many people. They are liable to be severely disappointed unless a firmly realistic attitude is taken.

Detailed examination reveals that the Chinese biogas programme, where it is working, does so because of a complicated set of circumstances particular to that country. In areas where many digesters have been built, a high degree of commitment by the local leaders has perhaps been the most important factor. Biogas digesters also require considerable masonry skill as well as institutional support, not just for initial construction but for long-term maintenance.

Other essential prerequisites appear to be a moist tropical climate, high pressure on land and resource use, concentrated animal husbandry, a tradition of composting and systematic use of organic fertiliser, and a capacity for communal action which can be deployed for the benefit of individuals in the building and operation of digesters. Where any one of these is missing, large-scale dissemination of biogas technology is unlikely to occur. It is also fundamental to the Chinese system of biogas production that it serves the triple ends of fertiliser production, sanitary disposal of faecal wastes, and energy production. Without a firm commitment to all three, rather than energy alone, the programme would not have been so successful.

In addition, biogas production is restricted by the availability of feedstocks. Ultimately it depends upon the solar flow of energy and its progression through photosynthesis and human and animal biological systems. The yield of biogas will depend upon the proportion of that flow which can be diverted into the digester. The Chinese, with an almost fanatical dedication to making use of every available morsel of land and a willingness to use human excreta as well as animal waste, have succeeded in making individual family biogas pits possible in the most densely populated and cultivated areas. The less intense land use and a smaller range of available feedstocks in other countries drastically limits their potential for biogas production.

Similar constraints apply to gasification by partial combustion. Feedstocks must be available in both the quantities and the time sequence to match the operating load on the gasifier. Before a gasifier can be installed with any confidence it is necessary to know the seasonal availability, cost, and practicability of storing different types of feedstocks. Competing uses have to be considered, as does the sustainable yield. These factors determine the number of gasifier units which can be installed in a particular area as surely as the availability of fodder determines the number of draught animals an area can support.

FERTILISERS AS ENERGY

Fertilisers are often the most important commercial input to subsistence farming and are considered as an energy input or cost by many of the authors in this volume. Indeed, the scope of energy inputs could also be widened to include the feedstocks and energy used in the manufacture of pesticides and herbicides, and even the energy used in the manufacture of farm machinery. There is no objection to this provided it is done on a logical and consistent basis, but the results tend to be of little operational value and may be confusing.

Chemically identical fertilisers arriving at a farm may have very different energy costs depending on their method of manufacture - and the conventions by which the energy costs are calculated. The effects on crop yields are, however, not changed by substituting one such fertiliser for another. It is the financial rather than

the energy cost which is of relevance. It is therefore
more useful to treat fertilisers as a demand upon the
farmer's financial budget, competing with other uses for
cash, than as a component in the total energy expended
in farming.

The only case where it is perhaps useful to count
fertilisers as an energy cost is when they are indige-
nously manufactured from natural gas or petrochemical
feedstocks which would otherwise go into the national
fuel supply. In this case the use of fertilisers is a
direct energy cost to the country and it may be informa-
tive to consider the relative productivity of using
petrochemicals as fertiliser feedstocks or as fuel.

TOWARDS NEW ENERGY STRATEGIES

It is now abundantly clear that there are no large-
scale energy solutions to the energy problems of the
subsistence areas of the world. In many cases there are
no energy solutions at all. Within the complex of
problems of rural poverty little evidence has, in fact,
been produced to show that energy supply is worthy of a
higher priority than adequate food, water, and housing.

The most clearly indicated direction for energy
policy is that which contributes to a comprehensive
economic development. This requires that a positive
attitude is taken to the productive potential within the
subsistence sector. Too often subsistence agriculture,
with its limitations, problems, and needs, is seen as a
drain upon the national economy. In fact, even at its
weakest, subsistence production of basic foodstuffs
fulfills an indispensable national need by providing, at
a minimum, food for those engaged in it; often it
furnishes a good portion of the food supply for the
urban labour force as well. It has the potential to
increase its output and efficiency. Enhancing the productive capacity of the subsistence sector may be one of
the more effective ways of dealing with balance of
payments problems in countries which import both oil and
food. Korea's import bill for grain in 1979, for example, came to $945 million, or 60 percent of what the
country paid for oil.

Within such a general strategy oriented towards the
economic development of the subsistence sector, specific
energy problems begin to become identifiable. It is
essential that these are each seen clearly within their
own particular context. Operational distinctions must be
made, such as those between non-productive and productive consumption, between non-commercial and commercial
fuel supply, and between energy used in merely
maintaining subsistence and that needed to achieve a
transition beyond it. Policy and action require a clear
idea of what is required for what purpose, and the

practical constraints which affect each particular case.

The question of time scales needs to be considered. Rural energy problems emerge, are recognised, and find implementable solutions within widely different time frameworks. The clearest example is the fuelwood shortage. In many areas the availability of large standing stocks of wood conceals the amount by which sustainable yields are being exceeded by current consumption. By the time scarcity is apparent it is too late to begin the process of replenishment with any hope of restoring the previous position, and there may be no option but to resort to emergency measures.

This is closely linked to the problem of whether, at a particular time, the need for a technical improvement is locally felt, and thought worth the effort of satisfying. For example, improved stoves can achieve considerable savings of woodfuel, but the conditions under which they can be successfully introduced may be related to factors other than wood consumption. Where, for example, their method of house construction has not advanced beyond simple mud-and-pole structures, it is unlikely that any significant effort will be devoted by people themselves to stove dissemination. It is far more likely that improvements in the efficiency of domestic energy use will occur as part of a general upgrading of housing quality or as a product of a broadly-based programme of technical training in the rural areas. The combination of factors which enables a technological initiative to become popularly self-sustaining is difficult to identify; but without it, progress at a rate commensurate with that at which energy problems are worsening is virtually impossible.

What all this amounts to is not a grand design for new energy strategies but rather a possibility of identifying a large number of small attackable energy problems. These will vary enormously between countries and regions. Those appropriate in Latin American countries such as Brazil, with a population density of 14 people/sq.km. will be very different from those in Asian countries where the density is 1 000 people/sq.km. They will differ in accordance with access to financial resources, skills, and the climatic and resource endowments of different countries.

Among such possibilities for action are small commercial fuelwood plantations run on a communal or individual basis; improved charcoal-making methods linked to fuelwood plantations; improved forest management and utilisation of forest wastes; improved stove designs and more efficient use of agricultural waste products by compression or pelletising; gasifier installations; biogas generation; small-scale hydro and windmills; solar drying devices for crops and fish; subsidisation and dissemination of kerosene stoves, and kerosene itself; introduction of coal, or bottled gas; and rural electrification. None is appropriate outside a narrow and precisely definable set of circumstances and efforts to promote these initiatives must be based upon a thoroughly realistic assessment of what is possible, and where it would fit within a locally perceived set of priorities.

Many international aid agencies now have a mandate - albeit often a restricted one - for directing resources to the solution of rural energy problems. The task of identifying appropriate opportunities for technical intervention is just as complicated for these agencies as it is for the countries they are trying to assist. In most cases it will require a meticulous, and expensive, step by step identification and resolution of small problems which have shown themselves impervious to large-scale solutions. In order to accomplish this, it will be necessary for them to rely increasingly on the recipient institutions for guidance. The difficulty, as times become more stringent, is that this puts a greater and broader call upon their resources if they are to achieve anything of significance. It is essential that this point is brought home to those in the higher decision-making positions in both technical assistance agencies and recipient countries: the energy problems of the poor rural areas of the developing world are complex, highly varied, and slow, difficult, and expensive to resolve.

Among all the case-studies presented here only that of Korea records a deliberately planned and executed series of rural energy transitions. It shows what is possible by integrating rural energy in the approach to national energy development. From being almost entirely dependent upon wood two decades ago, the Korean farming community has acquired a versatile and diversified energy base. Because a mechanism existed - in this case the State - for investing in the rural sector, it has been possible to raise energy consumption to a level at which almost total rural electrification has occurred. Rural energy development and the solution of the energy problems of subsistence agriculture cannot occur without investment. For each country the task remains of finding ways of making this possible.

REFERENCES

1. Leach, G., Lewis, C., Romig, F., van Buren, A., Foley, G., 1979, A Low Energy Strategy for the UK, Science Reviews, London.
2. FAO, Committee on Forestry, March 1980, Secretariat Note Wood for Energy.
3. FAO, 1981, Map of the Fuelwood Situation in the Developing Countries.

4. Hardin, G., December 1968, "The Tragedy of the Commons", Science, Vol.162, pp. 1 243 - 1 248.

5. FAO Forestry Department, December 1980, A Global Reconnaissance Survey of the Fuelwood Supply/Requirement Situation.

6. Barnard, G.W. and Hall, D.O., April 1981, Biomass for Developing Countries, Report for Solar Energy Research Institute.

2
Energy Technologies
for Rural Development

Hubertus E. M. Stassen
Willibrordus P. M. van Swaaij

During the past ten years a lack of adequate energy
supplies has increasingly hampered the development of
the rural sector of many developing countries; at times
it has even threatened their very survival. Two principal aspects of this shortage of energy can be distinguished.

In the first place, the demand for fuelwood, the
most important source of traditional energy for uses
such as cooking and heating, has grown far faster than
supply. Therefore many people, especially in the rural
areas, face an energy crisis, the magnitude of which is
immense. At the moment, the forests of the developing
countries are being consumed at a rate of 10-15 million
hectares or 1.3 percent of the total forest area each
year. Deforestation is most serious in semi-arid and
mountainous regions, where serious problems of erosion,
desertification, and siltation are being encountered.
As fuelwood supplies are exhausted, animal and crop
residues are burned, thus depriving the soil of valuable
nutrients and organic conditioning material.

In the second place, the development of the rural
sector in the past has relied heavily on relatively
cheap commercial fuels. The rising prices of petroleum
products since 1973 have seriously affected the balance
of payments position of many oil-importing developing
countries, thus limiting their ability to supply their
rural areas with the imported energy needed for development.

In order to counteract these trends, the best approach is to promote rural self-sufficiency in energy by
increasing energy production, and by encouraging the
substitution and more effective use of indigenous and,
preferably, renewable resources.

ENERGY FOR SURVIVAL

Experiments with cooking rice (1) show that the

21

quantity of energy necessary to bring the water to its boiling point, and then boil away the requisite amount, is about 2 500 KJ/kg rice (about 17.5 percent of the energy content of the rice). Assuming that other food-grains behave in the same way, that an adult, on average, needs about 10 000 KJ/day, that 80 percent of this energy intake is in the form of food-grains, and that 75 percent of the energy spent in preparing meals is used for grain cooking, the effective energy need can be estimated at about 0.73 GJ/person/year. Actual fuel consumption data which separate cooking from other fuel uses are scarce but a few surveys (2,3,4,5) present data ranging from 5.7 GJ/person/year (Bangladesh) to 11.2 GJ/person/year (Upper Volta), indicating that the overall cooking efficiency, in actual circumstance, varies between 6 and 12 percent.

Whether this efficiency can be increased significantly remains to be seen. Although for "improved" woodstoves fuel efficiencies of up to 25 percent are often claimed, these numbers only make sense when the efficiency is measured under a well-defined set of standardised conditions. Because cooking is a complicated process, involving different periods of temperature raising, boiling, simmering and so on, and because cooking habits differ regionally, there is not always a clear relation between measured and actual efficiencies. It is because of this that an intimate knowledge of local cooking habits is necessary for the development of appropriate "improved" woodstoves; a stove that performs well in one region does not necessarily reduce fuel consumption in another.

Apart from the more efficient end-use of firewood, increased production and efficiency in the logging operation are also necessary. Additional possibilities are to be found in the more efficient management of existing fuelwood resources, the introduction of high-yielding species, the stimulation of village woodlots and energy plantations, and the processing of logging wastes. Improvements in the energy-wasteful traditional methods of charcoal manufacture can also be sought.

Nevertheless, the dimensions of the fuelwood crisis are such that it is unlikely the above measures will be sufficient to solve the short-term problems. Emphasis, therefore, needs to be placed on the development and introduction of alternative fuels, either as a temporary measure or as permanent replacements for exhausted supplies. Possibilities range from the introduction of conventional fuels like coal, through biomass-based fuels like charcoal, ethanol, methanol, and biogas, to the direct conversion of solar energy to heat.

Charcoal Manufacture

Charcoal is produced as a result of the chemical reduction of organic material under controlled circumstances. Although the techniques differ widely, the basic principle is common to all manufacturing processes. Three types of appliances are used:

- kilns, in which the partial combustion of part of the charge is used to initiate carbonisation;
- retorts, in which the charge is heated by means of an external source of heat applied to the outside of the container;
- continuous furnaces, through which the charge is mechanically driven.

The carbonisation process can be divided into four stages:

- combustion (kilns only): part of the charge is burned in the presence of ample oxygen. This creates an "ignition zone" in which a small fraction of the charge reaches a temperature of about 600 C. The air supply is then reduced, but the heat for driving the next stage continues to be generated in the ignition zone;
- dehydration: in this stage the free water contained in the main body of the charge is driven off. The average temperature rises gradually to about 270 C;
- decomposition: once the water has been evaporated, an exothermic carbonisation reaction begins in the main body of the charge. This is accompanied by a rapid rise in temperature to about 600-700 C. Distillation products (chiefly methanol, acetic acid, and tars) are carried away. At the end of the decomposition stage, which is indicated by a change in the colour and quantity of the smoke, the kiln must be closed;
- cooling: the cooling rate depends on the thickness and radiation capacity of the walls of the apparatus.

Charcoal yields depend primarily on the type of equipment used, but other variables are important. For example, dry wood (20-30 percent moisture content) produces higher yields than wet wood (above 60 percent moisture content) and slow carbonisation at low temperatures tends to produce higher yields than fast carbonisation at high temperatures. Table 1 shows typical yields and efficiencies obtained with different manufacturing processes.

In general, timber from hardwoods, softwoods, and palmtrees can be converted to charcoal, but hardwoods tend to produce a stronger charcoal than do softwoods. Charcoal strength is important when considering the

24

abrasive wear which occurs during transport.

Table 1. Charcoal processes

Type of apparatus	Charcoal production t/yr (GJ/yr)	Thermal value of charcoal (GJ/t)	Conver-sion effic. dry wt. (%)	Thermal conver-sion effic. (%) *
Earth kiln (6,7)	12 (310)	25.5	10-20	13-27
Mark V kiln (6)	72 (1 950)	27	25	35
Slope kiln (7)	100 (2 400)	24	30	38
Bee-hive kiln (7)	200 (4 800)	24	30	38
Missouri kiln (6)	310 (9 300)	30	25	39
Lambiotte retort	9 000 (27 000)	30	30	48

*assumption: dry wood: 19 GJ/t

Ethanol Manufacture (8,9)

Ethanol is produced in the anaerobic conversion of sugars by micro-organisms. Feedstocks can be selected from among the many plants which produce sugars directly or from those which produce starch and cellulose. The initial processing can differ considerably, but some features are universal:

- simple sugars must be extracted from the plants that produce them directly;
- starch must be hydrolysed from its basic form by enzyme attack;
- cellulose, like starch, can be hydrolysed by mineral acids or enzymes, but differences in its chemical structure make this more difficult;
- a large amount of research has been carried out on the hydrolysis of wood to sugars, using mineral acids. The process aims at maximising glucose production and obtaining lignin as a by-product. The resistance of the lignocellulosic complex in wood, however, requires the use of high temperatures and acid concentrations which cause decomposition of the sugars. The process must therefore be interrupted when the sugar yield has

reached its maximum, which is 50 percent of the weight of the cellulose.

Sugar solutions ferment readily to ethanol, with energy efficiencies of 85-90 percent. After completion of the fermentation the mash is distilled to yield ethanol (with a strength of 96 Gay Lussac) as the end product. The ethanol yields from different feedstocks are shown in Table 2.

Table 2.   Ethanol yields

	Biomass yield (t/ha/yr) (10,11)	Ethanol yield (t/ha/yr)
Potato	27.0	2.6
Wheat	4.5	1.6
Maize	5.6	1.7
Cassava	15.0	2.2
Sugarbeet	45.0	3.5
Sugarcane	55.0	3.1
Wood	12.0	2.5

An important concern in ethanol production is the Net Energy Ratio (NER), or the final yield of energy in useful products divided by the total energy inputs. Within the literature, wide variations occur in the values quoted for the NER. These differences stem from the approach taken: especially whether all inputs and outputs are given an energy equivalent value, or whether the total energy inputs are compared to the ethanol output alone, or whether the energy inputs are apportioned to the various end-products.

It is clear, however, that a net energy gain will occur in those cases where the fermentation and distillation are powered by burning the crop waste, as is the case with sugarcane where the reported NER varies from 2.4 to over 7. For most starch crops and sugarbeets the value is close to or below one. Very low values for NER are found for cellulose fermentation using existing hydrolysis techniques. In addition to the question of the net energy yield, attention must also be given by energy planners to the competition which can arise between using land for energy or for food.

Cost estimates vary greatly. The Biomass Technical Panel of the UN Conference on New and Renewable Sources of Energy (12) found a variation of $8-37/GJ. A study in 1979 (13), however, costed ethanol derived from sugarcane and cassava in Brazil at $9.03/GJ and $9.39/GJ respectively. The average production capacity per unit in Brazil, at the moment, is 19 000 cu.m./year; newly planned units have an average production capacity of 34 000 cu.m./year(14).

Methanol Production

Methanol was originally produced on a limited scale as a by-product from charcoal manufacture. In the 1920s a process was developed to produce methanol by passing a mixture of hydrogen and carbon monoxide (synthesis gas) over a catalyst at high temperature and pressure. This synthesis gas can be made by reacting steam with coke or charcoal, by reforming natural gas, or by gasifiying coal or biomass with oxygen. Methanol production from natural gas is by far the most economic method at the moment.

The Biomass Technical Panel (12) estimated methanol costs from biomass at $13-24/GJ. Harris (11) lists the production costs in 1979 in New Zealand, for facilities producing 393 000 t/year and 31 500 t/year, at $10.8/GJ and $11.6/GJ respectively.

The overall thermal conversion efficiency of the process can be taken as 50 percent. If methanol is used for cooking this means that an area of 0.027 ha of wood per person is needed, assuming a cooking stove efficiency of 30 percent and a production capacity of 12 oven-dry tonnes of wood/ha/year. The minimum methanol-producing facility which can be economically envisaged has a wood input of 200 t/day (95 t methanol/day). This means that the wood plantation to keep it supplied has a minimum area of about 55 sq.km.

Biomethanation

Biomethanation, or anaerobic digestion, is a process which produces energy (chiefly methane) from wet biomass. The conversion of complex organic matter consists of three successive steps (15):

- hydrolysis: organic polymers are hydrolysed to their individual monomers by enzyme attack;
- acid formation: hydrolysed compounds are converted by a group of "acid forming" bacteria to simple compounds such as volatile fatty acids, ammonia, carbon dioxide, and hydrogen;
- methane fermentation: simple compounds from the preceding step are converted to methane and carbon dioxide by a group of strictly anaerobic bacteria. Only a very limited number of compounds, carbon dioxide, hydrogen, acetic acid, and methanol can be used directly by the methane bacteria. Fermentation of higher

volatile acids and alcohols needs the assistance of a group of acetogenic bacteria.

In a well-balanced digester the above three steps proceed simultaneously. But biological reactions are very sensitive to shocks, such as rapid fluctuations in temperature, acidity level, and rate of feed addition (16), and are therefore more difficult to operate on a steady basis than chemical reactions. This makes it difficult for a farmer to obtain a constant supply of fuel from his biogas unit since it is subject to all the variables of the weather and to the lack of uniformity of the feed material.

The prerequisites for successful biogas application include a moist tropical climate, ⌐high pressure on land and resource use, concentrated animal husbandry, and a tradition of composting and systematic use of fertiliser. It is significant that the primary justification for the introduction of biogas in China is the production of fertiliser and the sanitary disposal of human and animal wastes, with energy regarded as a somewhat optional extra (see Chapter 1).

In practice, the gas produced consists of 55-60 percent methane, 40-45 percent carbon dioxide, and minor amounts of hydrogen, nitrogen, organic sulfides, and higher hydrocarbons. The average thermal value of the gas is about 20 MJ/cu.m. The process can be operated on almost any type of organic waste with a low lignocellulose content. The total solids content in the digester is generally kept below 10 percent. An important advantage of the process is the retention of the fertiliser value of the waste, although about 10 percent of the nitrogen is lost if the residual slurry is dried. There seems to be some agreement of opinion that, outside China, biomass digestion is applicable mainly on a communal scale.

Cost estimates for biogas differ enormously. The Biomass Panel (12) gives figures ranging from $1.70-18.00 (1980)/GJ for small-scale units and $2.20-12.50 (1980)/GJ for larger units. As these values were calculated for the U.S. and New Zealand, they seem of little relevance to developing countries. Parikh and Parikh (17) quote costs in India varying between $1.21 (1980)/GJ* and $2.33 (1980)/GJ* for a privately-owned plant (1.8 cu.m./day) and a village-scale plant (170 cu.m./day), respectively.

---

* $0.91(1976)/GJ and $1.75(1976)/GJ

Solar Cooking

Solar energy comes in the form of electromagnetic radiation with wavelengths varying between 0.22 and 10 microns. A distinction must be made between beam and diffuse radiation; the former reaches the receiving surface in a straight line from the sun, while the latter is reflected in the atmosphere by clouds and dust particles. The quantity of radiation, as well as the division between beam and diffuse radiation, is extremely variable, depending on such factors as geographical location, time of day, season, meteorological condition, and altitude. In practice, under the very best circumstances, the total (beam and diffuse) radiation will seldom surpass 1 000 W/sq.m., and 200 W/sq.m. (6.3 GJ/sq.m./year) can be taken as a representative average value over 24 hours.

In principle, two types of equipment for the conversion of solar energy to heat are available. These are the non-tracking flat-plate collectors which convert the total available solar radiation, and the tracking focusing collectors which convert only the beam radiation. Flat-plate (evacuated tube) collectors can reach temperatures of up to 150 C, which would make them suitable for boiling but unfit for frying. Simple focusing collectors can reach temperatures of 350-500 C.

Table 3. Solar cookers

Type	Efficiency (%)	Costs (18) 1980 $/ sq.m.	Surface area sq.m./ cap.	Cooker cost $/cap.	$/GJ
Flat-plate collector	20	150	1.4	210	78
Focusing collector	50	200	0.55	110	41

Note: The above calculations are based on the following assumptions:
- incident solar radiation during cooking time: 500W/sq.m.
- daily cooking time: 4 hours
- interest: 10 percent
- depreciation: 5 years

Table 4.   Comparison of cooking technologies

Fuel	Therm. value (MJ/kg)	Therm. conv. effic'y (%)	Fuel cost ($/GJ)	Effec. energy cost ($/GJ)	Total wood use (kg/MJ)	Transp. cost ($/GJ.km) ++
Wood:						
trad.	15	9	1-4	11-44**	0.58	0.067
improved		20		5-20**	0.26	
Charcoal:						
trad.	28	20	3-15	15-75**	1.66 + 0.88	0.036
improved		30		10-50**	1.11 + 0.55	
Coal	30	30	4.3	14.3**	-	0.033
Kerosene:						
trad.	42	30	6.2	18-21**	-	0.024
improved		35				
Ethanol	27	30	9.0*	30**	0.59	0.037
Methanol	20	30	11.0	37**	0.35	0.05
Biogas	20 (MJ/cu.m.)	60	2.35	3.9**	-	-
Solar cooker (flat-plate)	-	20	-	78	-	-
Solar cooker (focusing)	-	50	-	41	-	-

Notes: *   sugarcane Brazil
          ** cost of stove not included
          +   thermal efficiency of charcoal kilns: tradi-
              tional 20 percent, improved 40 percent
          ++ calculated on the basis of 1 tonne/km

     The costs of solar cookers are tabulated in Table
3. It must be emphasised, however, that a number of
promotional demonstrations of solar cookers in the past
have failed. The factors responsible were the high cost
of the cookers, lack of storage facilities for supplying

heat for cooking during evening hours, unreliable designs which could not withstand rural conditions, and inadequate social acceptability. Any renewed introduction of solar cookers is bound to fail unless adequate solutions to these problems are found.

A summary comparison of all the above cooking technologies is given in Table 4. The following conclusions can be drawn:

- given the appropriate technical, environmental, and social circumstances, biogas is by far the most preferable choice;
- the introduction of appropriate woodstoves is next best; and the improvement of these woodstoves is worthwhile;
- charcoal manufacture should be discouraged because it is expensive and wasteful of wood. Only in cases where fuel has to be transported over large distances might an economic benefit become apparent to the user;
- in the case of exhausted wood supplies the introduction of imported coal should be considered;
- ethanol and methanol manufacture show good total wood usage comparable to present direct combustion techniques; however, their costs are too high to justify their introduction for cooking purposes only; transport costs are also relatively high;
- solar cookers are unfeasible for economic reasons.

ENERGY FOR DEVELOPMENT

The installed shaft-power required for cultivating a hectare of land varies with the crop, the soil condition, and the method of agriculture. That for land preparation can range from 0.4-2.8 GJ/ha/year. By assuming that half of this has to be provided in a fixed period of 200 hours, the installed power requirements can be estimated at 0.3-2.0 kW/ha. This figure is given some confirmation by data from Makhijani and Poole (19) for rice agriculture in different countries. Their figures range from 0.5 kW/ha (China) to 1.2 kW/ha (USA).

The quantity of water needed for irrigation-water varies with factors such as the soil-type, crop, climate, and irrigation method, but 50-100 cu.m./ha/day is a reasonable estimate for most circumstances (20). Assuming daily irrigation for 10 hours, the effective power needs for different heads and varying water amounts can be easily calculated. Some examples are shown in Table 5.

The energy need for threshing is best measured in relation to the weight of cereals processed. An ITB Bandung study (21) estimated a shaft-energy requirement of about 1 GJ/t for ricemilling. The installed power varied from 10-150 kW. In order to judge the applica-

bility of different energy choices, it is necessary to
know the average installed power requirements of typical
rural industrial activities. Table 6 which is taken
from an Indian study (22) in Andhra Pradesh, provides
this information for several types of rural industries.

Table 5. Power needs for irrigation

Head (m)	50 cu.m./ha/day	100 cu.m./ha/day
5	0.11 kW/ha	0.23 kW/ha
10	0.23	0.45
15	0.34	0.68

Note: Based on

$$P = \frac{9.8}{3600} \times \frac{Gh}{n}$$

where
P= pump installed power (kW)
G= volumetric water flow (cu.m./hr)
h= well depth (m)
n= pump effic'y (%) assumed 60%

Table 6. Average effective shaft power of small
industries by type

Type of industry	Average effective shaftpower (kW)
Rice mills	14.0
Flour mills	7.0
Oil mills	16.0
Groundnut shellers	14.0
Cotton gin mills	35.0
Saw mills	10.0
Power looms	2.2

Energy needs for transport are best measured in
terms of tonne-kilometres. The shaft energy required
depends on the road and vehicle condition, as well as on
the vehicle size and type, and on the method of operation. The effective shaft-energy needs for road transport can be taken to average 1.6 MJ/t-km (23), while for
rail transport this decreases to 0.5 MJ/t-km (24). Most
rural transport in developing countries is small-scale

and short distance. Animal-drawn vehicles are likely to be economical for loads up to 2 tonnes and distances up to 40 km. Especially in operations involving long loading and unloading times and relatively low levels of utilisation (50-100 days/year), they seem preferable to lorries which need a 5 tonne load, long-distance runs and a high utilisation level (250-300 days/year) to be economical.

POWER SOURCES

At present, rural mechanical energy needs of 3kW and over are usually met by diesel engines. Smaller energy needs are met by petrol engines and draught animal power. A wide range of possibilities for substitution of alternatives or improvements in existing methods of supplying energy already exists, and further developments are taking place.

Draught Animal Power

The power that can be generated by a draught animal depends on numerous factors including its species, body-weight, state of health and nutrition, its training and management, and its working environment. FAO estimates (25) give an average sustained output by draught animals, such as bullocks and buffaloes, of 0.3-0.6 kW. This means that for practical purposes the "installed engine capacity" is limited to about 1 kW (one pair of bullocks). The efficiency of use of draught animal power is often very low, as shown in Table 7.

Table 7. Traditional water-lifting devices

Type	Power source	Max.water depth	Efficiency
Dalou	1 bullock	50 m	45%
Persian wheel	2 bullocks	10 m	50%

The quickest way to improve efficiency is to use light-weight modern equipment with low friction and an appropriate harness. Improving the motive force is a longer-term activity.

The costs of animal power are difficult to assess. From data gathered by Odend'hal (26), the overall efficiency of a bullock can be calculated at about 10 percent. If all the energy input to the animal is provided in the form of cereal - which is seldom the case -

it will need about 6.7 kg/day. Taking the cost of
cereal at $0.15/kg, running costs would amount to
$1.00/day or $100/GJ.

Windpower

Small windmills are a traditional energy technology
in many parts of the world, and are used for water-
pumping and other applications where an irregular output
can be tolerated. A number of low-cost designs suitable
for fabrication in many developing countries have been
developed in recent years. Large-scale introduction has
been hampered by problems of reliability, but these are
now getting full attention and are slowly being overcome.

The power output of windmills depends on the average windspeed, and on the size and efficiency of the
mill. Because locally manufactured windmills with rotor
diameters of more than 5 m cannot easily be envisaged,
the maximum installed power can be estimated at about
160 W taking an average wind speed of 4 m/sec and a mill
efficiency of 20 percent. It is generally agreed that
windpower becomes unpractical for average windspeeds
below 3 m/sec. Because of their dependence on the wind
regime, the costs of windpower are difficult to generalise. The Windpower Panel of the UN Conference (27)
estimated the shaft-power energy costs of small windmills at $50-125/GJ.

Solar Mechanical and Electrical Power

Solar radiation can be converted to mechanical
energy by using a thermodynamic cycle with a hot source
provided by solar collectors and a cold source normally
provided by the water of a well. Several water-pumping
systems based on low temperature flat-plate collectors
have been installed in developing countries but, because
of their very low efficiency, have not proved cost-
effective. More efficient small systems based on suntracking reflectors or fresnel lenses are under development. In practical rural circumstances, however, the
need for suntracking will probably severely limit their
utilisation.

Solar cells, usually in the form of thin films or
wafers, are semi-conductor devices that convert 5-15
percent of the incident solar radiation directly into DC
electricity. Their efficiency depends on the illumi-
nation-spectrum intensity, solar cell design, semi-
conductor material, and the temperature. A solar cell
behaves much like a low voltage (about 0.5 V) battery
whose charge is continuously replenished at a rate proportional to the incident radiation.

The extraordinary simplicity of photovoltaic cells, makes them a highly desirable energy system for developing and industrialised countries alike. Attractive features include the absence of moving parts, very slow degradation of properly sealed cells, extreme simplicity of use, and the possibility of using modular systems starting from a few watts and extending up into the megawatt range.

Because of their modularity, solar cell systems show very small economies of scale. But because their fuel costs are nil and maintenance and repair costs are small, the cost of photovoltaic energy is very sensitive to the values chosen for interest and life-time. The World Bank (28) currently estimates the cost of energy from small solar cell systems, including battery storage, at $275-835/GJ, based on system investment costs of $20 000-30 000/peak kW. Major price reductions of $8 000-10 000/peak kW within 2-3 years are foreseen, but as the cost of solar cells falls, total costs are likely to be dominated by the "balance of system" costs. These include the cost of storage, except for uses such as water-pumping, where the application has an inherent storage potential.

External Combustion Engines

Because the economic size of steam engines is generally too large for rural energy needs, the discussion here will be limited to Stirling engines. These are external combustion heat engines which utilise air or other gases as working fluids. They are capable of using any source of heat, such as wood, agricultural waste, coal, or solar thermal energy.

Invented in 1816 by Robert Stirling, they were competitive with the steam engines of the day, and in the early 1900s thousands were sold as coal-burning water-pumps that produced from 50-500 W of delivered power at about 2 percent overall efficiency. Large-scale crank-type Stirling engines - especially for automotive use - still present a number of difficult design problems which remain to be solved, but free-piston type linear motion engines avoid many of those problems. Power is removed from these engines by linear motion pumps or alternators. Current data on Stirling engine technology indicate that overall thermal efficiencies of 17.5 percent (furnace 50 percent; engine 35 percent) are possible.

Although there is no significant commercial manufacture of Stirling engines as yet and therefore a certain amount of technical and economic uncertainty, tentative calculations (7) show that such engines may soon become competitive with petrol or petrol/gasifier engines in the very small power range of less than 2 kW.

Gasification

The complete conversion of solid fuels into a combustible gas is a well-known process which has been successfully used to provide fuel for internal combustion engines in many countries during periods of oil shortage. A number of different gasification technologies such as the fixed-bed, fluid-bed, entrained-bed, and molten-bath exist. These use different gasification agents such as air, oxygen, or steam and produce a variety of low to medium thermal-value gases (29). For the purposes of the present discussion, the most relevant is the fixed-bed gasifier, using air for partial combustion of the fuel, and producing a low thermal-value gas. Two types of fixed-bed gasifiers can be distinguished.

Co-current, or down-draft, gasifiers produce a clean low-thermal-value gas (45-50 MJ/cu.m.) – sometimes called producer gas – that can be used directly in internal combustion engines. The efficiency of the process varies between 60-80 percent.

Present systems are limited to a maximum output of about 200 kW (mech.). They can use biomass fuels, provided these have a relatively low moisture content – less than 25 percent – and ash content of less than 6 percent. Among suitable fuels are woodchips and blocks, pelletised sawdust, maize cobs, coconut shells, palm-nut kernels, different types of fruit pits, and others. Rice husks and straws are inappropriate because of their high ash content.

Small-scale down-draft gasifiers are capable of being manufactured locally in many developing countries. Investment costs range from $250/kW (mech.) for imported models to $125/kW (mech.) for locally manufactured ones (30). A few manufacturers offer co-current gasifiers in the 15-200 kW range.

Counter-current, or up-draft, gasifiers produce low to medium thermal-value gas (55-60 MJ/cu.m.), which can only be used as an engine fuel after elaborate cleaning. Because of the cost of the cleaning equipment, systems are generally designed with an output above 100 kW (mech.). Counter-current gasifiers can use all types of biomass fuels (including rice husks) with a moisture content below 40-45 percent. Renewed interest in counter-current gasifiers has led to their commercialisation. Investment costs are around $300/kW (mech.).

Internal Combustion Engines

Ethanol can be blended up to 20 percent with petrol and used without any changes in present-day spark-ignition engines. For 100 percent ethanol-use engine modifications are required. These entail a modified carburettor, a heated inlet manifold, a corrosion-resistant tank and fuel delivery system, a modified ignition system, and a modified cylinder head. Special engines have been developed in order to use 100 percent ethanol as a fuel.

The main disadvantage of ethanol is its lower thermal value compared to petrol (22 MJ/kg vs 32 MJ/kg). This disadvantage is, however, partly offset by a higher thermal efficiency (up to 30 percent vs 22 percent).

In diesel engines, the fuel requirements are largely dictated by the fuel ignition quality. Up to 7 percent ethanol can be used as a diesel-fuel extender without engine modification. For larger amounts of ethanol, fuel-additives or complicated engine modifications are necessary.

The same remarks also hold for methanol, except that because of its lower thermal value the energy output per unit of volume is even lower than with ethanol.

Spark ignition engines can be run on producer gas. Because of the low thermal value of the gas, maximum power output is reduced by 30-50 percent, depending on engine characteristics and the average piston speeds. Diesel engines, without modification, can only be run on producer gas in a "dual fuel" mode, and about 20 percent of the normal diesel fuel is needed to ensure ignition. The reduction in the engine maximum power output is normally limited to about 15-20 percent (31).

Petrol engines can tolerate a wide range of methane-carbon dioxide ratios and thus can be run on biogas. The presence of carbon dioxide causes a reduction in the maximum engine power output, but this may be beneficial to engine life (32). Thermal efficiencies of up to 30 percent can be achieved.

Diesel engines can run on biogas in a "dual fuel" mode. It is technically possible to use 90 percent biogas - 10 percent diesel fuel mixtures, but to date it has only been feasible to achieve a 2:3 maximum mix over the long term (7).

Vegetable oils like sunflower oil, rape seed oil, and palm oil, can be used either pure or blended with diesel fuel in diesel engines. The maximum power output of engines running on 100 percent sunflower oil falls by up to 4 percent and the fuel consumption increases by 5-10 percent. Gumming of the vegetable oils, as well as coking of the fuel injectors present problems that could possibly be overcome by converting the oils into their ethylesters (33,34).

Conclusions

It is difficult to make general remarks about the application "slots" of the technologies described above. Among the factors that strongly influence the system

choice are the site specificity of system costs, technical maturity and local adaptability, scale of production
of equipment, fixed charge rates, and legal and
jurisdictional matters such as subsidies or other financial incentives. Nevertheless, in order to give some
insight into application possibilities the following
observations can be made.

- In the fractional kW range (up to 1 kW), draught animal power and windpower (especially for water-pumping)
seem to be the only reasonable choices. If price
reductions in photovoltaic cells come about, they will
probably make their first inroads in this power range.

- In the small kW range (1-3 kW), the only presently
viable alternative to the petrol engine is the biogas
engine. Small Stirling engines are barely commercial
and not yet economically competitive, but could soon
become so if liquid fuel costs continue to rise and
the economics of production in larger numbers reduce
investment costs. It is difficult to see gasifiers
making an inroad into this power range because of the
relatively high fixed costs compared to those of small
petrol engines.

- For applications in the higher power range (5 kW and
above), gasifier diesel engines appear suitable, with
exceptions only when diesel-fuel prices are extremely
low or the number of yearly operating hours is very
low. Application of co-current gasifiers is especially
attractive in the 5 - 200 kW mechanical range; counter-current gasifiers deserve attention for larger
power needs.

- Biomass-based fuels like ethanol, methanol, and vegetable oils present technically sound alternatives to
petrol and diesel fuel. However, the matter of the
Net Energy Ratio (with the exception of sugarcane) as
well as straight costs presently prevent their world-
wide use. Nevertheless, because of the lack of competitive alternatives, some market penetration in the
transport sector is foreseen, especially in countries
in a position to produce ethanol from sugarcane or
molasses.

REFERENCES

1. Revelle, R., 1976, "Energy Use in Rural India",
   Science, 192.
2. Ernst, E., 1977, Fuel Consumption among Rural
   Families in Upper Volta, Peace Corps, Ouagadougou,
   Upper Volta (West Africa).
3. Bailey, J., 1979, Firewood Use in a Sri Lankan

Village: A Preliminary Survey, University of Edinburgh, England.

4. Bangladesh Energy Study, 1976, UNDP project BDG/73/038/6/01/45.

5. Weatherly and Arnold quoted by Ad Hoc Expert Group on Rural Energy, UN Conference on New and Renewable Resources of Energy.

6. Earl, D.E., 1974, A Report on Charcoal, FAO, Rome.

7. Meta Systems, Inc., 1980, Potential of Fuelwood and Charcoal in the Energy Systems of Developing Countries, US Department of Agriculture, Forest Service, Contract No.53-319R-O-137.

8. SERI, 1980, Fuel from Farms, A Guide to Small-scale Ethanol Production.

9. Coombs, J., 1980, Ethanol - The Process and The Technology for the Production of Liquid Transport Fuels, Energy from Biomass Symposium, Session III/k2, Brighton, England.

10. Bernhardt, W., 1980, Fuels from Biomass - Future Automative Fuels, Energy from Biomass Symposium, Session VII/kl, Brighton, England.

11. Harris, G.S., 1980, Planning for Transport Fuels from Biomass: The New Zealand Experience, Energy from Biomass Symposium, Session VII/k3, Brighton, England.

12. Technical Panel on Biomass Energy, 1981, UN Conference on New and Renewable Sources of Energy.

13. Anon., 1979, The Brazilian Alcohol Programme, Int. Mol. Rep., Special Edition, F. O. Licht, Germany.

14. Trindade, S.C., 1980, Energy Crops - The Case of Brazil, Energy from Biomass Symposium, Session I/k2, Brighton, England.

15. Lettinga, G., 1980, Anaerobic Digestion for Energy Saving and Production, Energy from Biomass Symposium, Session III/k2, Brighton, England.

16. Bene, J.G., Beall, H.W., Marshall, H.B., 1979, Technologies for Converting Biomass into Energy: A Survey. International Development Research Center, Ottawa, Canada.

17. Parikh, J.K. and Parikh, K.S., 1977, "Mobilization and Impacts of Biogas Technologies", Energy, 2, pp.441-455.

18. Technical Panel on Solar Energy, 1981, UN Conference on New and Renewable Sources of Energy.

19. Makhijani, A. and Poole, A., 1975, Energy and Agriculture in the Third World, Ballinger Press, Cambridge, Mass.

20. NAS, 1974, More Water for Arid Lands, Washington D.C.

21. ITB, 1979, Prefeasibility Study on Gasification, Bandung, Indonesia.

22. SIETI, 1977, Impact of Electrification on Rural Industrial Development; A Study in Andhra Pradesh

and A Study in Kurnout District of Andhra Pradesh, Hyderabad, India.

23. US Government, 1975, Energy Alternatives: A Comparative Analysis.

24. FEA, 1976, Comparison of Energy Consumption.

25. FAO, 1976, Farm Implements for Arid Tropical Regions, Rome.

26. Odend'hal, S., 1972, "Energetics of Indian Cattle in Their Environment", Human Ecology, 1.

27. Technical Panel on Wind Energy, 1981, UN Conference on New and Renewable Sources of Energy.

28. World Bank, 1980, Energy in Developing Countries, Washington, D.C.

29. van Swaaij, W.P.M., 1980, Gasification - The Process and The Technology, Energy from Biomass Symposium, Session IV/k1, Brighton, England.

30. Stassen, H.E.M. and Zijp, T., 1980, The Gasification by Partial Combustion Project in Tanzania, Progress Report, Small Industries Development Organisation (Arusha, Tanzania) and University of Twente (Enschede, Netherlands).

31. Stassen, H.E.M., 1979, Utilisation of Producer Gas in Small Diesel Engines, in Beenackers, A. (Ed.), Chemical Technology for Developing Countries, International Conference of the Nigerian Society of Chemical Engineers, Zaria, Nigeria.

32. Picken, D.J. and Fox, M. F., 1980, Uses of Biogas for Electric and Mechanical Power Generation, Energy from Biomass Symposium, Session VII/14, Brighton, England.

33. Bruwer, J.J., 1980, Sunflower Oil as Diesel Fuel, Energy from Biomass Symposium, Session VII/14, Brighton, England.

34. Hall, D.O., Vegetable Oils for Diesel Engines, (to be published).

Country Case-Studies

3
Mexico

Oscar Guzman

Mountains cover 86 percent of the surface of Mexico. Two ranges cross the country from north to south and come together in the state of Oaxaca. Between these lies the Central Plateau which is, itself, further divided by another two mountain ranges. On the mountain slopes leading down to the Pacific and the Gulf of Mexico, the land is suitable for agriculture. In all only about 30 million ha, or 15 percent of the country, is arable.

The Tropic of Cancer divides the country almost exactly into two broad climatic zones, moderate in the north and tropical in the south. The great range in altitude, with less than one third of the territory under 500 m above sea level, produces a wide variety of climatic conditions, from equatorial heat in the woodlands of Tabasco to the cold of the mountains. About 60 percent of the country, however, is dry, and only 13 percent has abundant rainfall throughout the year. Thus the agricultural area is limited by climate as well as topography. The most favourable conditions are on the Gulf Coast where 96 percent of the land has a climate conducive to agriculture.

There are three varieties of forest vegetation. The desert type is found in most of the northern part of the country where there is very little rain. Tropical vegetation occurs in the southeast and consists mainly of ordinary hard and softwood, but also includes some highly profitable cedar and mahogany. The third type is the coniferous, mostly pine, hemlock, common juniper, white cedar, and, frequently, holm-oak. The total forest area is estimated at 32 million ha, of which 19 million are highly productive coniferous woods and 13 million are tropical.

DEMOGRAPHIC AND ECONOMIC CONTEXT (1950-1980)

Mexico's population growth of 3.4 percent is one of

the highest in the world. From 35 million in 1960, the
country's population had almost doubled in 1980 to 67
million (Table 1). Most of these people are concentrated in the centre of the country, where densities of
over 70 inhabitants/sq.km. were registered in 1970. The
urban population has increased particularly rapidly.
The proportion living in centres of over 2 500 inhabitants rose from 42.6 percent in 1950 to 58.7 percent in
1970. As a consequence, the population economically
active in the primary sector fell from 54 percent of the
total in 1960, to 40 percent, or just 5 million people
by 1970, while the secondary and tertiary sectors
reached 23 and 38 percent.

Table 1. Total population, growth rates, urban percentages, and average density, 1950-1980

Year	Total population	Average annual growth rate in preceding decade	Urban population	Average density inhab/ sq.km.
1950	25 791 017	–	42.6	13.2
1960	34 923 129	3.06	50.7	17.8
1970	48 225 238	3.28	58.7	24.6
1980	67 395 826	3.40	–	34.4

Note: Population centres with less than 2 500 inhabitants are classified as rural.
Source: 1950-1970: DGE, SIC Censo General de Poblacion,
Resumen General.
1980: SPP X Censo General de Poblacion y Vivi-
enda, Resultados Preliminares.

From the 1940s onwards, Mexico, like other Latin
American countries, based its hopes of economic development on the expansion and diversification of its own
industries through import substitution, a process which
had, in fact, begun earlier. In the first phase the
growth of manufacturing was based on light industries
such as food, textiles, and clothing. The Government
promoted this process by expanding the industrial and
agricultural infrastructure and by introducing protec-
tionist measures to facilitate the growth of these new
industries.
This relatively "easy" phase of import substitution
drew to a close by the end of the 1950s. In order to
continue industrialisation and achieve a self-sustaining

developmental process, it became necessary to expand
the production of consumer durables and, above all, to
create a national capacity to produce intermediate
equipment and inputs. The long period of growth then
beginning in the industrialised world created a favourable international climate. Capital was available in the
world market, and markedly mobile. The Mexican economy
entered a phase of so-called stabilised development with
increasing capital formation. The Government played a
significant role throughout, using monetary, fiscal,
financial, commercial, and external trade policies, and
creating public and semi-public enterprises to produce a
wide range of services to back up industry.

This prolonged growth with very low inflation
lasted until the 1970s. Gross Domestic Product (GDP)
rose at an annual rate of 6.3 percent from 1960 to 1976
- faster than population increase. Growth, however, was
unequally distributed between industry - which expanded
at 7.7 percent and rose from 29 to 36 percent of GDP -
and agriculture which only attained a 2.9 percent growth
and fell from 15 to 9 percent of GDP. This shift was
clearly reflected in the composition of exports. In
1960 these were dominated by agriculture which contributed 48 percent of the total, and the extractive industries with 21 percent; by 1975 manufacturing accounted
for 43 percent, and livestock and agricultural activities only 23 percent. The growth, moreover, was uneven
between regions as well as sectors. Conditions for
production deteriorated in certain parts of the agricultural sector and increased the migration to the cities.

Meanwhile, there had been a worsening external disequilibrium, to which the loss of dynamism in the agricultural export sector contributed an increasingly significant burden. These emerging internal limitations to
growth, together with the worsening international economic environment, led the country into economic and
financial crisis in 1976.

Then vast oil reserves were discovered. Their
rapid exploitation and export allowed Mexico to overcome
one of the most serious restrictions on its economic
development: access to foreign exchange. The economy
was gradually reactivated out of crisis, and by 1979-
1980 it had re-established a growth rate of 8 percent.
Hydrocarbons rose to 66 percent of total exports in just
a few years. Oil has thus become a fundamental factor
in Mexican development, making it possible to proceed
further with opening the way to the next stage of industrialisation and the establishment of an integrated
production system. In this, oil has come to play a role
similar to that of agriculture during the earlier phase
of import substitution - as the generator of the foreign
exchange to finance industrial development.

THE CRISIS IN AGRICULTURE

From the time that the industrial sector was made the centrepiece of national development in the 1940s, the other sectors were to a large extent subordinated to its requirements. In agriculture itself, the objective of policy was to accelerate growth in productivity. Rapid and prolonged modernisation began and continued until the mid-1970s. For nearly three decades agriculture provided an essential support to industry - through its exports, which generated finance for investment and economic growth; through its supply of low-priced foodstuffs and raw materials to the domestic market; and through its continuous provision of labour over and above the absorption capacity of the other sectors.

During the first stage of agricultural growth from 1945-1955, new lands were brought under cultivation and public investment in irrigation systems increased. As a result, the irrigated area was extended, especially in the northwest, and production grew by 5.8 percent per year. Growth was sustained at the high rate of 4.2 percent annually over the following decade (1955-1965). Technical improvements such as the use of fertilisers and better seeds were introduced during this period, raising the yield of both traditional export crops such as cotton, and crops for the internal market, particularly maize and beans. Thus, for twenty years Mexico's growth in agricultural production exceeded its population growth and the country's nutritional level improved progressively with the increasing availability of food.

Commercial agricultural enterprises* were made the agents of growth in the rural development strategy, and it was upon these that the majority of public sector stimuli, in the form of irrigation, improved techniques, inputs at subsidised prices, and support for experimental research and development, were focused. These enterprises responded and used their land to produce the most profitable crops whether for export or for the domestic market. The peasants ('ejidatarios' and 'comuneros'**), however, did not share in the benefits of this government support, nor in the Green Revolution. Yet they held half the land as a result of the earlier Land Reform, and produced the bulk of the country's staple foods. As the real prices for its products

---

* Commercial agricultural enterprises or commercial agriculture is the definition given to private production units that operate capitalistically and aim at maximum profit.

** The term 'ejidos' originated during the Land Reform

fell***, the income of the peasant sector gradually
decreased. Given the restriction in rural investment by
the commercial agricultural enterprises and the fact
that for the majority of rural producers the conditions
for technical improvement were non-existent, agriculture's 25 year growth, and its supportive function for
industry, eventually came to an end.

In 1965 there was a radical change in the trend in
agricultural production. Growth in the entire primary
sector in the period from 1965 to 1979 slowed to just 1
percent per year, and agriculture to only 0.8 percent,
although livestock production maintained a 4 percent
annual growth. In subsequent years the composition of
agricultural output showed a significant shift towards
livestock feed (sorghum, soy bean, alfalfa), to the
detriment of staple foods. This was because the commercial enterprises were finding enormous incentives to
produce livestock and agro-industrial inputs in response
to the growing demand of the middle class and the livestock requirements of the United States market.

By the beginning of the 1970s domestic grain production had fallen and the stagnation in agriculture,
compounded by fluctuations in the world grain market and
climatic problems in the country, resulted in a severe
reduction in the domestic food supply. From being a
substantial international exporter of agricultural products Mexico began, in 1970, to import large quantities
of food. This crisis appears to have been one of the
primary causes of the ensuing ruin of the previous model
of development.

According to the 1970 Census the 'ejidos', rural

---

and denotes a particular form of ownership and organisation. The land is collectively owned and integrated
around a farm nucleus but usually subdivided into parcels for personal use.

The communities are mostly made up of indigenous
groups on whom the Land Reform conferred ownership of
their land, but who did not accept its subdivision into
parcels and continued their traditional methods of communal exploitation.

In Mexico, the extension of private properties is
not allowed beyond a certain area; in this way accumu-
lation is restricted but increased production is not
impossible, because it can be carried out on land rented
to the farmer in parcels beyond the limits established
by legislation.

*** Guaranteed prices for maize fell in real terms
during the 1960s and were revised at the beginning of
the 1970s.

communities, and small private production units (of less
than 5 ha) accounted for 58 percent of the total cultivated area and 51 percent of the total value of agricultural production (Tables 2 and 3). Nearly 70 percent of
'ejidos' and rural community lands were less than 10 ha
in size, and most of these were without irrigation. The
'ejidos', the rural communities, and the small private
production units produced more than two-thirds of the
nation's maize, beans, sesame, and rice. The private
production units larger than 10 ha dominated the production of wheat, forage, sorghum, soy bean, alfalfa, vegetables, fruit, and the other export crops.

Table 2. Classification of lands in the 1970 Census

('000 ha)

	Total area in census	Worked area	Irrigated area
Country	139,868	23,138	3,583
Total private production	70,144	10,385	1,822
Over 5 ha	(69,263)	(9,675)	(1,734)
Under 5 ha	(880)	(710)	(88)
'Ejidos' and communites	69,724	12,752	1,760

Source: V Censos Agricola, Ganadero y Ejidal 1970,
Direccion General de Estadistica, Mexico 1975.

These larger private production units were the
principal employers of permanent labour. Families supplied 73 percent of the labour in the remainder of the
agricultural sector, but some supplementary labour from
outside the family was also employed on a temporary
basis in 24 percent of the 'ejidos' and rural communities, and 80 percent in the small private production
units.

Mechanisation and fertilisers had spread to all the
smaller production units by 1970. Their average expenditure on fertiliser, however, was only half that of the
larger private units. This again illustrates the dual
structure of the rural economy with its widespread
occurence of 'minifundios', or small plots of inherited
land, on which live the poor farmers forming the rural
subsistence sector.

Table 3. Distribution of land and type of production by
          size of exploitation

	% of cul-tivated area	% total agric. & forest prod. value	Distribution of value (%) between crops, cattle & forestry		
			Crop	Cattle	Forest
Country	100.0	100.0	100.0	100.0	100.0
Private production	44.9	57.2	48.7	58.2	73.3
Over 5 ha	(41.8)	(48.6)	(44.7)	(53.8)	(53.6)
Under 5 ha	(3.1)	(8.6)	(4.0)	(4.4)	(19.7)
'Ejidos' and communities	55.1	42.8	51.3	41.8	17.7

Source: based on V Censos Agricola - Ganadero y Ejidal,
          1970, Mexico, D.F., 1975.

CHARACTERISTICS OF SUBSISTENCE AGRICULTURE

The peasant economy can be viewed as one which is
essentially mercantile but which does not pass beyond
simple reproduction. This is because within it there is
no means of accumulating capital. The farmer scarcely
manages to replace his tools, much less improve or
augment them. Whenever there is any economic surplus it
is systematically transferred to the other sectors with
which the farmer has established trade. Secondly, labour is predominantly provided by the producer and his
family. This does not exclude the possibility of
employing workers outside the family to cover requirements during specific periods of production. Nor does
it exclude family members taking work outside the farm
to supplement family income. Finally, the volume of
produce sold is related to amount consumed by the family. The peasant farmer's products are not simply goods
for sale; they must first satisfy the consumption needs
of the family. These features, which define the subsistence economy, are particularly evident on farms
smaller than 5 ha in non-irrigated zones, where maize is
the main crop. They can also occur on larger units and
with other crop types, but it is on the maize 'minifundios' that the majority of subsistence farmers can be
found.

In 1970 only 13.9 percent of the 3.2 million farm families had more income than was necessary to subsist (Table 4)*.

Table 4. Distribution of income and land-ownership (1970)

| | Number of farms | | | |
Annual level of production (pesos)	Over 5 ha	Under 5 ha	'Ejidal' plots	% share in national agric. prod.
- 1 000 (sub-subsistence)	148 400	458 430	777 198	2.3
1 000 - 5 000 (subsistence)	89 626	121 562	895 910	13.0
5 000 - 25 000 (family)	96 313	26 780	259 259	15.0
25 000 - 100 000 (medium multifamily)	35 909	1 920	253 487	39.4
100 000 - (big multifamily)	18 144	231	-	30.3
Country total	388 392	608 932	2 185 854	100.0

Source: Centro de Investigaciones del Desarollo Rural; in Erasto Diaz, 1977, "Notas sobre el significado y el alcance de la economia campesina en Mexico", Comercio Exterior, Vol.27, no.12.

The other 86 percent had, at best, just enough to maintain the family at subsistence level. It was estimated that only 24.8 percent were able to support the family unit, while the rest - predominantly 'ejidal' and small private farms - showed greater poverty. In addition to those engaged in subsistence farming, a further 2.5 million agricultural workers have no land. The entire subsistence sector therefore contains approximately 4.5 million workers and their families (1).

*Farms producing 5 000 - 25 000 pesos yearly (US$1.00 = 22.89 pesos, 1980) are considered to have sufficient income to cover the family needs (Erasto Diaz, 1977).

Despite the variation in the characteristics of subsistence farms in different regions, particularly in their internal division of labour and their external relations, there is a vast zone of concentrated sub-sistence agriculture that can be considered one entity (2). This includes the states of Oaxaca, Puebla, Tlax-cala, Hidalgo, Queretaro, San Luis Potosi, the Mixteca and Costa Chica parts of Guerrero, eastern Morelos, southern central Mexico State, and northwestern Guana-juato. This zone has no irrigation. In a large part of it water is lacking and the land is overused. The population densities are the highest in the country. In 1970 this zone held 24 percent of Mexico's total popula-tion.

While it covers 13 percent of the country's total area and 19 percent of the cultivated land, it contains 43 percent of all agricultural production units. It is the most important 'minifundio' region in the country, with 72 percent of the 1 ha farms and 58 percent of the 1-5 ha size. In this zone, 80 percent of the units are smaller than 5 ha. Of the total labour employed in 1970, family labour supplied 73 percent and temporary workers 24 percent. The region provides work for 37 percent of the population economically active in agriculture and constitutes an important labour reserve for the other sectors of the economy.

In this zone are found nearly half of all farms categorised as sub-subsistence in 1970 - those whose sales bring less than 1 000 pesos or $100 yearly. The producers in this area, almost half of the country's total, account for only 17 percent of all agricultural capital. Production techniques reflect their lack of resources and their very limited capacity for improving their usage of land. In 1970 only 8.4 percent of the zone and 5 percent of the farms with less than 5 ha used agricultural machinery. Investments and salaries per worked hectare were considerably lower than the national average.

This description reveals the limited capacity of subsistence producers to break out of the apparent equi-librium of the peasant economy and accumulate a surplus, however small. In fact, subsistence agriculture has undergone a distinct deterioration over the last de-cades, as a consequence of some of the characteristics the model of development followed since the 1940s. Not only were capital, technology and human resources trans-ferred selectively to industry and commercial agricul-ture, but other factors also worked against the peasant economy. Price limits and guarantees favoured the com-mercial agricultural enterprises; marketing systems were inadequate; conditions of credit were extremely tough; and there were deficiencies in land distribution policies. There was also restricted access to the tech-

52

nological advances made in agricultural practice since
these were based on a production system different from
that of the peasant economy (3).

The inadequacy of income from the traded portion of
their harvest led peasants to take on extra work outside
the farm. Family members became temporarily employed in
industry, in agricultural enterprises, or in services in
the region, in more distant places, and even abroad. It
is thought an estimated 10-20 percent of the population
economically active in agriculture have obtained additional income from migrant farm work in the United
States (4). Thus the peasant economy reproduces and
sustains a labour force that benefits other sectors
which need it only temporarily. This is being worsened
by the increasing use of technology in the agricultural
enterprises, which diminishes their capacity to absorb
the rural labour force.

The migration of male workers for long periods -
sometimes for 10 months of the year - significantly
affects labour roles and family relations. In the peasant family it is common for the men and boys to tend
crops and undertake temporary jobs. Women are in charge
of domestic activity, including the supply of water and
firewood, in which children assist. When the man mi-
grates for work, the woman takes over the entire management of the farm, replacing the man in all tasks and in
the external relations necessary to maintain production.
The remaining male children work with the mother, while
the daughters take over her previous tasks. All family
decisions are made by the farmer's wife until he returns
and resumes his role as head of the family. Alterna-
tively, the farmland may be rented, leaving the women in
charge only of domestic work.

The importance of men and women in decision-making
can vary considerably from one community to another,
depending on social and cultural patterns which lack
strict economic rationality. The complexity and variety
of interpersonal relations within and between communities makes it impossible to generalise about family
roles. Non-economic factors are also reflected in the
cooperation and solidarity between community members
which lead them to share risks and chores beyond blood
relations.

In view of the fact that agricultural development
had ceased, and maize was having to be imported, the
Government began to look for ways to restore the position of agriculture in the 1970s. Throughout the decade
it revised guarantee prices, subsidised investment,
increased public investment, regulated systems of commercialisation, and promoted collective 'ejidos'.

The set of policies recently formulated as the
Mexican Food System (SAM) reinforces this orientation of
agricultural policy. (5). The goal of SAM is to achieve

self-sufficiency in food production. A strong element
of government participation is proposed to support SAM's
alliance with peasant organisations, and to subsidise
producers by means of investments to increase the
productivity of land. The way has also been opened for
legalising association between 'ejidatarios' and private
producers for joint land use. This offers not only the
possibility of a quantitative increase in production,
but also some measure of security in the face of the
peasants' need to make capital bring a rapid return.
The future of the peasant economy is thus closely tied,
as it was in the past, to the current agricultural
development strategy.

ENERGY IN AGRICULTURAL PRODUCTION

Mexico has ample energy resources which enable it
to maintain high rates of economic growth and assure its
energy supply for the immediate future. Energy development received a strong stimulus in the 1970s, particularly since 1976, with the verification of the country's
large hydrocarbon resources. In 1976, proven reserves
of oil and natural gas were 10 300 mboe; by 1980, these
had been revised upwards by a factor of six to 60 000
mboe, putting Mexico fifth in world oil reserves. Other
resources are also considered important: solar; geothermal; and uranium, with proven reserves of 10 000
metric tonnes in 1980, sufficient to begin the development and installation of nuclear power stations.

In 1980 hydrocarbons supplied 90 percent of primary
energy demand, hydroelectricity 5 percent, coal 4 percent, and geothermal less than 1 percent. Of total
primary energy in 1979 (79 million toe), 34.5 percent
was consumed within the energy sector, 24.9 percent in
manufacturing industry, 23.7 percent in transportation,
and only 0.7 percent in agriculture. To understand this
last figure, it is necessary to take a closer look at
productive and domestic energy consumption in the rural
areas.

Most studies of energy demand in the agricultural
sector deal solely with commercial energy use in production (6), that is, with oil and electricity, leaving
aside all "non-commercial" forms such as fuelwood and
vegetable wastes.

Between 1970 and 1978 the Mexican economy increased
its energy consumption by 7 percent per year. Energy in
agriculture grew at only 3.8 percent annually, so that
its low share in national consumption was even further
reduced. Although electricity consumption showed a
better performance, growing rapidly and reaching 5.3
percent of total electricity use in 1978, the demand for
oil products fell in absolute terms, in parallel with
the economic performance of agriculture over that period

54

(Table 5). Electricity is particularly used to power
water pumps in irrigated areas, while diesel and kerosene are used for tractors and other agricultural machinery.

Table 5. Estimated energy consumption by the agricultural sector and its share in national consumption

	Petro-leum products ('000 toe)	% of nat'l con-sump'n	Elec-tricity ('000 toe)	% of nat'l con-sump'n	Non-commer-cial energy ('000 toe) (1)	Total con-sump'n ('000 toe) (2)	% of nat'l total
1970	246	1.3	116	5.1	2 280	2 642	6.4
1973	239	0.9	150	5.0	2 140	2 529	5.1
1975	193	0.7	194	5.5	2 043	2 430	4.4
1976	184	0.6	210	5.6	2 043	2 437	4.2
1978*	233	0.5	253	5.3	n.a.	n.a.	-

Notes: *preliminary data
(1) The OECD energy balance attributes this
consumption to the agricultural, commercial,
public service, and residential sectors.
(2) The consumption of non-commercial energy is
assumed to correspond to the rural areas. This
total is obtained from the sum of total
commercial energy and non-commercial energy in
the agricultural sector.
Source: Secretaria de Patrimonio y Fomento Industrial;
-Estudios sobre programacion industrial 2. El
sector de energeticos; estadisticas basicas y
balances de energia, 1970-1977, Mexico 1978.
-Boletin Energetico, 1979, Vol.3 no.8.
-OCDE, 1978 Statistiques et Bilans Energetiques.

Statistics give details of the energy used in irrigation, tractors, mowing and threshing machines. These
all characterise the more advanced sectors of agriculture, but are almost completely absent in peasant production. In this, plowing is carried out with a wooden
plow drawn by an animal or by the peasant himself, on
poor, non-irrigated and often steeply sloping land.
Although the use of animals has decreased over the last
two decades, they can still be found even on farms with

modernised techniques; Table 6 gives an energy profile of one such farm.

Table 6. Annual energy consumption on the 'Ejido de Arango' (northern Mexico)

	Delivered energy		Useful energy	
	toe	%	toe	%
DOMESTIC CONSUMPTION				
Non-commercial energy (a)	150	84	7.5	44
Commercial energy (b)	29.2	16	9.6	56
Sub-total	179.2	100	17.1	100
Consumption per person (kgoe)	426		40	
CONSUMPTION FOR PRODUCTION				
Direct energy (c)	275	64	19	18
Indirect energy (d)	82.5	19	82.5	78
Animal energy (e)	75	17	3.8	4
Sub-total	432.5	100	105.3	100
Total	611.5		122.4	
Consumption per ha (kgoe)	790		19	

Notes: (a) Firewood and vegetable wastes.
(b) Gas, kerosene (70% and 30% respectively) and electricity. Kerosene is used for lighting.
(c) Petroleum products for agricultural machinery, and electricity for irrigation pumps.
(d) Corresponds to fertilisers.
(e) 20% of the area is worked by animals.
Characteristics of the 'ejido':
- population: 420 people;
- work area: 550 ha, of which 380 irrigated;
- crops according to planted area: wheat (40%) cotton (35%), corn (20%), bean (5%).
Source: Makhijani, A. and Poole, A., 1975, Energy and Agriculture in the Third World, Report of the Energy Policy Project of the Ford Foundation, pp.49-51.

The predominance of human and animal energy in subsistence farming is reflected in the breakdown of energy required to produce subsistence crops. The human and animal energy used in cultivating maize, beans, and sesame in 1975 was 22 percent, 48 percent, and 65 percent, respectively (7). Although these crops exceeded wheat, sorghum, and alfalfa, which are the typical crops of the agricultural enterprises, by an average of 40 percent in their consumption of muscular energy, the reverse is true when only the energy in fertilisers and machinery fuel is considered*. The substitution of muscular energy by electricity and fuel through the introduction of agricultural machinery is, however, not within the economic means of the subsistence sector and often technically difficult, given the topography of the areas in which subsistence farming is found.

DOMESTIC ENERGY CONSUMPTION

When the non-commercial fuels used in domestic activity are added to the energy used in agricultural production, the rural zones can be seen to account for a larger proportion of total energy demand in Mexico: rural energy demand becomes 4-5 percent of the national total instead of the previous 0.7 percent (Table 5). This estimate does not account for electricity, oil, or gas used domestically, since existing statistics do not distinguish between urban and rural households.

During the 1960s energy in the domestic sector grew faster than in industry and transport, and changed its composition. The number of people using liquefied gas or electricity rose rapidly but, while the number of woodfuel users remained almost constant, their share of the total domestic energy demand fell from 64.8 percent to 43.1 percent (Table 7). In 1970, domestic consumption of commercial energy was dominated by liquefied gas (50 percent) and kerosene (34 percent). These percentages had varied slightly by 1977 because of an increased use of natural gas and electricity, and slower rate of growth in kerosene.

---

*It is important to note that mechanisation is not always possible and depends on the kind of crops. The estimates presented refer to Mexican agriculture as a whole and not to subsistence agriculture in particular; there is no intention of proposing a definitive description of the energy characteristics in this sector.

Table 7. Breakdown of domestic energy consumption by
fuel and number of users, 1960 and 1970

Fuel	1960 inhabitants ('000)	%	1970 inhabitants ('000)	%
Wood or charcoal	22 617	64.8	21 379	43.1
Kerosene*	6 180	17.7	5 669	11.4
Liquefied gas or electricity	6 126	17.5	21 308	43.0
Natural gas	-	-	1 261	2.5
Total	34 923	100.0	49 617	100.0

Note: *This is locally referred to as 'petroleo diafano'.

Source: Mexico, Secretaria de Industria y Comercio, VIII and IX Censos de Poblacion, 1960 and 1970 Mexico, D.F.

The absolute amounts of energy consumed in Mexico's rural sector are impossible to ascertain accurately. An estimate made for the year 1975 was that total rural consumption amounted to 5.4 million toe. This was about 10 percent of the total national consumption estimated in the OECD energy balance for the same year. Table 8 is based on the above estimate and gives an approximate distribution of fuel use in three different zones of the country. It can be seen that fuelwood, with animal and vegetable wastes, supplied around 80 percent of the total, while charcoal supplied 6-7 percent.

Table 9 gives a considerably more detailed breakdown of energy consumption per head, by income group and end-use for each of the above three zones. In the lowest income groups, which comprise 64 percent of the rural population (8), over 80 percent of the fuel is used for cooking, while only in the coldest region of Zone 1 was a small proportion (4 percent) used for warmth and water heating. It can be seen that in the higher income groups the proportion used for cooking falls and that used for other heating purposes rises correspondingly. It has, however, been shown that in the lowest income group cooking takes place over an open fire, using three or more stones. This gives an efficiency of energy use of only about 5 percent (9).

58

Table 8. Energy consumption by source in the rural
          domestic sector, 1975

(%)

	Fuelwood, animal & vegetable waste	Conventional oil-based fuels	Electricity	Charcoal	Total
Zone 1	77.2	14.8	1.7	6.3	100
Zone 2	79.1	14.0	–	6.9	100
Zone 3	87.2	6.0	0.8	6.0	100

Note: The three zones include the following states:
         Zone 1: Baja California, Sonora, Chihuahua,
         Coahuila, Nuevo Leon, Tamaulipas, Durango,
         Zacatecas, San Luis Potosi, Aguascalientes,
         Guanajuato, Queretaro, Hidalgo, Tlaxcala, Pue-
         bla, Mexico, and Morelos. Zone 2: Sinaloa,
         Nayarit, Jalisco, Colima, Michoacan, Guerrero,
         Oaxaca, Chiapas y Yucatan. Zone 3: Veracruz,
         Tabasco, Campeche y Quintana Roo.
              The division between these three zones is
         based on weather, topography, and vegetation as
         well as socio-economic criteria, trying to
         group them according to similarities in energy
         use.
              In the energy consumption estimate, human
         energy used in fuelwood and vegetable wastes
         collection is included.
Source: Instituto de Economia Energetica, 1979, prepa-
         ratory for Estudio sobre los requerimientos
         futuros de fuentes no convencionales de energia
         en America Latina, Bariloche, Argentina, Table
         V-14.

Even on farms above the level of subsistence, wood
and vegetable residues are an important source of domestic fuel. This was seen, for example, in the case of
the 'Ejido de Arango', in Table 6, where these sources
provide 84 percent of the primary energy used for domestic purposes.

A recent study in the northeast of Pueblo revealed
that domestic use accounted for 93.6 percent of the wood
consumed in the area (10). This area has similar
characteristics to other parts of the region of concentrated subsistence agriculture (2) and may be considered
representative of the whole of it.

Table 9. Energy consumption in the rural domestic sector according to end use, income level and
zone, 1975

(%)

Income level	Zone 1			Zone 2			Zone 3		
	Low	Med	High	Low	Med	High	Low	Med	High
Cooking	82.6	58.5	50.3	85.4	79.7	57.6	83.3	82.6	48.9
Water htg	2.0	9.1	34.0	-	10.5	36.7	-	4.3	42.2
Heating	2.2	24.0	15.5	-	0.5	5.5	-	3.4	8.7
Other heat	4.3	8.4	0.2	9.1	9.3	0.2	7.0	9.7	0.2
Fuel stock	8.9	-	-	5.5	-	-	9.7	-	-
Total (kgoe/ person)	269	237	193	212	184	138	221	176	192

Source: Derived from IDEE internal documentation.

The study showed that per capita consumption of
fuelwood and charcoal was an average of 548 kgoe per
year, which is 3.6 times the average urban consumption.
It also showed that direct wood use was much greater
than the use of charcoal. In this area, wood is also
employed as the fuel for small industries such as pot-
teries, bakeries, lime kilns, and brick-making, but this
use is very small in comparison with domestic consumption, and amounted to only 4.6 percent of the total.
The remaining 1.8 percent was used in small wood industries.

An average of the annual domestic fuelwood consumption in both rural and urban areas is 392 kgoe, or
nearly 3 kg of fuelwood per person per day. This is
close to consumption levels in Peru, Nicaragua, and
Costa Rica and seems to indicate a significant regional
similarity.

In the northeast of Pueblo, forest resources are
rapidly diminishing as a result of tree-cutting and a
lack of replanting. It is estimated that the natural
rate of replenishment replaces only 17 percent of the
wood used annually. As a result, peasants are forced to
go from 2-8 km to collect firewood. This task is carried
out usually by the women, and sometimes the children,

but as distances increase it is transferred to the men.

Although the levels of firewood and charcoal
consumption found in Pueblo cannot be applied to the
rest of the country because of climatic, economic, and
social differences, they can be regarded as typical of
subsistence farming. If the consumption of the whole
region of concentrated subsistence farming (2) is taken
as being the same as in Pueblo (548 kgoe per head per
year), then the total annual domestic energy consumption
of the region is equivalent to about 70 000 barrels of
oil per day. If the quantity is reduced to an equivalent 7 000 barrels per day of useful energy, it would
require a mere 0.25 percent of Mexico's present oil
production of 2.75 million barrels per day to replace
it.

For the whole country, there are several different
estimates of fuelwood consumption. According to government statistics (11), the consumption of wood for fuel
accounted for 15.9 percent of total wood consumption in
the country in 1970 and amounted to 253 000 toe, but by
1979 this had dropped to 6.2 percent and amounted to 151
000 toe. These figures, however, appear to leave out
rural domestic consumption. Other estimates place woodfuel consumption at about 9 million cu.m. or 2.5 million
toe; this is close to the OECD figure shown in Table 5.
Yet higher estimates of 4.16 million toe have been made
by the IDEE research, with consumption mainly concentrated in Zone 1. Even if this high figure is considered as the true fuelwood consumption in the Mexican
rural sector it would require only 15 000 barrels of oil
per day to replace it. This is only 0.5 percent of the
country's present production. Nevertheless, these figures may be underestimates, given the fact that for a
great proportion of the rural population their actual
consumption of energy is less than their needs.

According to Table 8, commercial petroleum-derived
fuels accounted for less than 15 percent of rural domestic consumption. Of these, kerosene is probably the
most important since its use has been widespread for
several decades, and its price has consistently been
lower than that of liquefied gas, which is the only fuel
with a distribution system which would allow it to
compete. The availability of kerosene to the subsistence sector is, however, limited not just by the low
incomes there, but because part of the supply has been
channelled to non-domestic uses, especially industry,
precisely because it has been subsidised.

Mexico's widely scattered rural population makes
the supply of energy, like other goods, difficult. The
existence of a large number of dispersed villages, each
with a small number of people, has acted as a constraint
on rural electrification. Nevertheless, the Federal
Government has maintained a policy of expanding the

rural electricity supply, and a rapid growth in consumption has occurred. During the period 1960-1974, the growth rate of consumption by the lowest income rural families was 11.3 percent per year, compared with 9.9 percent per year for the corresponding urban groups.

There is, nevertheless, a vast sector of the rural population without access to electricity. In 1978, it was estimated that 32 percent of farm dwellers - nearly 10 million people - were outside the reach of the grid. These, it should be noted, lived in small villages, which had less than 500 inhabitants, and were irregularly dispersed across the country. The extent of rural electrification in the various states of Mexico, in fact, is related to the degree of concentration of sites and the number of inhabitants in each. It is not possible to say exactly what proportion of the subsistence sector has access to electricity, nor how much it consumes. Isolation and subsistence are, however, closely linked and it is reasonable to assume that this applies to a majority of the 10 million people without electricity.

ELEMENTS OF ENERGY POLICY

The main areas in which energy policies have addressed the rural areas are in electrification and fuel-pricing. One of the objectives of recent programmes has been the extension of energy supplies to the isolated and marginalised parts of the country. Another aspect of policy has been the subsidising of kerosene for domestic use. But other than these, Mexico has not had any official policy aimed at interpreting and resolving the energy problems of the rural areas, much less those of the subsistence sector.

In 1980, the Secretaria de Patrimonio y Fomento Industrial introduced an Energy Programme, the first of its kind in Mexico. This defines long-range energy policies which are in accordance with the National Development Plan, and the National Industrial Development Plan. The Energy Programme covers the use of energy in the rural areas and emphasises the use of electricity, and the need to ensure that its supply is both reliable and economic. The objectives are to increase agricultural production by expanding the capacity to pump water for irrigation, and to encourage the development of small commerce and industry; a further aim is to expand the electricity service to communities which have not yet had access to it (12). In order to achieve these goals it is proposed to rationalise the rural electrification programmes and give them major support while coordinating them with the programmes of the Mexican Food System (SAM).

Since the expansion of energy distribution systems

to isolated communities would involve high costs and technical inefficiency, the present policy is that these programmes should concentrate on decentralised supply systems. These are to be based on the use of small-scale technology which is appropriate to the rural environment and takes into account the degree of population dispersal. Priority is therefore being given to gasoline and small hydroelectric generators, which have hardly been used up to now in Mexico. The Programme also expresses interest in using solar energy in the rural areas to heat water for domestic or commercial applications, and to dry agricultural produce. The contribution of solar energy to the country's total energy supply in both the short and medium term is, however, expected to be marginal.

The Energy Programme asserts that it will protect the weakest sectors by means of specific subsidies. Its orientation, however, remains within the boundaries of existing energy policy. Vegetable fuel, the central feature of rural energy use, is not considered. The underlying idea is that in a country with such abundant energy resources, petroleum products and electricity must be made to penetrate the rural areas. The small proportion of national oil production that would be needed to replace the consumption of vegetable fuels would tend to support this view. Nevertheless it must be pointed out that even after several decades of self-sufficiency in oil, with abundant supplies and low prices, other forms of energy are still the predominant fuels among the peasantry, and these should not be ignored in the formation of an energy strategy.

Equally, the Programme makes no provision for ensuring energy supply to rural areas or for replenishing vegetable fuels. Neither does it specify the steps by which non-conventional energy sources will be developed. The gesture it makes to acknowledge them therefore runs the risk of being unfounded in reality and doing damage to the intended beneficiaries.

In accordance with the criteria on which it was based, the implementation of the Energy Programme should be coordinated with that of the Mexican Food System (SAM) with which it interacts. The energy requirements of the subsistence sector were, however, not taken into account in formulating the SAM, despite the fact that it had been given a central role in reactivating the production of basic grains*. In the technological package proposed by the SAM, fertilisers are the foremost

---

* It should, however, be pointed out that, recently, the SAM has, in fact, affirmed the need to deal with energy aspects of agricultural production.

means for increasing agricultural output. The route proposed for escaping agricultural stagnation is, it should be noted, an energy intensive one; progressive mechanisation and the improvement of farm equipment will presumably also accompany the increase in fertiliser use, but these aspects are left unspecified in the plan.

Despite the absence of an official rural energy policy, various technical groups have been developing non-conventional energy sources for rural application in different parts of the country. Progress in research, technology, and diffusion has mainly been in anaerobic fermentation and certain applications of solar energy (13).

Mexico now has the capability for a massive diffusion of biogas digesters producing 11 cu.m. of gas per day, and the ability to build larger units to produce both gas and fertiliser. This could become an important source of fertiliser for augmenting peasant agricultural productivity. The country also possesses the scientific, technological, and economic capability to produce solar water heaters, grain and fish driers, water distillers, and stoves. The potential significance of solar energy can be seen in the role it might play in reducing the losses of grain from lack of drying methods, which are currently estimated to be about 30 percent.

Experiments to promote biogas and solar energy have, however, not always been successful. In some cases difficulties have stemmed from the attempt to introduce a technology that is not yet under full control; in other instances, the units proved technically inadequate for the purpose intended. In some places these difficulties have been aggravated by a lack of acceptance of a new energy source on the part of the local population. The reasons for rejection are many and frequently reside in the method of introduction. Lack of interest in the alternative offered, the degree of participation in the implementation of the project, and the knowledge obtainable from it appear to play an important role in determining whether a new technology will be incorporated into local habits of production and life-style (14). Diffusion has also been hindered by a shortage of financial and human resources and by the lack of integration and coordination between the different groups working in this field.

It is possible that the existence of a centralised energy supply system, and the preferential allocation of resources to hydrocarbon and nuclear energy development, will prevent the emergence of options for alleviating rural energy problems. This remains to be seen. A strategy to satisfy the full energy needs of the peasant sector - and its most impoverished portion in particular - will, however, have to begin with a detailed picture

64

of the existing energy position in the different regions
of the country. It will have to be based upon an understanding of the diversity of forms in which energy is
used: commercial, non-commercial, conventional, or new.
Its proposals must take into account the customs and the
kinds of energy used by peasants, and evolve a plan to
ensure a continuous supply of these fuels at prices that
will allow the entire rural population access to energy
consumption. Such a goal will be difficult to achieve
unless the energy policy is part of a wider strategy of
agricultural development that gives the farmer the
opportunity to retain for himself the surplus of his
production.

REFERENCES

1.   Bartra, A., 1979, "El Panorama Agrario en los 70",
     Investigacion Economica, Vol.38, no.150, octubre-
     diciembre, Notas sobre la cuestion campesina (Mexico
     1920-1970), Mexico.
2.   Burgos, G.S., 1980, La Region Fundamental de Econo-
     mia Campesina, Mexico.
3.   Consejo Nacional de Ciencia y Tecnologia, 1976,
     Lineamientos para el Desarollo de un Plan Nacional
     de Alimentacion y Nutricion, Mexico.
4.   Warman, A., 1975, "El Neolatifundio Mexicano: Expan-
     sision y Crisis de una Forma de Dominio", Comercio
     Exterior, Vol.25, no.12.
5.   Oficina de Asesores del Presidente, marzo 1980,
     Sistema Alimentario Mexicano.
6.   Such is the case in the Energy Balances of the
     Energy Commission, and the study by the Mexican
     Petroleum Industry, 1975 Energeticos Demanda Sec-
     torial, Analisis y Perspectivas, Mexico.
7.   Internal Document, Instituto de Economia Energetica
     (IDEE), 1979, Bariloche, Argentina.
8.   Income groups were categorised as follows: Low   -
     that proportion of the total population which re-
     ceived 25 percent of the national income at the
     lowest levels; Medium - the proportion receiving 50
     percent of the income; High - the proportion re-
     ceiving 25 percent of the income at the highest
     levels. UNDP, OLADE, 1979, Future Requirements of
     Non-conventional Energy Sources in Latin America
     (synthesis of a UNDP study) p.50.
9.   Instituto Nactional de Nutricion, 1976, Encuestas
     Nutricionales en Mexico, Vol.II, Mexico; Instituto
     Nacional Indigenista, Informe Personal.
10. Internal document, Subsecretaria Forestal y de la
     Fauna, 1980.
11. IV Informe de Gobierno, Sector Agropecuario, p.64.
12. Secretaria de Patrimonio y Fomento Industrial; Co-
     mision de Energeticos, Programa de Energia. Metas a

1990 y proyecciones al 2000.

13. For a more detailed interpretation of the actual development of the non-conventional sources of energy, see _La Energia Solar en Mexico, Situacion Actual y Perspectivas_, 1980, Alfonso Castellanos y Margarita Escobedo, Centro de Ecodesarrollo, Mexico.

14. These conclusions are derived from the experience of private and public institutions, amongst which the Programa de Ecodesarrollo Xochicalli can be singled out in its development and application of biogas digesters and waste-processing systems, to achieve better and more complete use of the resources available in rural zones.

4
Guatemala

Roberto Caceres

The Republic of Guatemala is the most northerly
country of Central America. It is also the largest, and
has an area of 106 360 sq.km. It is bounded by Mexico,
Honduras, and El Salvador. Two branches of the Andes
mountains cross the country; their different altitudes
produce a wide variety of climatic conditions, and three
broad ecological zones can be distinguished.

The tropical strip includes both moist, dry, and
very dry tropical forests. It covers 62 000 sq.km. or
about 57 percent of the country's total area and rises
to about 300 m above sea level on the Pacific coast and
500 m on the Atlantic. The average temperature exceeds
24 C. The moist tropical forests of the Izabal region
on the Atlantic coast, and the Peten, in the north, have
considerable economic potential. Much of the timber in
the dry forests has, however, already been cut for
export.

The sub-tropical strip covers one quarter of the
country. It extends from the low tropical land on both
coasts, up along the mountain slopes to 1 500 m altitude
on the southern side and slightly less on the northern,
and it includes both dry and rainy areas. Few forests
remain, although dense pine woods can be seen where
slash-and-burn cultivation has not yet been introduced.
The intensity of past agricultural use has impoverished
the soil, but the more humid forest areas still produce
most of the coffee which is the country's most important
export crop.

The mountainous tropical strip includes 20 200
sq.km. of the Guatemalan High Plateau (Altiplano). This
is the most densely populated area of the country. The
land is very productive and the climate favourable. The
soil is mostly of volcanic origin, with a satisfactory
balance of carbon and nitrogen up to the 1970s. During
the last three decades the pressure of population growth
has made land increasingly scarce. Settlements have
been forced onto steep slopes, and erosion is

67

increasing. Some coniferous and fruit trees are found in this region, in small woodlots used by communities of smallholder subsistence farmers. A further small zone of 800 sq.km. rises to an altitude of 3 000 - 4 000 m. This is the cold region of Guatemala with average annual temperatures of less than 17 C.

The dry season extends from November to May and the lowest temperatures occur in January. The highest temperatures, especially in the low lands, are registered just before the rainy season, which extends from May to November.

Between 1950 and 1964, the population grew from 2.8 to 4.3 million people. By 1979 it had reached 6.8 million, of which 4.3 million, or 64 percent, were rural. There, the annual growth rate was 2.8 percent, and the density was 64 inhabitants per sq.km. Table 1 gives an estimated distribution of rural and urban population for the main regional divisions of the country.

Table 1. Estimated population distribution for 1979

('000)

	Main urban centres	Other urban centres	Rural	Total
Western High Plateau	91	329	1 776	2 196
Central High Plateau	1 175	246	432	1 852
Southern Low Lands	100	190	744	1 034
Eastern Low Lands	52	201	881	1 132
Verapaz - El Peten	-	98	498	597
Total	1 418	1 064	4 331	6 811

Note: This distribution is based on that given in the 1973 census when the total population was 5 161 000. The 1979 total population is from Bank of Guatemala statistics.

From 1950 to 1964 the area of land under cultivation increased at 3.4 percent per year, from 1 477 000 ha (including fallow land) to 2 190 532 ha, by encroaching on natural grazing lands and forests. The censuses of 1950 and 1964 show that land occupied by forests and non-agricultural uses diminished from 44.6 percent to 22.8 percent. By 1964, it was already evident that reserves of arable land were diminishing and this was forcing an increasing intensity of land-use. However, it is estimated that some 66 percent of the national territory, or about 7 million ha, is land with agricultural potential. Extending the agricultural frontier to realise this potential on a large scale could be damaging to the agro-forest balance in the long-term.

ECONOMY

In 1979 the GDP of Guatemala was 6 886 million Quetzales*, the highest in Central America. The industrial sector, with an output of Q488.4 million was also the largest in Central America. In the previous ten years its GDP grew fivefold, and brought per capita income to Q888 in 1979.

The economy of the country is divided regionally. The Central Plateau, where the capital city is located, has the highest urban and industrial concentration. The Western High Plateau, with 41 percent of the population, is where the greatest concentration of subsistence agriculture is found. This, and the East, with 20 percent of the population, are the two most densely populated regions. The East contains the majority of the country's sharecroppers, and there is a zone of economic potential on the Atlantic coast. These two regions of subsistence farming are the basis for the peasant agricultural sector of the economy, and produce the staple food crops of beans, maize, and rice.

The South Coast and, to a lesser extent, the Atlantic coast are where the large farms which produce the agro-export commodities are located. Verapaz is the oil-producing area and here large infrastructural projects are under way related both to oil and the expansion of the agricultural frontier. El Peten is a huge sparsely inhabited zone to the north of the country with large forests, and oil reserves.

Agriculture is the most important sector of the economy and produces over 25 percent of the GDP. It is also a major source of export earnings. In 1976, the principal export crops were coffee (Q243 million), sugar (Q110 million), cotton (Q84 million), bananas (Q41 million), meat (Q21 million), and processed agricultural products (Q13 million).

In recent years the minerals sector has become important and nickel has begun to be developed for export. Oil production has reached 8 thousand barrels per day, and this has justified the construction of a

*Q1.00 = US$1.00 (1980)

pipeline to the Caribbean port of Puerto Barrios.

The formation of the Central American Common Market (CACM) gave rise to a rapid increase in the manufacturing sector, particularly in food processing, clothing, footwear, textiles, chemical products, and non-metal minerals. Many of these industries are affiliated with multinational enterprises. Two-thirds of the labour force are, however, employed in small enterprises operating at low levels of productivity.

While the CACM has allowed the manufacturing sector to grow and diversify its exports, the recent difficulties within the CACM over tariffs and political questions have slowed the growth of exports. Tourism, which has been a growing source of foreign exchange, also decreased in the last year. If these trends continue the balance of payments could deteriorate seriously over the coming years. Guatemala, in fact, still relies heavily on its agro-exports, especially coffee, which provides 33 percent of its export earnings.

In 1979, 11.4 million barrels of oil were imported, 50 percent crude, and 50 percent in products, at a total cost of Q250 million. This was slightly more than the value of coffee exports, at high prices. It is estimated that oil imports in 1982 will cost Q700 million.

The rapid rises in oil prices have affected cost structures, the balance of payments, and GDP growth rates. The foreign exchange flows needed to cover the imports of fuels and lubricants have been higher than those projected in the 1974 Operative Plan of the Ministry of Planning.

The inflationary impact on household budgets has been estimated to be 3.4 percent, in addition to the current rate of inflation of 11 percent. Within the productive sector, the industries most affected have been transport, whose costs have risen by 2.6 percent, and electricity, where they rose 6 percent. The nickel and cement industries were also affected. The impact on small industries and subsistence agriculture was more severe, with increases of 8 percent on top of those arising from the current inflation.

Between 1973 and 1979, however, Guatemala's external trade position improved considerably, particularly because of the high prices for coffee, sugar, and cardamom during that time. The rise in oil prices had a moderate adverse effect, but sufficient reserves of foreign exchange remained to maintain the prospect of external solvency. In the last two years, heavy capital drains, because of high external interest rates and the political events of the region, have somewhat modified this outlook.

Nevertheless, the prospects for economic growth, in spite of the above difficulties, remain favourable. The country's low foreign debt, its important agricultural potential, the increase in indigenous energy production, and the high level of investment make an annual economic growth rate of 6.7 percent not inconceivable over the next decade. If, however, the restrictive policies of the industrial countries, and the decrease in demand because of the world economic crisis both continue, this potential will probably not be realised.

The pessimistic view of the future is that within the next five years there will be a major social crisis with extensive repercussions. This could lead the country into a position similar to that of El Salvador at the moment where GDP growth rates are lower than those of population.

ENERGY RESOURCES AND NATIONAL POLICIES

Guatemala possesses a wide range of energy resources. It has considerable hydroelectric potential. It also has hydrocarbon reserves, geothermal resources, large biomass resources in its forests, and potential for both solar and wind.

The country has only recently begun to exploit its hydroelectric potential. The need to develop this has been recognised since 1952, but a variety of obstacles has prevented progress being made. The total theoretical hydroelectric capacity is about 11 000 MW, of which 101 MW have been already installed. At present, there are plans to have 390 MW installed in the near future, and a total of 3 600 MW by the year 2000. A series of building problems and cost difficulties have slowed these programmes, but it is hoped to have them back on target by 1983.

To date, Guatemala is the only Central American country with known and published reserves of oil. The proven reserves amount to 10 million barrels, and probable reserves are 20 million barrels. Present production is 8 000 barrels per day. Gas reserves amount to 240 million cu.m. Guatemala has one refinery, in the south of the country, with a capacity of 15 200 barrels per day. There are plans by private enterprise to use the gas which is now flared.

Geothermal resources exist in Zunil and Moyuta. These are still in a preliminary stage of exploration, but INDE (National Institute of Electrification) has plans for the installation of a 55 MW plant by 1985.

There have been large private and public sector investments in energy projects over the past few years. The return on these has, however, been delayed, especially in the case of hydroelectricity. This has increased the country's debt servicing ratio from 1.9 percent in 1975 to 7 percent in 1981. Of these total investments, estimated at Q7 100 million by 1982, Q1 900 million will have been invested by the public sector, and Q5 200 million by the private sector. This, however, depends on the degree to which investors have confidence in the political and social stability of Guatemala.

Table 2. Energy supply breakdown by fuels 1978 and 1979

('000 barrels oil equivalent and % of total)

	('000 boe)		(% of total)	
Supply	1978	1979	1978	1979
Production:				
Fuelwood	14 079	14 264	53.6	51.5
Bagasse	1 744	1 604	6.6	5.8
Oil	221	571	0.9	2.1
Hydro	172	166	0.7	0.6
	16 216	16 605	61.8	60.0
Imports:				
Crude oil	5 829	5 724	22.2	20.7
Oil products	4 203	5 341	16.0	19.3
Total supply	26 248	27 670	100.0	100.0
Less				
Changes of stocks and export	(178)	(664)	0.7	2.4
Available for domestic use	26 070	27 006	99.3	97.6
Losses				
Electricity generation	(2 517)	(2 809)	9.6	10.2
Losses in refining	(119)	(121)	0.4	0.4
Available final use	23 434	24 076	89.3	87.0
Final supply				
Fuelwood	14 079	14 264	60.1	59.2
Bagasse	906	834	3.9	3.5
Crude oil	197	192	0.8	0.8
Oil products	7 276	7 699	31.0	32.0
Electricity	976	1 087	4.2	4.5

Source: Annuario Estadistico, July 1980, Secretaria de Mineria, Hidrocarburos y Energia Nuclear (SMHEN).

The strategic goal is to develop oil production to the level at which it can substitute a third of the present imports. In addition it is intended to end the use of oil as the main fuel for electricity generation by bringing the hydroelectric projects on the Chixoy River into operation. These will supply 270 MW to the country's electricity system.

Table 2 gives a breakdown of the total energy supply for Guatemala in 1978 and 1979. Table 3 gives a sectoral breakdown for end uses according to each fuel.

Table 3. Energy final use by sector and fuel, 1979

('000 barrels oil equivalent and % of total)

Product	Final use	Residential	Industrial	Mining	Transportation	Energy industries	Bunkers & non energy uses
Total	24 076	14 271	4 485	545	3 776	331	668
% of total	100	13.3	27.4	6.1	42.0	3.7	7.5
Fuelwood	14 264	13 075	1 189	-	-	-	-
Bagasse	834	-	834	-	-	-	-
Oil	7 891	800	2 069	404	3 776	174	668
Hydro	-	-	-	-	-	-	-
Electricity	1 087	396	393	141	-	157	-

Source: Annuario Estadistico, July 1980, Secretaria de Mineria, Hidrocarburos y Energia Nuclear (SMHEN).

RURAL SUBSISTENCE SECTOR

This sector covers all agricultural production in which the land-holding is worked by family labour alone, or with a certain amount of employed labour. Taking this as the basic definition, subsistence agriculture can be divided into two categories of holdings.

The 'minifundio' is a small farm that cannot absorb the full working capacity of a rural family, assuming that two adult labourers, using the technology typical of the 'minifundista' region, work most of the year upon it. Since their labour capacity cannot be fully ab-

sorbed, farmers seek work on the large agro-export farms
of the south and the Atlantic coast in order to comple-
ment their income. In the 1964 agricultural census
there were about 365 000 'minifundios'; this amounted to
87 percent of the total number of farms in the country.
The total area of 'minifundios' was 642 000 ha or about
18.7 percent of the total farm area.

The average 'minifundista' family has six members
with a total labour capacity of 600 man-days per year.
If the land holding is less than 2 ha it is impossible
to have the whole family working on it for the whole
year. According to a poll by CIDA, the 'minifundios'
of the high lands generally require less than 110 days
work per year per holding, but this goes down to 60 or
70 days in the most impoverished areas of Totonicapan
and Solola. The 'minifundios' of the coast, where the
climate and soils are more favourable and holdings larger, absorb up to 128 days of work per year. It is
considered by some observers that 3 ha is the minimum a
rural family with no other important source of income
requires for subsistence. This is provided soil erosion
does not worsen and the price of fertilisers remains
within the scope of the family budget.

Above the 'minifundio' in size, but still classified as subsistence, comes the family farm. This can
absorb the whole labour of a rural family. At a national level, the average size of family farms is between 7-
45 ha.

Table 4. Distribution of agricultural land in the
western region by type of holding

Type of holding	Hectares	Each type as % of total no.	Each type as % of total area
Minifundios:			
microfarms	0.0- 0.7	33.90	3.1
small subfamily	0.7- 3.5	45.88	17.8
medium subfamily	3.5- 7.0	10.20	11.0
Family farms	7.0- 44.8	8.60	22.5
Medium multifamily	44.8-448.0	1.30	22.3
Large multifamily	448.0-	0.20	23.3

Source: Adapted from Molina Cabrera, 1964, Vol.II,
"Diagnostico Sector Agricolo", Plan de Desarollo Regional de Occidente, Datos Censo Agropecuario.

Table 4 shows the distribution of landholdings in the western region using data from the 1964 census. This is the principal area of subsistence agriculture in the country. It can be seen that land holdings of less than 7 ha accounted for 90 percent of the total number, yet they accounted for only 31.9 percent of the total farm area. The high proportion of microfarms with holdings of less than 0.7 ha should also be noted. While these constituted almost 34 percent of the holdings in the western region in the same census year, they accounted for just over 20 percent of the total number of farms in the whole country. Recent studies show that on the northwestern High Plateau the average size of subsistence farms has decreased slightly since 1964, but that of multifamily farms has increased about one third, from 137 ha in 1964 to 184 ha in 1978.

Land tenure and usage take a variety of forms. On the microfarms, owner-occupation, usufruct, communal hiring, and sharecropping predominate. In subfamily farms, the method of tenure is mainly owner-occupation and usufruct; family farms are generally owner-occupied or communally owned.

In the family, men are mainly in charge of clearing the land, preparing it for sowing, and harvesting; carrying wood, especially that obtained in the form of cut logs; some community tasks; small industry, such as pottery, furniture-making, lime-making, and bakeries; house-building; and care of draught animals.

Women bring water, cook, raise children, harvest, grow vegetables, sell them in the market, do handicrafts such as weaving and basketry, fetch fuelwood from around the house (generally dry branches and small pieces of wood), and take care of small domestic animals. The family participates together in the organisation of celebrations, small commercial and educational activities, and grain storage. With the influence of the mass-media, transport, and education, the younger generations, in particular, are tending to leave the community to look for non-agricultural jobs and acquire a measure of economic independence.

In the microfarms, capital consists of traditional and rudimentary tools and utensils, such as machetes, hoes, axes, and files. There is no space for pasture or cattle sheds, and there is no money to buy animals. In the subfamily farms, while capital investment is generally greater, that invested in draught animals is extremely low, and amounts to only 2.5 percent of the total agricultural capital; animal traction, in fact, has not been adequately disseminated. Family farms have the largest investments, especially in methods for increasing coffee production. Total yearly capital investments in working equipment are between Q20-30 for microfarms; between Q30-50 for subfamily farms; and between Q100-200 for family farms.

Over the past few decades, the position of subsistence agriculture has deteriorated severely, and widened the economic gap between the urban and rural areas. The price paid for the food products of subsistence farming has steadily fallen, while that of all commercial products used in the rural areas, salt, sugar, fertilisers, tools, construction materials, and domestic items has risen. Transport has become particularly costly because of the increase in fuel prices.

The shortage of land has reached the dimensions of a national problem. The agricultural frontier is being extended to the north and many families have migrated to those lands to try to make them arable. Nevertheless, this migration has not been sufficient to ease the present shortage of land, especially in the High Plateau and the East.

In general, the average size of 'minifundios' has decreased and they are close to the limits of atomisation. They are increasing in numbers, to the detriment of the family and subfamily farms, and especially communal farming. The 'minifundios' and the large farms, or 'latifundios', now exist in an economic symbiosis. The 'minifundios' form an efficient labour reserve from which the large farms on the South Coast can draw the cheap labour they need for periods of peak agricultural activity. The wages paid give the 'minifundistas' the small amount of cash they need to purchase the industrial products they need.

Until recently, the minimum wage in the rural areas was Q1.20 per day. This was raised to Q3.20 per day after massive strikes. As a consequence, much of the labour has been made redundant to compensate for these wage increases, which were the first in 22 years. On the large farms which have already been mechanised and can benefit from high export prices for products such as cotton, sugarcane, and cattle, wages are higher than on the more traditional farms devoted to coffee. This is rapidly leading to a proletarisation of the migrant farmers, manifesting itself through labour demands, unionisation, and salary claims.

All these reasons have contributed to an exodus from the country to the city which was increased by the earthquake of 1976 which severely afflicted the areas of subsistence agriculture. In the urban areas, these migrants, in the midst of an already large number of unemployed, have great difficulty in finding even menial stable jobs. The rural-urban migration actually takes place in several stages. First, people move from the villages to small towns, then to larger towns, and finally to the capital. An increasing number of those unable to find work in the capital have now begun to emigrate, particularly to the United States.

ENERGY USE IN THE SUBSISTENCE SECTOR

Fuelwood is still the country's most important indigenous resource. Thirty years ago it supplied three quarters of all the energy used in Guatemala. With urbanisation and industrialisation, the consumption of oil products has grown rapidly so that oil now predominates in sectors other than the residential. Fuelwood has retained its dominance in the domestic sector (Table 5). It is also used in small industries and commercial enterprises. In the rural areas it is used by 94 percent of the population, and even in the main urban centres it is used by 46 percent of the population.

Table 5. Consumption of fuelwood and wood in Guatemala (1979)

('000 cu.m.)

	Fuelwood			
	Domestic	Small industry	Non fuel uses	Total
Central Plateau	1 345	285	70	1 700
High Plateau	3 685	780	585	5 050
South Coast	1 640	350	110	2 100
East	1 800	380	450	2 630
Verapaz	830	180	455	1 465
Sub-total	9 300	1 975	1 670	12 945
El Peten	125	25	1 930	2 080
Total	9 425	2 000	3 600	15 025

Source: FAO, CEMAT

In Table 2, it can be seen that fuelwood accounted for almost 60 percent of the national final energy supply; and Table 3 shows that it accounted for 92 percent of the total final residential demand. A survey of cooking fuels made in 1979 showed that 60 percent of the population used fuelwood as their sole cooking fuel, and a further 20 percent used it in conjunction with kerosene or propane. Of the remaining 20 percent, 12 percent used propane, 7 percent used kerosene, and only 1 percent used charcoal. Table 6 is based on this survey and gives details on a regional basis of the fuels used for cooking, in both urban and rural areas.

78

Table 6.   Summary results of cooking fuel study

(% of families)

	Pro-pane	Kero-sene	Fuel-wood	Fuel-wood & kero-sene	Fuel-wood & pro-pane	Char-coal	To-tal
Western High Plateau							
Main urban centres	8	–	31	–	61	–	100
Other urban centres	17	–	60	6	17	–	100
Rural	–	–	92	5	3	–	100
Total	3	–	85	5	7	–	100
Central High Plateau							
Main urban centres	36	20	32	–	10	2	100
Other urban centres	27	29	30	–	–	14	100
Rural	26	24	45	3	–	2	100
Total	31	22	36	1	3	4	100
Southern Low Lands							
Main urban centres	30	13	30	–	27	–	100
Other urban centres	15	–	56	7	22	–	100
Rural	1	1	72	23	3	–	100
Total	7	2	65	18	9	–	100
Eastern Low Lands							
Main urban centres	45	–	44	–	11	–	100
Other urban centres	13	–	65	10	13	–	100
Rural	3	2	61	26	8	–	100
Total	7	2	61	22	9	–	100
Verapaz – El Peten							
Main urban centres	–	–	–	–	–	–	–
Other urban centres	21	21	50	8	–	–	100
Rural	–	1	99	–	–	–	100
Total	3	4	91	1	–	–	100

Table 6 (ctd')

	Pro-pane	Kero-sene	Fuel-wood	Fuel-wood & kero-sene	Fuel-wood & pro pane	Char-coal	To-tal
All areas							
Main urban centres	35	17	32	–	14	2	100
Other urban centres	19	8	52	6	12	3	100
Rural	3	3	79	12	3	–	100
Total	12	7	66	8	6	1	100

Source: Bogach, V.S., 1981, A Fuelwood Policy for Guatemala, van Meurs & Assoc., Ltd., W.G. Matthews
Assoc., Ltd., Canada.

Although fuelwood is the principal source of fuel
for subsistence farmers, almost half of them purchase
it. Table 7 shows the regional distribution of households purchasing fuelwood. It can be seen that it
varies widely. In the densely populated subsistence
areas of the Western High Plateau it is almost 90 percent, whereas in Verapaz and El Peten it is just 16.5
percent.

Table 7. Estimated number of households that buy fuelwood, 1980

('000)

	Urban	Rural	Total	%
Western High Plateau	54.0	89.0	143.0	36
Central High Plateau	88.5	17.0	105.5	27
Southern Low Lands	33.0	39.0	72.0	18
Eastern Low Lands	20.5	28.0	48.5	12
Verapaz - El Peten	9.5	16.5	26.0	7
Total	205.5	189.5	395.0	100

Source: Bogach, V.S., 1981, A Fuelwood Policy for Guatemala, van Meurs & Assoc., Ltd., W.G. Matthews
Assoc., Ltd., Canada.

Prices to the consumer in 1979 varied widely, from Q10 per solid cu.m. in El Peten and some other rural areas to Q19 in parts of the Central High Plateau, and Q23 in Guatemala City; in 1980, the price in Guatemala City had risen to Q30. The average outlay per family using fuelwood as the exclusive cooking fuel was Q175 in 1979.

The annual consumption of fuelwood per head is estimated to be about 750 kg but this decreases to about 500 kg in the case of families which use kerosene and propane as supplementary cooking fuels. The total esti- mated forest stock of Guatemala is about 927 million cu.m. of which 673 million cu.m. are in El Peten. In El Peten itself fuelwood consumption is small, and amounts to about 150 000 cu.m. per year with an additional 2 million cu.m. being used for other commercial purposes (Table 5). In the rest of the country fuelwood consump- tion is the main use of wood and amounts to about 9.3 million cu.m. with small industries and other uses bringing the total to about 13 million cu.m. per year. Natural replenishment is estimated at 5.2 million cu.m. per year. This means that the average depletion rate is about 3 percent per year, but this varies considerably between regions. On the South Coast it is 12.5 percent, and in the Central High Plateau it is 8.5 percent. If firewood consumption continues to rise in parallel with the growth in population, Guatemala's forests outside El Peten will have virtually disappeared by 1988.

As shown in Table 6, propane and kerosene are the other two major cooking fuels. Their use, however, is almost entirely confined to the urban areas and only 3 percent of rural families use either as their exclusive cooking fuel. A somewhat higher proportion use kerosene to supplement fuelwood. The average annual consumption per head of kerosene, when it is the exclusive cooking fuel, is about 53 litres, and about 17 litres when it is used as a supplementary fuel. Where propane is used as the sole cooking fuel, annual consumption per head is about 34 kg, and about 14 kg when it is used as a supplementary fuel.

About 30 percent of rural families still use kero- sene for illumination, but this has been diminishing with the extension of electricity services, particularly in the Central Region, Central High Plateau, and on the South Coast near the cities. The average annual per capita consumption of kerosene for lighting is about 9 litres.

About 80 percent of the families using fuelwood for cooking do so on an open fire. This may be directly on the ground, or it may be placed on an earth or brick platform, or on top of a barrel. Even in the urban areas over half the families using fuelwood employ a metal plate over the fire as a support for the cooking

pot.   The   use   of metal or Lorena stoves is   rare   and
almost   entirely confined to the urban areas.   Table   8
shows a regional breakdown of cooking methods with fuelwood for urban and rural areas.

Table 8.   Families using different cooking methods with
           fuelwood

(%)

	Open fire on the ground	Open fire on a bench or barrel	Fire on bench with plate cover	Other
Western High Plateau				
Urban	–	35	63	2
Rural	20	51	29	–
Central High Plateau				
Urban	25	53	22	–
Rural	33	55	12	–
Southern Low Lands				
Urban	6	71	19	3
Rural	14	76	9	–
Eastern Low Lands				
Urban	–	69	31	–
Rural	1	91	8	–
Verapaz – El Peten				
Urban	–	83	17	–
Rural	7	91	2	–
All areas				
Urban	7	55	37	1
Rural	14	69	17	–
Total	13	66	21	–

Note: "Urban" includes main urban centres and others.
          "Others" includes Lorena stoves and all   metal
          stoves.
Source: Bogach,   V.S.,   1981, A Fuelwood Policy for Gua-
          temala, van Meurs & Assoc., Ltd., W.G. Matthews
          Assoc., Ltd., Canada.

    As   the stock of fuelwood diminishes its price will
increase.   Many rural families will begin to use   kerosene   for   cooking.   This is already happening in   the
critical zones in the East and the South Coast and in 20
years it could be the case throughout the   country.   If
this   happens,   a renewable domestic resource will   have

been replaced by an imported non-renewable one. Table 9
summarises the present average annual fuel consumption
per person for the different fuels and fuel-combinations
most commonly used. It also shows approximate family
expenditures on fuel.

Table 9. Annual consumption and cost of domestic fuels

Fuel and use	Average annual use per person	Average annual cost per family of 6 (Q)
Fuelwood		
As sole cooking fuel	750 kg (oven-dry)	175.00
With other cooking fuels	511 kg	120.00
Kerosene		
As sole cooking fuel	53.0 l	74.00
With fuelwood	16.7 l	26.00
Lighting only	9.5 l	14.20
Propane		
As sole cooking fuel	34.0 kg	85.00
With fuelwood	13.7 kg	34.00

Source: Bogach, V.S., 1981, A Fuelwood Policy for Guatemala, van Meurs & Assoc., Ltd., W.G. Matthews
Assoc., Ltd., Canada.

PAST AND PRESENT POLICIES

In 1974, the impact of the oil price rises was most
clearly seen in the balance of trade figures. It was
also calculated that the costs of agricultural production would increase by 5 percent, and that the growth in
GDP would be reduced by 1 percent.
The following series of policies was adopted by the
Government in response:

- restrictions on sales and increased gasoline prices;
- restrictions on electricity use;
- promotion of an aggressive reforestation campaign
  throughout the country;
- promotion of energy from geothermal sources;
- acceleration of the hydroelectric project at Chixoy;
- grid interconnection with El Salvador for better use
  of electricity surpluses;
- feasibility studies to produce fuel alcohol from
  sugarcane;

- feasibility study to substitute oil tank-trucks by
pipelines.

At that time the full measure of the impact of the
energy crisis on the rural areas was not taken into
account. The main emphasis was placed on the supply of
energy to transport and on electricity for the urban
areas. Later, and in view of the increasing difficulties of the rural areas, a programme of rural electrification to increase the national coverage by 8.2 percent
was designed. In 1980, a programme of rural electrification to extend coverage to the critical areas in the
Western High Plateau was commenced.

The delayed installation of the hydroelectric plant
has, however, meant that fossil fuel consumption for
electricity generation has increased. At present prices
this amounts to Q2.5 million per month. Nor has the
decision on the grid connection with El Salvador been
finalised. Significant increases are therefore expected
in electricity tariffs with consequent problems for the
rural areas.

Experimentation with non-conventional sources of
energy in the rural areas on a larger scale, however,
began in 1976, as a result of the earthquake and the
reconstruction this required. Projects included:

- small-scale biogas digesters;
- firewood-saving stoves;
- solar energy devices;
- nurseries for reforestation;
- development of windmills;
- experiments with fuel alcohol.

Private development of biogas, in fact, began in
1953, especially on the South Coast where 14 plants were
built. Support for a national programme of diffusion
was, however, lacking because of the low price of oil at
that time, but Guatemala now has a valuable body of
experience in the production of biogas and biofertili-
sers. There are about 20 digesters of various capacities functioning and there is sufficient technical capability for a strong drive to promote biogas throughout
the country. The main failures have been because promotion and follow-up have been carried out in an isolated
and partial manner. The experience of OPINA, CEMAT,
ICADA, ICAITI and the Engineering Faculty at San Carlos
University of Guatemala, however, constitutes a basis
for future coordination.

Since the rural population is finding it
increasingly difficult to obtain its traditional supplies of fuelwood, there has been a corresponding increase in the interest shown in improved woodstoves,
such as the Lorena. This is being promoted by techni-

cal extension groups such as ICADA, CEMAT, XELAC, and
more recently by INTECAP and ICAITI, who are finding
that it is readily accepted by the rural population.
The efficiency of these stoves has been demonstrated,
and in San Pedro La Laguna, Solola, and other towns
around Atitlan as well as in Cantel and Quetzaltenango
they are now widely diffused.

Nevertheless, and in spite of such successes, fuel-
saving stoves have not been given wide distribution.
The main cause has been a lack of inter-institutional
coordination which would permit official organisations,
as well as non-governmental and private institutions, to
participate on an equal footing in the work of diffusing
energy-saving stoves throughout the country.

The Centro Agronomico Tropical de Investigaciones y
Ensenanza (CATIE), in collaboration with the Government
Forest Agency INAFOR, have identified the critical zones
of deforestation and are now engaged in a reforestation
programme. They are selecting fast-growing species and
are identifying different methods of achieving community
participation in forest production. It is clear that a
large-scale reforestation programme will require an
increasing level of community engagement, but this is
difficult to achieve in view of the rural unrest in
several areas. The present approach has relied upon
distributing seedlings in plastic bags to be sown by the
recipients, but there is no follow-up whatsoever.

The Government, through INAFOR, is sponsoring a
replanting programme for the period 1978-1982. The goal
is to plant a total of 100 000 ha, but during the first
two years a total of only 32 000 ha was achieved.
Assuming that this rate continues, it would mean 65 000
ha would be planted by 1982. This would result in an
increase in the standing stock of wood of just 3 million
cu.m. by the year 2000.

The feasibility of alcohol production has been
studied but no decision has yet been reached on whether
to proceed. The experience of Costa Rica could be relevant to this. There, a plant yielding 240 000 litres per
day has been built. Experiments are being conducted on
the use of this in automobiles.

One of the major limitations on the development of
non-conventional energy programmes is the lack of adequate financial resources. Some of these technologies
are new and difficult to finance using conventional
criteria for granting credit. In addition, credit in
general has been more difficult to obtain because of the
financial stringencies of recent years.

FUTURE POLICIES

Subsistence agriculture in Guatemala is now going
through a transition. Rapid changes are taking place as

a result of the combined effects of the energy crisis, accelerated demographic growth, scarcity of land, inflation in the price of the industrial products used, and increased unemployment, and underemployment, because of low agro-export prices.

As far as energy is concerned, the most critical element is the future supply of fuelwood. Forest exploitation is on an ascending logarithmic curve which could lead to the virtual exhaustion of wood resources by the year 2000. The critical zones in the country, in order of priority, are the Western High Plateau, the East, the Central Plateau, and the South Coast.

The Western High Plateau contains most of Guatemala's small subsistence farms. In this area, population pressure has created the worst fuelwood deficit in the country. In the north there are still some forest reserves but they are being rapidly exhausted as a result of the 3.1 percent annual growth in the number of consumers.

Up to the 1940s and 1950s, the agricultural system had maintained a state of equilibrium. Since then problems arising from the increased demand for farming land have accumulated. Subsistence agriculture is expanding into forest areas, and upwards on to high and steeply-sloping land. This creates a vicious circle of deforestation, erosion of fertile lands, diminishing returns, decrease of agricultural income, increasing need for chemical fertilisers, and a growing indebtedness of the rural economy. To all these problems should be added the fact that large areas of native conifers are coming under the attack of pine weevil (Dendroctonus). It is precisely in these areas on the Western High Plateau that fuelwood has begun to become scarce.

The East, with its large numbers of family and sub-family farms, is another critical area in relation to its natural energy endowment. Climatic factors affect an important part of this zone, and drought is the most serious problem. Deforestation as a result of the increasing wood-consuming population is also important. The exodus from here to the capital city is proportionally the most intensive in the country. The area of Izabal, in the northeast of the region, contains economically important forest reserves, but these are, however, rapidly being exhausted by wood exports.

The Central Plateau, where Guatemala City is located, has a large forest deficit. Studies show that over 30 percent of the urban population and 45 percent of the rural population still use fuelwood as their principal cooking fuel (Table 6).

The South Coast is where the most important agro-export farms are located. This is the most deforested region of the country. It is estimated that the forest stock will last only 8-10 years at present rates of consumption. Small centres of population are usually located within large estates, and the land belongs to the estate owners. This prevents families from making any investments in improving their domestic living conditions. The luxuriance of the vegetational growth, however, may prevent an energy crisis occurring in this region.

For a variety of reasons, the magnitude of the rural energy problem is less clearly defined, and the pressures to resolve it are less important for legislators than those related to oil. For example, although the general dimensions of the rural energy crisis are known, quantitative, specific, and reliable data are scarce. In addition, the organisation of programmes of action is difficult, given the existing institutional framework.

In comparison, infrastructure projects, such as the building of hydroelectric plants are more tangible and more manageable. The attractiveness of strengthening the "modern" urban and industrial sectors of the economy also helps to divert attention from rural energy problems. If the relative political advantages of satisfying the urban, industrial, and commercial electorate are added to these considerations, it is easily understood why accelerated efforts to deal with rural energy needs are a matter of second priority.

Although numerous activities are taking place, energy policies for the subsistence sector have not been systematised. There are no specific programmes, nor a definition of priorities. Coordinating the disparate activities of different government and private agencies is probably the first necessity.

Because of the strategic importance of the energy problem in subsistence areas, policies should be made at the highest level and implemented by the intermediate government institutions with the active participation of non-government, private, and community organisations. Critical elements in such policies would include:

- institutional coordination and restructuring;
- training staff;
- compiling statistical data to obtain detailed energy balances;
- setting-up specific energy programmes for the subsistence sector;
- assigning priority to the more economical use of fuelwood and the diffusion of more efficient stoves;
- increasing the use of new energy resources: biogas, solar, mini-hydro, methanol, mini-alcohol plants, draught animals, wind energy, etc., and evaluating and reassessing the potential of these resources;
- supporting the formation of rural energy demonstration units;

- creating revolving funds to invest in these technologies;
- massive education and information programmes;
- incentives for commercial application of new technologies;
- giving technical assistance through support for institutions already promoting new technologies and the exchange of experiences;
- increasing the number of woodlots, communal forest units, fuelwood-production farm units, agro-forestry units, and natural vegetation units, especially in the critical zones;
- extending the national electricity system to rural areas.

In implementing such policies at a practical level, scientific and technical institutions which conduct energy research relevant to rural energy needs will need to be supported. Future strategies should give support to existing networks of organisations concerned with rural energy problems, including, for example, the following:

- the Latin American Energy Organisation (OLADE), which coordinates the efforts of institutions in the energy sector, and has already made an inventory of resources and needs, and begun to train national staff;
- networks of NGOs, such as the Coordinating Committee for Appropriate Technology for Latin America (COCOP), Latin American Association of Development Organisations (ALOP), the International Network for Appropriate Technology (TRANET) etc.;
- research networks such as the Bioenergy Association, the Associations for Applied Microbiology, Forest Sciences, etc.;
- information and documentation centres on energy sources for rural areas.

Financial and technical assistance will be needed by the national focal points of such international networks, once they are established, and by the official institutions which collaborate with them. In Guatemala, these would include:

- the Ministry of Mining, Hydrocarbons, and Nuclear Energy which is the main institution for energy matters in Guatemala;
- the Energy Office of the General Secretariat of the National Council of Economic Planning, which is in charge of coordinating and promoting the use of new energy sources;
- the National Reconstruction Committee which, following the 1976 earthquake and reconstruction work in the

rural areas, has demonstrated a dynamic style of coordination with non-government and private organisations
which work directly with the grassroots;
- the National Forestry Institute (INAFOR) which is
promoting forestry units which permit a better management of national forests;
- the Technical Institute of Training and Productivity
(INTECAP), which trains middle-level and operative
staff.

THE ROLE OF INTERNATIONAL AGENCIES

The world-wide difficulties experienced in coordinating efforts on critical problems of development, such
as the environment, the role of women and children,
science and technology, and others, would appear to
indicate that this should be the first item to which
international agencies give their attention, to avoid
the creation of programmes with no local justification
or relevance. It is essential to prevent that duplication of efforts or, in the worst case, inter-institutional rivalry, which can block the dynamic implementation of programmes which international agencies are
trying to support.

It is also clear that, in spite of the fact that it
has an extremely precise technical dimension, the rural
energy problem has important political components. It
is therefore necessary to ensure that an equilibrium is
maintained, and that support for official institutions
is balanced by support for non-governmental institutions, support for research centres by that for groups
diffusing techniques at the grassroots, and that concrete local programmes are promoted as well as general
activities. The fundamental criterion, however, is
whether a programme has been able to reach the base
levels of the rural community, and become both self-
managed and a generator of local energy self-
sufficiency.

The energy crisis is too important to leave solely
in the hands of technologists. The participation of the
communities affected is extremely important, and every
effort which can be made to involve them, no matter how
small, is a contribution to the resolution of the problems from which they are suffering.

5
Brazil

Adilson de Oliveira
Luiz Piugnelli Rosa

GENERAL DESCRIPTION

Brazil is one of the largest countries in the world. It covers 8.5 million sq.km. and most of its territory lies between the Equator and the Tropic of Capricorn. Its climate is fairly diverse and the vegetation tends to vary widely across its regions. Among the many climatic zones which may be distinguished the following are among the most important:

- humid and super-humid Amazon: this covers almost the whole of the northern region across the total width of the country, and extends southwards into the northern part of the midwest region;
- 'Cerrado': this is typical of areas with a tropical and semi-humid climate, and a dry season of 4 to 5 months; it covers almost all of the Central Plateau, and extends to parts of Minas Gerais, the west of Bahia South, the southeast and east of Maranhao, and the midwest of Piaui;
- 'Caatinga': this has a tropical and semi-arid mild climate, whose dry season may last from 6 to 11 months. It covers the whole northeast, with the exception of areas close to the eastern littoral, the mid-west of Piaui and Maranhao, and parts of the north of Minas Gerais;
- sub-humid vegetation of the interior: this lies in a narrow belt in the south of the state of Bahia, between the humid and dry zones. It widens considerably in the states of Minas Gerais, Espirito Santo, Rio de Janeiro, and covers all of the state of Sao Paulo;
- the Swamps complex: this is a mosaic of vegetal formations which exists in the area of the Mato Grosso, where a hot and semi-humid tropical climate dominates;
- open lands: these are closely related to local ecological conditions. Among the most important ones, some regions which are easily flooded, such as parts of

Maranhao and Para, the Meridional Plateau, the 'Gaucha' openlands in the Rio Grande do Sul, and those to the south of Mato Grosso do Sul stand out;
- coastal: these are quite diverse, and are directly influenced by the environmental conditions. The beaches, sand-dunes, sand-banks, and the mangroves are most noticeable.

This immense territory is not all cultivated. The productive area is estimated to be nearly 309 million ha, of which only 40 million or 13 percent were cultivated, either with permanent plantations (8 million ha) or with temporary plantations (32 million ha) in 1975 (1). There is, thus, a large agricultural frontier still to be conquered in the country, and not always very far from the big consumption centres.

The Brazilian population is estimated to be 122.2 million with a growth rate of 2.8 percent per year*. The demographic density is extremely low at the national level (14.2 inhabitants/sq.km.), although, regionally, this can reach much higher levels. One of the principal demographic features of the past decade has been a substantial migration to regions at the economic frontier, such as the midwest and the south of the northern region.

The process of urban concentration in Brazil has accelerated since 1950. The rural population is at present growing very slowly and is estimated at approximately 47 million inhabitants, while the urban population is growing faster and is estimated to be 75.2 million inhabitants. However, the picture at the national level is different from that in the five major regions of the country. In the southeast, the rural population is falling, but in all the other regions it is growing. Of the total population, 53 percent were classified as economically active (over 10 years old) in 1977, and of this percentage, 63 percent were in the urban areas.

The Gross National Product (GNP) of Brazil reached a total of approximately $230.5 billion in 1980, which corresponds to a per capita income of $1 886. Table 1 shows that the Brazilian GNP went through a phase of fast growth (10.5 percent) between 1967 and 1973. From then on, the growth rate slowed somewhat, but it is still high by international standards (7.1 percent). The distribution by sectors of the GNP shows a predominance of the services sector (53.5 percent), while the

---

*The census of 1980 seems to indicate a drastic reduction in that growth rate. However, the official figures have not been published yet.

industrial sector is second (39.2 percent) and the agricultural sector comes last (7.3 percent).

Examination of the trends in the sectoral distribution of GNP shows a distinct change in the Brazilian
productive structure, with the contribution of the agricultural sector shrinking from 14.5 percent to 7.3 percent between 1965 and 1980, while that of the industrial
sector rose from 33.5 percent to 39.2 percent. It is
worth noticing, however, that this structural shift was
accompanied by a fairly strong growth rate of 3.6 percent per year in the agricultural sector throughout the
period (2).

Table 1. Growth of total real Gross National Product

(%)

	Rate of growth				Sectoral distribution	
	1967/ 1973	1974/ 1976*	1977/ 1980	1974/ 1980	1965	1980
Total real GNP	10.5	8.1	6.3	7.1	-	-
Agriculture	5.3	5.3	4.5	4.8	14.5	7.3
Industry	11.7	8.9	6.7	7.6	33.1	39.2
Commerce	11.1	7.1	5.7	6.3	52.4	53.5
Transport & communicat'n	10.7	10.6	8.4	9.3	-	-

Note: *preliminary data
Source: Conjuntura Economica, Fevereiro 1981, vol.36
no.2, Encarte Anuario Estatistico, p.VI.

As far as the current account is concerned, international trade experienced a very rapid growth in the
seventies. Brazilian exports rose from $2.9 billion in
1971 to $20.1 billion in 1980, while imports grew from
$3.2 to $23.0 billion in the same period (3). The rise
in oil prices had a major impact on the Brazilian current account. Imports of oil and oil products jumped
from $280 million in 1971 to $2.8 billion in 1974, and
$9.4 billion in 1980. Oil, which accounted for 8.6
percent of Brazilian imports in 1971, grew to 22.3
percent in 1974, and 41.0 percent in 1980. Between 1972
and 1980, the Brazilian external debt rose from $9.5 to

$54.4 billion, and debt servicing grew from $2.6 billion in 1973 to $12.9 billion in 1980; this was a growth rate of 25.8 percent per year. Since exports grew at a substantially lower rate (18.3 percent per year), the proportion of exports used for debt servicing rose from 41.6 percent in 1973 to 64.0 percent in 1980.

Faced with this growing disequilibrium, economic policies were designed to preserve the confidence of the international financial system, and a two-stage set of policies was directed towards obtaining a medium-term surplus in the current account. The strategy required both export stimulation and import substitution. In the short term, the emphasis was put on the production of agricultural surpluses for export and opening new markets abroad for manufactured products, through negotiations with the multinational firms with subsidiaries in Brazil. During the period 1974-1978, non-oil imports fell substantially, but further reductions became more difficult to achieve. The increase in the price of oil in 1979 pushed the Government to propose a set of fairly ambitious goals aiming at a substitution of oil imports through increased production of national oil (from 10 to 25 million tonnes a year) and the use of alternative energy sources for 25 million tonnes of oil equivalent (toe).

THE ENERGY STRUCTURE

Table 2 shows that, although seven primary sources of energy are currently used in Brazil, only three of them - oil, hydroelectricity, and wood - account for 86.5 percent of total energy consumption. Coal (5.5 percent) and sugarcane wastes (5.7 percent) account for more than 11.0 percent, while alcohol (1.5 percent) and natural gas (0.5 percent) play a marginal role.

The future of natural gas will be largely determined by the progress of the negotiations on importation from Bolivia and Argentina. The volumes in question reach figures of around 10 million cu.m./day, which would radically alter the present picture. In addition, a pipeline, with a capacity of 2.3 million cu.m./day, is currently being built to connect the oil basin of Campos with Rio de Janeiro (4). The markets for natural gas are in the large urban centres of the country, particularly for industrial use.

Alcohol is already a traditional energy source in Brazil, as it has been used as a motor-car fuel since the thirties. The low price of oil and gasoline, however, reduced the role of alcohol as fuel, though it continued to be added to gasoline during the whole post-war period in the sugar-region of northeastern Brazil. Now, the price of oil is bringing back alcohol as an energy source. The Government is planning a consumption of 7.1 million toe in 1985, which would be about 5.4 percent of the total energy consumption at that time (5). It is worth noting that this alcohol will be consumed almost exclusively by cars, and is therefore associated with a very specific and essentially urban market.

Table 2. Brazilian energy balance

	1969 ('000 toe)(2)	(%)	1979 ('000 toe)	(%)	1985(1) ('000 toe)	(%)
Oil	21 673	42.9	47 375	49.4	40 944	31.0
Natural gas	96	0.2	438	0.5	895	0.7
Coal	2 342	4.6	5 123	5.3	15 665	11.9
Oil shale	-	-	-	-	1 154	0.9
Nuclear (3)	-	-	-	-	331	0.2
Hydro electricity(3)	2 740	5.4	9 928	10.3	19 637	14.9
Alcohol	27	0.1	1 876	1.9	7 057	5.4
Bagasse	2 520	5.0	5 489	5.7	9 646	7.3
Wood (4)	21 153	41.8	25 852	27.1	35 758	27.1
Others	-	-	-	-	730	0.6
Total	50 551	100.0	96 471	100.0	131 897	100.0
Annual growth rate	-	-	-	6.7	-	5.4

Notes: (1) Consumption for non-fuel use is not computed.
(2) 1 tonne oil equivalent (toe) = 10 800 Mcal.
(3) For the conversion of hydro and nuclear electricity, the real equivalent (860 kcal/kWh) was used.
(4) Wood consumed in its original state and wood consumed as charcoal.

Source: Balanco Energetico Nacional.
Modelo Energetico Brasileiro.

Sugarcane waste, or bagasse, is a by-product of the sugar-alcohol industry; and its consumption as fuel is, at present, restricted to that industry. A significant proportion of the waste could, however, be allocated for other energy uses, since only 70 percent is necessary for supplying energy within sugar and alcohol factories, and the surplus is often simply burnt off. Several studies are now under way in an attempt to find profitable uses for this.

Coal is used today almost exclusively (92 percent) by steel mills (6) and, of this, 60.5 percent is imported because the country's own coal has a high ash-content which makes its transformation into coke difficult. However, after the second oil shock in 1979, a plan to substitute national coal for fuel oil in industry was drawn up. The aim is to raise the consumption of coal to a total of 15.7 million toe in 1985, which will correspond to 11.9 percent of total Brazilian energy consumption. The markets for national coal are primarily in the cement industry and oil refineries.

Hydroelectricity accounts for a substantial proportion of energy consumption and is responsible for 92 percent of the total electricity supply. The hydroelectric potential of the country is huge - 216 GW - of which only 24.2 GW (11.2 percent) were being exploited at the end of 1979. That means that for at least three more decades, hydroelectricity will be a source of energy growth for Brazil.

Electricity consumption is concentrated in three large sectors: urban residential (21.1 percent), industrial (55.5 percent) and commercial (12.6 percent). Rural consumption represents a much smaller fraction: only 1.6 percent of the total (7), and more than 41.2 percent of that is in Sao Paulo State, which is the most industrialised region in the country. The forecasts for the near future show a growth rate for total electricity consumption of around 9.6 percent per year. In 1985 the consumption of the industrial sector (57.3 percent of the total) will amount to 194.9 million MWh and the relative participation of the residential (18.8 percent) and commercial (11.5 percent) sectors will tend to decrease. A much more rapid expansion of rural consumption is forecast (20.5 percent per year) bringing it up to 4.9 million MWh in 1985, which will raise it to 2.5 percent of the national total. It is worth noting that this increase will be in the state of Rio Grande do Sul, which should by then account for 34.7 percent of consumption in the rural sector, with that in the state of Sao Paulo being 28.6 percent (7).

Oil is the dominant energy source in the Brazilian energy structure and is almost totally imported (84.7 percent). The country's refineries produce a wide range of oil products which are used in various sectors. Gasoline, diesel, and kerosene are used mainly in the transport sector and represent 60 percent of Brazilian oil consumption. The rural sector absorbs an insignificant portion (0.3 percent) of the oil, as gasoline or diesel fuel. Fuel-oil and other important derivatives, whose use is concentrated in the industrial sector account for 26 percent of consumption (6). A small amount of fuel oil is consumed in the agricultural sector for grain-drying. Liquid petroleum gas (LPG) and kerosene

are used in residential consumption. More than 98 percent of LPG is consumed in the cities, but the use of
kerosene is concentrated in the countryside, where 63
percent of the total is consumed (6).

Wood is another important energy source. Its share
in the total energy supply has been falling in the last
decades, but its annual consumption, in absolute terms,
has stabilised at around 26 million toe. Most of this
wood (79.3 percent) is consumed in its original state by
the rural (56.6 percent) and urban (15.4 percent) residential sectors, by the industrial sector (13.0 percent), and by the agricultural sector (15.0 percent).
The remaining 20.8 percent is transformed into charcoal
and is used mainly in steel mills (77 percent), with 16
percent used in urban and residential and 7 percent in
the rural sectors (6).

The Government plans to increase the role of wood,
in the form of charcoal, in the Brazilian energy
balance. Goals have been established to introduce it
massively as a substitute for fuel oil in the generation
of industrial steam. If these are met, the consumption
of wood, as charcoal, will reach a figure of 16.5 million toe in 1985. Total consumption of wood in that
year will then be 35.8 million toe, or 27.1 percent of
Brazilian energy consumption.

It can thus be seen that Brazilian energy policies
are centred on the substitution of oil by other energy
sources. Table 2 shows that a drastic reduction in the
proportion of oil in the country's energy supply is
being attempted, from 49.4 percent of the total in 1979
down to 31.0 percent in 1985. This will be accomplished
through the intensive use of four different energy sources:

- coal: which will more than double its share;
- hydroelectricity: whose share will rise by 4.6 percent;
- alcohol: together with sugarcane wastes will reach
  12.7 percent;
- wood: contrary to its historical downward trend, will
  increase its share by 0.4 percent during this period;
- other sources: oil shales, nuclear, and solar will
  be introduced during this period but their impact will
  be small, less than 2 percent of the total. It should
  be noted that while precise goals have been set for
  nuclear and shale, none exist for solar energy.

As can be seen, all these policies have been oriented towards providing the industrial and urban sectors
with substitutes for oil and its derivatives. The rural
sector, and more particularly, the rural residential
sector are not included in government plans. On the
contrary, a growing portion of wood, whose use is now

concentrated in the countryside, will be transformed
into charcoal and brought to urban centres for industrial consumption, making the supply of wood more difficult for the non-urban population.

THE RURAL SECTOR

Brazilian land tenure has been historically characterised by the domination of large monoculture estates
('latifundios'). Table 3 shows that, in 1972, close to
83 percent of the total cultivated land in Brazil
belonged to approximately 14 percent of rural owners.
On the other hand, 85.8 percent of rural owners had
properties with an area of less than 100 ha, together
representing only 17.5 percent of the total available
land. Between 1967 and 1972, it was noted that the
numerical relationship between large and small land-
holdings tended to reproduce itself, even when the agricultural frontier was expanding (8).

Table 3. Distribution of rural land holdings, 1972

Area (ha)	Number of properties (%)	Total area (%)	Average area (ha)
Less than 10	31.1	1.4	4.8
10-25	27.8	4.2	16.5
25-50	16.5	5.3	34.9
50-100	10.4	6.6	69.6
100-1 000	12.7	31.2	267.7
1 000-10 000	1.4	32.4	2 493.0
10 000-100 000	0.1	14.6	22 577.9
100 000 & over	-	4.5	198 468.2
Total	100.0	100.0	109.4

Source: da Silva, Jose Graziano, 1978, Estrutura Agraria e Propriedade, Hucilec, p.267.

An analysis of the value of production at that time
(1972) indicated that practically all the properties
with less than 10 ha had annual gross yields below the
minimum annual wage which was then Cr$3 000 (US$500).
Even among properties with an area of up to 100 ha, the
majority (85 percent) showed yields of less than four
times the minimum annual wage. It is also noteworthy
that a surprisingly large proportion of 'latifundios'

have extremely low annual yields. This can be explained by the fact that many 'latifundios' maintain large extensions of unexploited land as purely speculative investments.

As for agricultural labour, there is a clear predominance of family labour in the holdings of 50 ha and below. In the larger estates, there is a greater emphasis on temporary salaried labour. It is also important to note the significant presence of sharecropping and leasing in the large properties. This is no more than the reproduction of family labour within these properties. The tenants play a particularly important role in the regions of the agricultural frontier, where they do the initial clearing of the land, and after a brief period of cultivation, leave, whereupon the land is incorporated into the large properties as pastures.

Table 4. Analysis of agricultural labour force by age, sex, and size of holding

	Total (millions)	% men (% over age 14)	% women (% over age 14)	Paid and unpaid family members	
				% men	% women
Less than 10 ha	8.3	59.0 (45.8)	41.0 (31.3)	54.2	41.0
10-100 ha	8.4	63.1 (51.2)	36.9 (27.4)	48.8	33.3
100-1 000 ha	3.0	73.3 (63.3)	26.7 (20.0)	30.0	16.7
1 000-10 000 ha	0.5	79.7 (73.1)	20.3 (15.6)	12.8	6.1
over 10 000 ha	0.06	82.9 (77.8)	17.1 (12.8)	6.9	4.1
Total	20.3	63.6 (51.2)	36.4 (27.6)	47.3	33.5

Source: Censo Agropecuario do Brasil, 1979, IBGE, Rio de Janeiro.

Table 4 shows the distribution of the labour force in the agriculture and livestock sectors by sex and age. It can be seen that men account for two-thirds of the total labour force and more than half the adult labour force. Children account for more than 20 percent of the total labour force with an almost exact division between male and female. It is also noticeable that the unpaid members of the family supply up to 95.2 percent of the total labour on farms up to 10 ha.

Small-scale agriculture is responsible for the largest portion of food production in Brazil. Some 60 percent of the supply of basic crops, vegetables, and fruits is obtained from farms which are smaller than 100 ha. Since the yields in the smaller estates (50-100 ha) are superior to those in larger farms, and since a significant proportion of the area of the larger properties is exploited by sharecroppers and tenants whose production should be added to that obtained in small estates, small producers, in fact, are supplying most of the basic foodstuffs to urban and rural Brazil.

Agricultural policy contributes to this since it determines the prices for basic foodstuffs, which are profitable only with traditionally-established costs - that is, with an underpaid labour force. As a result, the large properties specialise in agriculture for export and in livestock; for these activities the Government has a pricing policy compatible with capitalist profitability.

Due to the system of tough conditions and guarantees required, small properties do not have access to the subsidised credits that the Government offers for the production of export commodities. Thus, small land-owners tend to rely on the kind of agricultural production which is not profitable to the large property owners. In order to guarantee a minimum profitability, small land-owners are also forced to incorporate the whole family into agricultural activities without paying the full value of their labour. This explains why 80 percent of the properties which produce basic foods use only family labour (8).

The example of three products which are part of the basic Brazilian diet (beans, manioc, and maize) illustrates the role of small-scale production in the national food supply. Properties of less than 100 ha are responsible for 72.8 percent of bean production, 89.2 percent of manioc, and 71.9 percent of maize. In the case of beans and manioc more than 40 percent of total production is provided by properties of less than 10 ha. This is in contrast with the production of sugarcane and soybean, in which properties of over 100 ha account for 82.5 percent and 55.2 percent of the respective totals. Moreover, a proportion of the beans and maize as well as nearly two-thirds of the manioc are self-consumed, which shows the importance of these foodstuffs in the rural worker's basic diet (Table 5).

Table 5 also shows that only a small proportion of basic food producers use modern production technology (irrigation, fertilisers and pesticides) and the majority of those who do, restrict themselves to the use of

pesticides. As a consequence there is low productivity
in these crops: 550 kg/ha for beans; 12 793 kg/ha for
manioc; and 1 504 kg/ha for maize (figures for 1975).

Table 5. Production of staple foods

	% of production self-consumed	Use of modern technology (%)	Use of pesticides only (%)
Beans	22.8	25.3	13.1
Manioc	60.8	26.3	17.6
Maize	35.4	36.5	9.7

Note: Modern technology means the use of irrigation,
         fertiliser, pesticides, or any combination of
         these.
Source: Censo Agropecuario do Brasil, 1975.

ENERGY USE IN THE RURAL SECTOR

     The distribution of rural energy consumption by
fuel and size of estate is given in Table 6.   It can be
seen that total consumption increases with the size of
estates. This is particularly noticeable in the case of
diesel oil which is 130 times higher in estates of over
10 000 ha than in those below 10 ha; and that of gasoline which is 23 times higher.
     Wood is the predominant source of fuel in the
smallest farms and supplies 55 percent of their total
energy consumption. Only 4.9 percent of these farms use
electricity, but 90.5 percent use kerosene. The use of
charcoal is comparatively rare and is used by 12.9
percent of the smallest farms and only 1.6 percent of
the largest.
     Up to recently, rural energy policy has been re-
stricted to introducing electricity to rural areas.   It
has been implemented directly by the energy companies,
or by a system of energy-users' cooperatives.   In the
first, the energy company builds a main line and it is
up to the farmers, either with governmental financing or
with their own resources, to build extensions to reach
their properties, and to set up the necessary voltage
transformers.   In the second system, the cooperative
receives energy from the companies and distributes it to
its members (9).   It is worth emphasising that farmers
belonging to these cooperatives are not typically small
producers nor is rural electrification yet very wide-

100

spread in Brazil. Only 5 percent of the 5.0 million
farms had electricity in 1980, and a large majority of
them are in the state of Sao Paulo.

Table 6. Average consumption+ of each energy source by
          size of estate

(kgoe)

	Size of estate (ha)				
	0-10	10-100	100- 1 000	1 000- 10 000	10 000 and over
No. of estates ('000)	2 075.0	1 680.8	397.1	36.2	1.7
LPG	125.8 *(8.1)	114.7 (17.9)	202.8 (14.9)	317.8 (21.0)	628.9 (23.1)
Charcoal	379.3 (12.9)	412.3 (4.2)	614.7 (3.4)	1 114.1 (2.2)	1 302.9 (1.6)
Wood	1 918.8 (83.6)	2 667.6 (90.6)	3 407.0 (85.7)	6 402.2 (83.2)	10 801.4 (76.5)
Kerosene	38.3 (90.5)	43.5 (82.6)	60.7 (76.6)	125.1 (68.5)	343.6 (64.5)
Diesel	347.1 (3.4)	1 350.0 (11.7)	5 450.0 (24.5)	16 983.8 (43.7)	45 404.0 (64.2)
Gasoline	541.9 (3.6)	665.4 (17.5)	2 120.4 (27.2)	4 572.5 (49.7)	12 604.8 (70.2)
Electricity	122.7 (4.9)	143.1 (10.0)	468.9 (11.9)	1 248.3 (20.7)	2 190.9 (34.2)
Ave. consumption all sources per estate	3 473.9	5 396.6	12 324.5	30 763.8	73 276.5

Notes: *Figures in brackets give the percentage of
        estates using each energy source.
        +Consumption figures are averages for estates
        actually using each fuel.
Source: Calculated from data in Censo Agropecuario do
        Brasil, 1975.

        After the second oil price shock, the Brazilian
Government began moves to intensify the use of non-
conventional energy forms in Brazilian agriculture. Its

policy is to encourage the technological development of these new sources within research institutes and to open credit lines and provide subsidies that will encourage their use.

After pilot project experience, 575 biogas digesters have now been constructed, and the plans call for 6 200 units to be built in several regions of the country by the end of 1981. The Government's objective is to reach an ambitious goal of 1.5 million digesters in the second half of this decade. This programme is based on an estimated energy potential of 60 million toe of various wastes (10).

As for solar energy, there is a large potential use in grain-drying, using a process developed by the laboratory of the University of Campinas (State of Sao Paulo). Promotion of this is encouraged by a law which forbids the use of fuel oil for grain-drying after 1982.

FURTHER PERSPECTIVES

Since 1973, with the first substantial increase in the price of crude oil in the international market, the price of oil products has continued its upward trend in the Brazilian economy. Up to that time, the price had been declining in real terms, since its increase was lower than the inflation rate (11).

Table 7. Evolution of oil product prices in Brazil (1973 = 100)

Year	GIP*	Gasoline	Diesel	Fuel oil	Kerosene	LPG
1973	100	100	100	100	100	100
1974	129	177	139	139	139	150
1975	164	314	211	208	189	199
1976	232	466	325	336	279	278
1977	331	612	480	448	403	373
1978	460	815	631	591	544	488
1979	709	2 194	1 646	1 326	1 721	631
1980**	1 127	2 913	1 852	3 094	1 889	864

Note: Prices at the end of each year.
* General Index of Prices.
**Until May 1980.
Source: Author's research.

Table 7 shows that from 1973 to 1978 the prices of all oil products rose more rapidly than the General

Index of Prices (GIP). However, it can be seen that there were differences between the various derivatives. LPG prices, for example, were very close to the GIP, which means that in real terms they remained practically constant over the period. But the price of gasoline grew much faster than LPG which seems to reflect a policy of making car users pay for the additional cost of oil products.

A growth in wood demand in the urban sectors as a result of rising oil-product prices could have put the energy supply for subsistence agriculture into jeopardy. This, however, did not occur, since the main use of wood in Brazil's urban sector - for the cooking of food - continues to be substituted by LPG; this and the fact that the price of LPG remained practically constant during the whole period, account for the rise in LPG consumption in Brazil.

After 1973, a number of measures were taken to increase the internal supply of energy products. Petrobras, up to then a state monopoly company, increased the number of exploratory drillings in 1974. As a result of this, a large offshore oil field was found which allowed oil production to grow to 10 million tonnes a year over the last decade, with an anticipated increase to 25 million tonnes per year in 1985. In 1975, the Government broke up the Petrobras monopoly and has since permitted multinational companies to explore for oil on Brazilian territory. After 5 years, the exploration efforts of the multinational firms are insignificant compared to those of Petrobas, and none of the wells drilled by them has produced oil. It is worth noting that 35 percent of any oil found would belong to the multinationals who will also receive interest on their investments, paid at rates equal to the Bank of America prime rate plus 1 percent (12).

In 1975, a National Alcohol Plan (NAP) was instituted. This was designed to provide protection for the Brazilian sugar industry which was then being threatened by an international sugar crisis. It was also part of the policy of oil import reduction.

In 1975 Brazil also signed an agreement with Germany for the construction of eight nuclear power-plants (PWR) of 1 300 MW each before 1990, and for the necessary fuel-cycle facilities. At the time the agreement was signed the estimated cost of the investment was $400/kW, but today it is around $3 000/kW (13). This is up to 200 percent greater than for the hydroelectric power-plants (including transmission), whose potential is sufficient to supply Brazilian electricity demand for the next 30 years (14). As a result, the original plan has been postponed and the construction of the eight power-plants has been left to the year 2000.

With the second price shock in 1979, the search for

national energy alternatives to oil was intensified and
a policy of increasing oil prices was adopted as a means
of making alternative sources economical. The price of
LPG underwent a reduction in real terms, but the price
of the other derivatives increased considerably. In
particular, the prices of gasoline and fuel oil rose
enormously in 1979 and 1980. In the case of diesel,
there was a huge increase in 1979 but the rate of increase was less in 1980.

At the same time several programmes were launched,
aimed at the substitution of oil products by alternative
sources including coal, shale oil, alcohol, charcoal,
and hydroelectricity. Others are studying the substitution of oil by the intensive use of biomass and one
even proposed the use of 80 million tonnes of vegetable
oil as a substitute for diesel (15). This, however, is
still at a preliminary stage, and there are serious
doubts about its economic viability.

NATIONAL ENERGY POLICIES AND SUBSISTENCE AGRICULTURE

These new national policies will deeply affect
subsistence agriculture in Brazil. Some effects are
already being felt while others can only be inferred.

The first, though not the most important, comes
from the increase in the relative price of oil products.
As a result of this, the percentage of diesel and gasoline users in the smaller farm groups will tend to
decrease since the income of these users is so low. As
only a small proportion of farms of less than 100 ha use
these oil products, this should not radically change the
present picture of subsistence agriculture in Brazil;
but it will act as a restraint on the dissemination of
mechanisation in this sector.

The second effect will be as a result of the charcoal plan. Today in Brazil, around 80 percent of charcoal is produced from wood extracted from natural forests. An intensification of charcoal production at the
rate proposed by Government will certainly generate
competition for the wood used now by subsistence farmers. As wood provides such a high proportion of the
energy used in this sector, the effects will be extremely severe unless an intensive programme of reforestation
is immediately organised. The experience and the technical knowledge for this already exist, since several
steel mills have been working for some decades with
charcoal furnaces (of up to 9 000 tonnes annual capacity) in the region of Minas Gerais, and already 10 percent of this charcoal is produced from forests created
specifically for this purpose. This, however, is not
sufficient on its own. Since charcoal from native forests is slightly cheaper today than from artificial
forests, it will be necessary to create the pre-condi-

tions for reforestation. Among the advantages of reforestation is the fact that it is carried out on land for
which alternative uses are difficult to find, and that
it creates employment. Each 50 ha of forest, in fact,
requires two permanent employees. Given, however, that
the price of charcoal from native forests is estimated
at about US$67.00/tonne (16), equivalent to US$15.00/
barrel of oil, and that the technology of charcoal
furnaces is extremely simple, there is a high probabili-
ty that the supply of wood for subsistence agriculture
will become critical in the short run.

The effect of the competition for agricultural
land, which will occur as a result of the 1975 National
Alcohol Plan (NAP), is probably the most important in
the long run. This had as its original goal the production of 5 million cu.m. of motor alcohol in 1985; its
production plan was increased to 10 million cu.m. in
1979, after the second oil price shock.

When NAP was launched, it had the following objectives:

- the reduction of foreign currency expenditures on oil
  imports through the use of alcohol as a gasoline
  substitute;
- the reduction of regional income inequalities through
  the installation of alcohol distilleries in poorer regions of the country;
- the reduction of individual income inequalities
  through the use of labour-intensive technology;
- the use of unexploited land and unemployed labour
  through the implementation of projects in areas with
  excess supplies of both factors;
- an increase in national production of capital goods,
  since the programme would be carried out with national
  technology.

Two crops traditionally grown in Brazil, sugarcane,
an export product, and manioc, a basic food, were proposed as raw materials for alcohol production;
saccharine-sorghum, a crop not grown in Brazil was also
suggested. As a result of this plan, the production of
alcohol in Brazil grew from 580 thousand cu.m. in 1975
to 3 676 thousand cu.m. in 1980 (Table 8). Up to 1980,
318 projects were approved, with a total production
capacity of 8.2 million cu.m. per harvest. Almost all
use sugarcane as their raw material and the great majority of them are concentrated in the state of Sao Paulo,
which is the richest region of the country. A careful
analysis of these projects (17) has shown that the type
of property involved in the NAP is the 'latifundio'
type, and that the jobs created are temporary. All this
completely contradicts the original objectives of reducing individual and regional income inequalities.

The objective of utilising unexploited land was
based on the assumption that the basic raw material for
the NAP would be manioc, since this is not very demanding in the type of soil it requires. It was intended that its production would be intensified in regions of the agricultural frontier such as the 'Cerrado'
of the Central Plateau. However, the few experiments in
large-scale manioc cultivation failed and sugarcane has
predominated as the raw material for alcohol production.

Table 8. Alcohol production by type and region

(million litres)

	1975	1976	1977	1978	1979	1980
North/						
northeast	115.8	100.0	144.8	249.7	594.4	621.7
Anhydrous	3.5	21.0	76.9	198.1	510.4	350.6
Hydrated	112.3	79.0	67.9	51.6	84.0	271.1
Central/						
south	464.3	542.2	1242.8	2086.5	2855.9	3054.5
Anhydrous	216.8	251.4	1011.0	1745.4	2321.6	1822.0
Hydrated	247.5	290.8	231.8	341.1	534.3	1232.5
Total	580.1	624.2	1387.6	2336.2	3450.3	3676.2
Anhydrous	220.3	272.4	1087.9	1943.5	2832.0	2172.6
Hydrated	359.8	369.8	299.7	392.7	618.3	1503.6

Source: IAA

Sugarcane, in contrast with manioc, is a crop which
requires good quality soils. A large part of this soil
is already being used for basic foodstuffs or export
crops. The NAP requires the allocation of 2.5 million
ha for the production of sugarcane by 1985, with an
optimistically estimated average production of 4 cu.m.
of alcohol per hectare (18). The establishment of the
great majority of the alcohol distilleries in Sao Paulo
has already created competition for land between sugarcane for alcohol and food export crops, and pastures.
Analysis has shown that between 1974 and 1979, the
initial phase of the NAP, more than 27 percent of the
area used for sugarcane plantation had been used before
for production of the basic foodcrops of rice, beans,
maize, and manioc (3). The completion of the new projects in progress, will intensify this process and, as a
consequence, Brazilian subsistence agriculture is likely

to be heavily affected.

In summary, it seems as though the pressure exerted by the charcoal plan on the wood-supply from small properties, together with the competition for agricultural land created by the NAP in the highly populated regions, will have a negative impact in the medium term upon the supply of subsistence products.

REFERENCES

1. Anuario Estatistico do Brasil, 1979, IBGE, Rio de Janeiro.
2. Conjuntura Economica, fevreiro 1981, Rio de Janeiro, vol.35, no.2.
3. Mattar, H., 1980, Programa Energetico Nacional: Possibilidades e Impacto, IPT, Sao Paulo.
4. Brasil Energy, 24/02/81.
5. Cavalcanti, G.A., 1980, "O Pro-Alcool e o Nordeste - Contribuicao a Analise dos Impactos da Politica Alcooleira na Regiao", Rio de Janeiro, Tese de Mestrado.
6. Seminario de Conservacao de Energia, 1977, FINEP, Rio de Janeiro.
7. Mercado de Energia Electrica: 1979-2000, 1977, Eletrobras, Rio de Janeiro.
8. Graziano da Silva, J., 1978, Estrutura Agraria e Propriedade, Hucilec, p.267.
9. Rabello, P.B., 1977, III Simposio de Eletrificacao Rural de Cooperativas, Brasilia.
10. Programa Biogas, 1979, MME, Brasilia.
11. Oliveira, A., 1977, "Internalisation du Capital et Developpement Economique: L'Industrie Petroliere du Bresil", Tese de Doctorat, 3eme cycle, Grenoble.
12. Oliveira, A., "Contratos de Risco: O Fim do Monopolio Estatal do Petroleo", PTC/06-80.
13. Oliveira, A., Contreras, E.C.A., Gomes, F.M., 1981, Evolucao do Custo da Electricidade no Brasil, 2 Congresso Brasileiro de Energia, Rio de Janeiro.
14. Rosa, L.P., 1979, Energia, Tecnologia e Desenvolvimento, Ed. Vozes, Rio de Janeiro.
15. Campos, C., 1980, Sugestao para Programa de Substituicao de Oleo Diesel, mimeo.
16. Borges, M.H., et al., 1981, A Producao de Carvao Vegetal no Brasil, 2 Congresso Brasileiro de Energia, Rio de Janeiro.
17. Anciaes, A.W.F., et al., 1979, Avaliacao Tecnologia do Alcool Etilico, CNPq, Brasilia.
18. This is obtained by estimating the productivity of sugarcane as 60 tonnes/ha, and the production of alcohol as 67 litres/tonne of sugarcane.

ACKNOWLEDGEMENTS

The authors would like to thank the economist Ivo Mauricio Bettega de Loyola for his helpful cooperation in data gathering and processing. They are also thankful to the economist Antonio Barros de Castro for his comments and suggestions. Grateful acknowledgements are also due to Daisy Vedovi Barreto and Lucia Helena Henriques de Azevedo for skillful typing and organisation of the paper.

APPENDIX

Small production in Brazil can be classified into four types (1):

- small production on the frontier: located close to the agricultural frontier, in particular in Amazonia, this plays an important role in the initial preparation of the land for large agricultural estates. These areas shift continuously and disappear with the establishment of large-scale agricultural estates;
- the formal peasantry: principally present in the regions of the south and southeast. The producer owns the land, but the product is completely tied to an agro-industrial capitalist enterprise. In this case, the decision on what and how to sow belongs to the capitalist;
- small commercial production: located mainly in the southeast and in some areas of the northeast. The producers own the land, control its production, and bring its products to the market. This guarantees them a relative autonomy in the choice of product and its destination;
- small commercial family production: in this mode of production, the farmer uses the labour of the whole family to produce its own subsistence on his own farm, where he also works on activities related to the extensive monoculture of sugarcane. The products are brought to the market. This type is disappearing due to the fact that since 1960 there has been a movement to dispossess temporary harvest workers.

6
Jamaica

Arnoldo Ventura

Jamaica is an island of 7 000 sq.km. situated in the Caribbean, about 18 degrees north of the Equator. Half the island is at a height of around 300 m, with a mountain peak rising to over 2 000 m in the northeast. About one third of the land is steeply sloping, and covered with a thin poor soil, especially in the lime-stone areas where water is also scarce. As a result, only about 31 percent of the land is cultivable, with 18 percent being used for crops, and 13 percent for pasture. Of the remaining area, 24 percent is under forests, 20 percent is shrub and woodland with patches of subsistence farming, 12 percent is permanently unproductive, 8 percent is unused but potentially usable for agriculture, and the remaining 5 percent is urban and built-up (1). There are about 4 300 km of main roads around the perimeter of the island but some of the inland areas, particularly in the hilly parts, are without adequate roads.

The annual daily temperature of the island fluctuates between approximately 27-32 C on the coast. The higher elevations, and the nights, are usually 5-10 C cooler. Rainfall on the windward side of the central mountain range is around 3 200 mm per annum in the northeast and a little less in the rest of the northern areas. The leeward side of the range is much drier, averaging some 750 mm of rainfall per annum. Contrasting periods of long drought and heavy rainfall, especially during the hurricane season, are characteristic of the island.

Jamaica has a population of 2.2 million. The average density is 191 inhabitants/sq.km., composed mainly of negroes and mulattos, with a small proportion of Caucasian, Chinese, and East Indians. Over one million, 55 percent, live in the rural areas and the majority of Jamaica's subsistence farmers are negroes. It is estimated that, between 1980 and 1990, the population will grow by 263 000 people, despite the reduction in the birth rate observed since 1972, and an expected 10 000 emigrants.

Soil erosion is a major problem as a result of indiscriminate clearing of the forests for lumber and charcoal. In areas where no soil conservation measures are practised, especially on sloping land, up to a centimetre of topsoil is lost each year. Lands which were fertile in the days of slavery and used for large plantations are now barren, or provide only a few tenants and squatters with a meagre subsistence.

ECONOMY OF THE ISLAND

Jamaica's economy is founded on traditional plantation agriculture; but, recently, bauxite and tourism have become the main foreign exchange earners and Jamaica is now the world's third largest producer of bauxite and alumina (2). This industry accounts for about two-thirds of the total foreign exchange earnings (3) and consumes nearly half the island's energy supplies (4). This makes Jamaica one of the highest per capita consumers of energy in the underdeveloped world. Tourism, the second largest foreign exchange earner, has suffered significant declines in the recent past due to bad North American and Western European publicity, coupled with political unrest on the island. Sugar is the major agricultural foreign exchange earner with rum and molasses as important by-products. Other important crops are bananas, citrus fruits, coffee, and tropical fruits. The economy relies on the export of food and primary products, and on the import of food, capital equipment, consumer durables, and a wide range of services.

The Gross Domestic Product (GDP) in 1979 was JA\$3.9 billion* and the per capita income was estimated to be JA\$1 698; on small farms, however, it has been estimated to be only JA\$400 (5). In 1977, over 60 percent of the labour force earned less than 19 percent of the national income, while the top 5 percent enjoyed 35 percent of the total revenue.

Agriculture generates 11 percent of the GDP, mainly in the production of sugar, bananas, cocoa, citrus fruits, copra, and in forestry and fishing. Approximately 19 percent of the GDP comes from manufacturing, including sugar-processing, and the production of rum, beer, clothing, and furniture; 19 percent comes from government services, 11 percent from real estate and business services, 16 percent from the distributive trade, 8 percent from construction, 8 percent from mining and refining, and the rest from transport, storage,

---

*JA\$1.00 = US\$1.78 (1980)

communication, financing, insurance, and a number of miscellaneous activities (3).

External borrowing is high and reached JA$3 440 million in 1979, with a debt servicing burden of US$368 million per month. Due to the poor state of the country's finances, and its association with the International Monetary Fund (IMF), Jamaica underwent an exchange rate devaluation in 1978. As a consequence, real wages were reduced by over 30 percent, and personal per capita consumption fell 13 percent below the previous year; unemployment increased from 23 percent to 26 percent, consumer prices increased by some 35 percent; the trade gap widened, and the balance of payments deficit grew as the foreign exchange cost of imported energy spiralled.

The total labour force in 1980 was 953 000 and unemployment was over 35 percent. It is estimated that 350 000 Jamaicans between the ages of 14 to 22 years are illiterate and unskilled, or inappropriately skilled. This is because the island finds it difficult to provide school places for the approximately 65 000 children born each year.

Industry is expanding slowly and has progressed from the processing of a limited number of agricultural products to the production of a range of consumer goods. The manufacturing and service operations in the urban areas are, however, incapable of providing jobs for the influx of peasant farmers and their children. It is noteworthy that the productive sector also has great difficulty in providing employment for the present number of graduates.

Agriculture employs approximately 30 percent of the total labour force. In contrast, the other major activity in the rural areas, mining and quarrying, employs only 1 percent of the population. Despite the unemployment in other areas, however, many jobs in agriculture remain unfilled; it is also significant that, although more than 50 percent of the Jamaican population is under 15 years of age, most of the farmers in peasant agriculture are over 50 years old (6).

During slavery, the lowlands of Jamaica were occupied by large sugar and cattle estates, while the hills were mostly left in forest and bush. After emancipation most of the slaves left the estates and set up small subsistence holdings in the hills. Today, this dichotomy between large estates and small peasant holdings still exists, with the peasantry obliged to cultivate the most inaccessible and infertile areas. It is estimated that 78 percent of the farmers work only 15 percent of the total agricultural acreage, with holdings of less than three acres (less than 1.2 ha) per farmer (6), mostly on steeply sloping terrain.

Historically, agriculture for local food production

has been assigned a much lower priority than agriculture for export. This has serious implications for nutrition on the island and occasions a food import bill of US$30 million per month. As a result of the maldistribution of the nation's wealth and food supplies, about 70 percent of the population are below the recommended daily nutritional allowance for both energy-foods and protein. Jamaica is gradually being forced onto international welfare, and its position will become steadily worse unless it can begin to feed its population to a much greater extent than at present (7). It follows that it is of paramount importance to enhance the economic well-being of the rural agricultural worker whose present per capita income is only one quarter of the national average.

Previous rural development programmes have been numerous, but largely unsuccessful. Their major objectives have been to increase agricultural production by improving the rural infrastructure through the provision of clean water, improved health and education, and electricity. Policies have also included the construction of feeder roads for marketing goods, the expansion and diversification of agricultural production, and the improvement of agricultural marketing. The specific long-term objectives have been to achieve self-sufficiency in domestic food supply, while at the same time increasing the potential for export, by promoting non-traditional export crops, and generally enhancing the living conditions in the rural areas. Many of these programmes have ended in frustration and failure of implementation.

THE AGRICULTURAL SUBSISTENCE SECTOR

There are no good estimates on the size of the subsistence agricultural sector, but a rough estimate is that 44 percent of the island's population or 80 percent of the rural population belongs to this group. Farming in this sector is conducted by the old and illiterate, without any specialised skills or formal training. They rely on archaic knowledge, and employ very simple general-purpose tools such as forks, machetes, and hoes (8). They use traditional methods of cleaning, cooking, and maintaining their homes and livelihood. They display a strong sense of pride, and stubbornly adhere to superstition and religious dogma. There is also a fair degree of distrust and apprehension about modern methods and scientific approaches.

The people in this sector eke out an existence on the island's sloping and relatively infertile lands with little assistance from their society. Their families are usually large and it is not strange to find up to ten people living in a one or, at most, three room wooden shack, without running water, electric light, or indoor sanitation. They are almost completely removed from the usual amenities of modern living, but they have access to rapid communication through radio and "bush telegraph". Most of the younger members of these households dream of escaping from the bondage of subsistence living, but seldom possess the wherewithal to do so successfully. The head of the household is often forced to seek employment on nearby estates, or in the tourist trade, if these opportunities present themselves. Most feel that these jobs are less rewarding than working their own land but lament the lack of planting material, artificial fertiliser, and tools.

Families who have cultivated a piece of land for a long time tend to become de facto owners. It is not exceptional to find that many of these families have no legal document of possession, while others have operated as tenants on the margins of estates for so long that they consider these acreages to be theirs. Thus, although most of the subsistence agricultural farms do not legally belong to the farmers who work them, there is a certain stability in their tenancy.

The roles of women and men in subsistence farming are to a certain extent distinct. Men are the undisputed heads of households and are expected to work the fields and cut firewood. Women and children take care of household chores such as cooking, cleaning, and washing. Occasionally the roles of the sexes coincide, especially during reaping and marketing. Women are usually responsible for taking produce to the markets and selling it there; but the selling of livestock or agricultural produce on site is undertaken by the men. Both the procurement of water, which can be an extremely laborious task, and the collection of the firewood, after it has been cut and left to dry in the sun by the men, are undertaken by women and children. Men are also likely to bring in some firewood after the day's work in the field.

The rearing of livestock is extremely important to the survival of subsistence farmers. It offers some flexibility in their budgets by generating a modicum of surplus to cope with buying fuel, clothing, medicines, salt, cooking-oil, and other indispensables. The rearing of these animals is therefore under the direct supervision of the head of the household, with the help of the children.

The men in subsistence farming work 15 hours a day, starting at four in the morning, tending livestock, and ending at seven in the evening with the sharpening and cleaning of their tools. Women also have a difficult life in these areas. Women who have lost their men (marriages are not usual among subsistence farmers) have to become fathers in addition to being mothers to a household of children. They receive little help outside their village and are neglected by the Government, not considered by national planners, and overlooked by urban women's organisations.

Subsistence farmers have developed a system of community cooperation to help each other in times of heavy work load, incapacitation, or death. They give and receive work days, and food is also shared in case of dire need. Once a collective decision has been taken, it can only be modified or rescinded by communal agreement. Laziness and impoliteness are abhorred. Nevertheless, nutritional deficiencies and the resulting disease and lethargy now plague those trapped in sub-sistence agriculture. Mental retardation and anti-social behaviour emerge with growing frequency in the descendants of this group. As the prices of staple commodities such as salted fish, flour, and kerosene increase, and supplies become irregular, the desire to leave these subsistence farms grows. The tendency is for people to flood the urban areas taking their frus-trations and animosities with them.

The fact that the land is still fertile enough to accommodate some unsophisticated, technologically back-ward production in the subsistence sector has led to the faulty deduction that this type of agriculture requires minimum skills and knowledge. This misconception is reinforced by the fact that the school garden is often used as a penal institute for the unruly and that acade-mic non-achievers are regularly shuttled into agricultu-ral training. The prevailing attitude is that farm production is a lowly endeavour not befitting people who can find alternative occupations and there is a lin-gering impression that agricultural pursuits are the remnants of slavery. Privileged urbanites and large land-owners regard small-scale agriculture as uncompeti-tive, yet they baulk at collective farming among the small farmers. Subsistence farmers have become, lite-rally, the rejects of society.

Although the old members of subsistence families doggedly remain and fight all the prejudices and hard-ships, fewer and fewer subsistence farmers are found each year and, because of this, the island has to import increasing amounts of food to survive. Furthermore, as the subsistence farms progressively lose their labour force, and as those who choose to remain get older, the efficiency of their operations decreases. In their desire to hold on to the farms, those who remain persist in their ignorance of better agricultural practices. Erosion, overuse of land, and overgrazing are rampant and the environment is despoiled by the pressures of poverty.

At the same time, some of the larger, once more prosperous farmers are falling into the ranks of sub-

sistence. These farmers have gradually become uncompe-
titive because of their insistence on using old, inefficient techniques, and their inability to adapt to new
market conditions. Many of those recently fallen into a
state of subsistence have used their savings to leave
farming altogether, and a large number have fled their
country for menial jobs abroad.

The former Government, in attempts to stem the
slide in agricultural production, encouraged cooperatives, acquired and leased arable land to subsistence
farmers, established pioneer farms for urban youths to
participate in agriculture, and created agricultural
loan schemes. These programmes met with mixed success
because of intense opposition to them by large land-
owners, backward thinking among the conservative elite
in Jamaican society, and political sabotage. Bureaucra-
tic indecision, corruption, and indolence, together
with the shortage of foreign exchange, often left these
schemes without water, fertiliser, indispensable tools,
planting materials, adequate transportation, storage,
and processing facilities, or accessible markets. The
hesitant attitude of the poor farmer, local backwardness
in science and technology, and the slow manner with
which urban youths adjusted to rural conditions also
contributed to the failure of some of these programmes.

There are indications that such programmes will now
be scaled down, profoundly modified, or dropped altogether under the new conservative Government. This may
well mean that the provision of attractive incentives to
larger more traditional farms will receive more attention - to the exclusion of the subsistence agricultural
sector.

JAMAICA'S ENERGY POSITION

Jamaica depends upon imported petroleum for 90 percent of its commercial energy needs; bagasse supplies a
further 9 percent, and hydropower the remaining 1 percent. The bauxite and alumina industry, together with
aviation and bunkering, consume about 55 percent of the
oil imports, but this is paid for by sources outside
Jamaica and does not constitute a charge on the country's foreign exchange. It is referred to as the
"international energy sector".

Of the remaining 45 percent of petroleum imports
used in the "inland energy sector", roughly a third goes
to make electricity, a third for transport, and a third
in industry and commerce. Including alumina and bauxite, the manufacturing sector consumes about 70 percent
of the energy used in the country. About 100 companies
are responsible for this high proportion of the total
energy consumption but, unfortunately, they employ no
more than a few thousand workers.

Household energy consumption accounts for about 1.3 million boe per year or 17 percent of the petroleum used in the inland sector (9). The fuels used in domestic consumption are electricity (51 percent), kerosene (28 percent), liquid petroleum gas (12 percent), charcoal (6 percent), and fuelwood (3 percent) (10). As far as end-uses are concerned, the major one is cooking which consumes 44 percent of the total, 15 percent is used for lighting, 14 percent is used for refrigeration, and the remaining 27 percent is accounted for by air-conditioning and miscellaneous appliances.

A recent household survey (10) has revealed a wide difference in energy use between different income groups. The lowest income group, which includes about 191 300 households, or 27 percent of the total, has a daily consumption of 28.2 MJ. The highest income group, which covers about 9 percent of the population, has an energy consumption about eight times as high, at 232 MJ per day.

For Jamaica as a whole, kerosene is the most popular cooking fuel and supplies about 47 percent of the total energy used for this purpose. Liquid petroleum gas supplies 26 percent, and charcoal and fuelwood together provide 17 percent. Charcoal, in fact, is more important than electricity as a cooking fuel.

The pattern of fuel use, of course, varies with income. In the lower groups, cooking occupies a greater proportion of energy use since few have access to electric light or refrigerators. Cooking fuels also assume a greater significance because they are used for a wider range of activity, such as the boiling of fruit and vegetable skins as fodder for livestock. Moreover, cooking fuels are used with a low efficiency, frequently in open fires from which the heat losses are up to 94 percent.

Charcoal retails at about JA$0.88 per kg. Its rate of use in a charcoal stove is estimated to be about 0.4 kg/hour. Wood consumption, on the other hand, is an almost totally non-commercial activity for which no reliable figures are available. The Forestry Division estimated that in 1974 about 300 000 tonnes of wood were cut, of which about 5 percent would have been used as domestic fuel. It is now felt that about 17 000 tonnes of wood are being used annually as domestic fuel.

ENERGY IN SUBSISTENCE AGRICULTURE

Precise information on energy use in subsistence does not exist. Some end-use data have been collected for agriculture but they do not include details of the subsistence sector. The few energy studies which have included subsistence have invariably handled only its commercial aspects. Reliable estimates of forest fuels and animal power are non-existent; neither are there figures for energy use in household industries, cooperatives, and informal fruit and other agricultural processing operations. Inferences have to be drawn from incomplete and subjective information, or gleaned from a few interviews.

The main energy use in subsistence is, of course, cooking. Lighting is provided by kerosene lamps, candles, torches, and other devices which make use of animal fats and vegetable oils. Water for irrigation and drinking is obtained by manual lifting, mostly from nearby streams, if no municipal water-mains or wells are in the vicinity. Land preparation, harvesting, and transport are carried out by muscle power, employing a range of simple tools, containers, and traditional vehicles drawn, for example, by donkeys.

Kerosene, however, is the mainstay of the subsistence sector and accounts for 42 percent of total energy consumption. As the cost of fossil fuels rises and hence local electricity prices increase, more middle-income people are turning to kerosene, which, until quite recently, carried a substantial government subsidy. As more kerosene is used in the higher income brackets, less becomes available for the rural areas. The poor have great difficulty in finding the money to pay for the small amounts they need, and with the rising cost - kerosene has increased in price by about 300 percent since 1973 - the government subsidy becomes less significant. The position is made worse by the fact that, even when sacrifices have been made to obtain it, kerosene often cannot be found. The unobtainability of commercial energy supplies in the rural areas is, in fact, a greater problem to subsistence farmers than the escalating price of fuels. The subsistence sector is consequently forced, more and more, to rely on wood fuels.

Attempts to increase rural productivity have also been frustrated by the rising costs of other essential products derived from fossil fuels, such as artificial fertilisers, herbicides, and insecticides. The situation has been further aggravated by the fact that hardship in the rural areas has prompted a spate of larcenies, forcing many farmers to cut back planting in certain fields, while others succumbed to the temptation of illegally cultivating and selling ganja (marijuana).

The potential of charcoal as as a partial substitute for kerosene may, however, not be realised by those most in need. This is because charcoal is inferior to kerosene in its efficiency of use. The increases in its price in response to rising demand may actually make it more expensive than kerosene, which is now being sold for JA$2.50 per gallon. It is therefore important to improve the efficiency of charcoal stoves by modifying their design.

The increasing reliance on raw wood as fuel has begun to have a number of negative social and environmental consequences. The effects of indiscriminate tree-cutting are well-known. In addition, many subsistence farmers have been forced to rifle other people's plantations for wood and run foul of the law, adding further misery to their existing difficulties. Furthermore, as reliance on wood increases, they are forced to go further and further to obtain it; walking two to three miles for firewood is not now exceptional. Also, as commercial fuel becomes scarce, farmers have to spend more time collecting wood (three to four trips per week) because raw wood does not store well and is quickly eaten by insects or decays by microbial action. Moreover, as this task becomes burdensome for adults, children become involved, and consequently spend less time productively on the farms , or in school. During the rainy seasons farmers are forced to stockpile wood. Some make use of small kilns fashioned from oil drums to make charcoal and thereby improve the storage life of their collection. As the difficulties in obtaining firewood become greater and farmers look for other combustible materials, they gravitate to the use of agricultural wastes, which robs the soil of fibrous materials and recycled nutrients.

The prospects for fuel supplies in the subsistence agricultural sector are thus gloomy. Although the island has a rural electrification programme it has been estimated that 35 percent of the rural population, even if they were reached, would be incapable of benefiting from it because of the price of the electricity (11), which at present is JA$0.30/kWh. It has been estimated that the cost per month per family would be up to JA$75 which is outside the financial capability of the rural poor. Furthermore, stocks of kerosene and LPG are being consumed elsewhere before they reach the farmers. This is forcing the subsistence sector towards a total reliance on wood and charcoal but, as explained above, the increasing demand for charcoal and its rising price are putting it out of reach of subsistence farmers. Wood is left as the only accessible fuel and it is becoming scarce.

PAST AND PRESENT POLICIES

Escalating prices and the dwindling availability of petroleum have induced all non-oil-producing nations to embark on strategies to find alternative forms of energy. Jamaica initially paid little attention to these developments but towards the end of the seventies, the Government was forced to respond. In a planning frenzy, various energy policies and programmes were devised.

Campaigns to promote energy conservation and to educate the unaware public about the global and local energy crisis were launched. Likewise, surveys to determine the nation's energy potential and end-uses, referred to as a National Energy Auditing System, were mounted. A few local scientists at the Scientific Research Council had, in fact, foreseen the consequences of the events in the early seventies, and had already begun examining renewable energy resources, with little or no government support. This facilitated the setting up of an Energy Division at the Council, and an Energy Section was added to the Ministry of Mining.

The studies soon revealed that the high energy-intensity of the island's industries limited their potential reduction in energy consumption in the manufacturing sector to only 10-20 percent. It was also clear that economic growth would require increased petroleum use. Not much consideration was given to agriculture in these early planning efforts and none at all to the subsistence agricultural sector. The previous Government, however, did introduce a subsidy for kerosene. Although this subsidy was substantial, at one stage almost 50 percent of the cost, the price of kerosene gradually increased and great hardship was caused.

Although there has been a steady worsening of the energy position on the island, those institutions which have been looking for alternative sources of energy to the fossil fuels are still not being given adequate support, and some are openly ignored. From the sudden concern for dwindling energy supplies a few years ago, the country has slowly retrogressed to the original misconception that the island's energy problem can be solved simply by finding ways to earn more foreign exchange to pay the oil bill. These trends are in stark contrast to the National Energy Policy and Programme promulgated in 1980 as part of the 1978-1982 Five Year Development Plan (12). Briefly stated, the plan was to:-

- reduce dependence on imported energy and diversify the present energy supply mix away from imported petroleum;
- accelerate exploration for indigenous energy supply sources and promote their development (in this case, oil exploration is, in fact, being vigorously pursued);
- reduce the energy intensity of the economy whilst seeking to sustain economic growth, especially non-energy-intensive export-oriented growth;
- cushion the impact of continually increasing energy prices on the low-income groups, while adopting pricing policies appropriate to the promotion of the first two objectives.

It is interesting to note that the plight of subsistence agriculture was not mentioned in this Plan and that, while there was a call for cushioning the impact of the island's energy problems on the poor, recommendations were made for the gradual removal of the subsidy on kerosene without providing any alternative to ensure that the poor could afford the fuels they need. Even today there is still no specific policy to ensure that adequate supplies of energy reach the poorest farmers. Much of the present emphasis is on the urban areas and the manufacturing sector and it appears that these farmers will continue to be neglected in national energy planning.

In the face of inadequate support and insufficient numbers of qualified personnel, work on renewable technologies has, however, continued. The Scientific Research Council, soon after the dramatic increase in the price of fossil fuels in 1973, began to explore alternative energy technologies. Originally, these projects were not necessarily designed with the subsistence sector in mind, but rather arose as part of the technological trends of the time. Biogas generation was started in the rural areas; energy farms and more efficient production of charcoal were introduced in conjunction with the Forestry Division; and a search for safer and more efficient charcoal and wood stoves for indoor use began. Wind energy for irrigation, and more efficient solar crop-drying techniques were also explored in collaboration with the University of the West Indies.

Results obtained so far nevertheless suggest that these technologies may well be the salvation of the subsistence agricultural sector, at least in the short run. However, the lack of manpower has not only slowed down the generation of results, but has also prevented the demonstration of relevant developments to those most in need. Subsistence farmers are still unaware that a small home-made biogas plant using the excrement from ten pigs, or about eighty chickens, could provide all the lighting and heating in a rural household; that windmills, which were used successfully in the earlier part of this century on the island, could lift water from wells for irrigation; and that simple solar dryers could permit longer storage of agricultural produce.

Since most of the research and demonstration centres are situated in the capital city and since transportation is often unreliable, contact with the remote villages has been infrequent or non-existent. Attempts by the Scientific Research Council over the last four years to inform people, through the mass media, of the importance of technological developments to their livelihood have met with some success, but actual demonstration of the practical aspects of the Council's work have been far less successful. Without convincing practical displays rural people remain reluctant to adopt these methods.

Clearly, the paltry energy allocations to this disenfranchised sector are incompatible with its proper development. If these problems are to be tackled successfully, the subsistence agricultural sector must become a point of special focus and concern for all the other sectors in the community.

FUTURE POLICIES

Exploration has revealed that peat is the most significant non-renewable indigenous energy resource in the country. It exists in two major deposits which are estimated to be capable of providing about 40 percent (60 MW) of the island's electricity, or about 7 perecent of the island's total energy for a period of thirty years (13). Oil and gas exploration are getting under way and the prospects are encouraging (14). The hydropower contribution may be increased to about 4-5 percent, although at great cost, and there is some room for improvement in the efficiency of the use of bagasse for fuel.

Solar energy, logically, should also play a significant role in the long-term energy strategy of the island, but this will depend on appropriate technological developments and Jamaica's willingness to harness them. However, the solar energy technologies which are available for heating, drying, and cooling, can substitute no more than about 2 percent of the island's present total energy demand. Biogas and biomass in general are still at the rudimentary stages of development and application and, in the near future, will not be able to supply more than 2 percent, at most, of the island's total energy needs.

In the short run, therefore, because of the energy-intensive nature of the Jamaican economy, and with the present capability of local energy technology, renewable sources of energy are capable of reducing the island's energy bill by no more than about 10 percent over the next five years; while conservation and more efficient generation of electricity could conceivably save at best a further 3 percent. If indigenous oil is not found, the island will therefore remain heavily dependent on imported fossil fuels, despite the fact that it is rapidly approaching a position in which it will not be able to afford to pay for such imports. The continuing neglect of institutions and personnel engaged in finding ways to furnish the nation with energy alternatives seems to indicate a lack of local comprehension of the full dimension of the problem, and suggests that the deeper problem of chronic technological indifference in the society has to be handled first (15).

Before proposing what steps might be taken to ease the energy plight in the subsistence agricultural sector, it is useful to outline current plans for solving the island's energy crisis. Under the short-term programme, conservation measures are given high priority. To this end, comprehensive energy end-use surveys and national publicity campaigns have been started with the aim of persuading domestic, commercial, industrial and public sector consumers to take simple conservation measures such as switching off lights. Other more incisive measures, such as improving the energy efficiency of existing uses, and projects to introduce solar, wind, or biomass energy have also been initiated.

Medium-term objectives largely focus on energy supply and demand diversification, on the basis of detailed technical studies. They include using coal and peat as alternatives for electricity generation, garbage as fuel, municipal sewage for methane gas generation, medium and small hydro-projects, and creating a national transport system in the rural areas.

In the long-term, institutional development, major energy projects, new and emerging renewable energy technology, and better energy planning and coordination are contemplated. The principal developments anticipated include exploration for oil and gas and the completion of all hydroelectric feasibility studies with the construction of all those projects found practicable.

Better coordination and control of the supply and demand of energy are being planned by the Ministry of Mining and Energy. To this end, laws are being enacted to afford more control over the import and use of energy by the private sector. Although these policies and programmes will have an impact on subsistence agriculture, they are being promulgated without a full appreciation of the needs of this sector. It is not unlikely that such a resolution of the energy problem for the rest of Jamaica, could cause a deepening of the energy crisis in the subsistence agricultural sector by widening the gap between it and the more privileged groups and reducing the likelihood of any trickle down of energy from the urban or industrialised sectors.

Subsistence farmers already make a significant contribution to the island's food requirements; and without further contributions from them, the often-mooted self-sufficiency in basic foodstuffs will be a long time in coming. Additional supplies of energy along with an upgrading of skills could transfer this sector into a more meaningful contributor to the national economy. But in order to introduce technical improvements, an active extension programme will have to be established and probably managed from rural outstations. Mutual respect will have to be achieved between extension workers and farmers, and a spirit of

collaboration will have to prevail for any rural extension programme to succeed. Subsistence farmers have
been victims of exploitation and deception for so long
that a special effort will have to be made to win their
confidence. This cannot be achieved from a position of
superiority and condescension. Certain programmes are
now facing this problem and have training components
specifically tailored to subsistence farmers (16).

Moreover, research and development work on alternative sources of energy which can be useful for
subsistence farmers will be of little or no avail unless
a concerted effort is made to include this sector as a
discrete and important component of national policy. It
is not sufficient to improve the nation's general status
with the expectation that, in time, this group's energy
needs will be satisfied. This did not happen in the
past when energy was cheap and abundant and we cannot
reasonably expect this to happen now, when energy is
expensive, diverse, and scarce.

Future policies to deal effectively with the energy
plight of the subsistence sector must be based upon
certain definite principles. The objective of introducing new technologies must be concerned with reducing
human drudgery, and thereby enhancing the quality of
life. It also appears necessary to replace commercial
fuels, which have become too scarce and expensive, with
energy from decentralised and more readily available
non-commercial sources. Actions which degrade the environment will have to be avoided. Basically, the total
quantity of energy available to the rural areas will
have to be increased significantly.

Policies will also have to be based on reliable and
current information, obtained from surveys of current
use patterns. The changes which will occur with economic growth will have to be anticipated. Decisions will
have to be made on whether to supply energy on an individual family or on a communal basis. The cost-effect-
iveness of each technology will have to be weighed. Any
policy will have to enlist the willing support and
enthusiasm of the farmers from the outset if it is to
succeed (17).

It should also be borne in mind that, while all the
studies of needs and resources are being conducted,
subsistence farmers are still in dire need of energy.
Actions should be taken to ensure that each family
receives a decent quota of kerosene, wood, or charcoal.
If this is not done, irreparable ecological damage will
ensue from the scramble for firewood.

In contemplating energy policies for the subsistence sector, it is worth remembering that it has
been in the grip of an energy crisis long before the
rest of society. Increasing commercial energy supplies
is of little avail to the poor farmers who rely on non-

commercial fuels for their survival. The one advantage is that, given the low per capita consumption and limited range of end-use requirements, relatively simple technical alternatives will be found useful; on the other hand, such unsophisticated technologies restrict production possibilities.

Turning now to more detailed technical considerations, certain renewable energy technologies appear suitable, as far as Jamaica is concerned, for providing energy to the subsistence agricultural sector. There is immediate scope both at the family and community levels for biogas generation. The Scientific Research Council is building and demonstrating community size biogas plants with capacities of around 60 cu.m. which can produce around 60 cu.m. of gas, with an energy value of about 300 kWh per day. The Council hopes to demonstrate that methane is capable of fuelling engines to generate electricity or power tools and thereby allow subsistence farmers to start up small agro-industries. However, the introduction of a biogas programme has to be coupled with an investment and risk capital scheme, and a technical extension service if it is to be successful. Even a simple single-family biogas plant is expected to cost JA$700, which is beyond the financial reach of subsistence farmers, and their present level of skill would not permit them to construct such a unit and operate it properly without instruction. Introduction of ferro-cement in the construction of such units is expected to reduce their cost and allow a certain amount of mass production (18).

Jamaica is an Arawak word meaning the land of wood and water and the island can still be so described today as it was in the pre-Colombian times. Because of this, biomass has been advocated by serious scientists as a long term solution to the island's deficiency in fossil fuels. It has been suggested that substantial amounts of energy could be obtained from silviculture, sugarcane farms, and ocean energy farms (19). Assuming that Jamaica will require some 0.154 quadrillion BTU (quads) per year by the year 2000 (excluding the bauxite industry), 150 590 ha of silviculture, 139 600 ha of sugarcane or 208 800 ha of ocean farms could satisfy the energy needs of the island.

One plan is to plant fast-growing trees which mature within five years - such as the Ipil Ipil, (Leucaena leucocephala), Quick Stick (Glivicidia sepium) and Calliandra (Calliandra calothrysus) - in areas of high demand for woodfuels. The Jamaican Forestry Department intends to establish fuelwood plantations at the rate of 40-200 ha annually over a 2-4 year period. It is estimated that, after 3 years, fuelwood can be obtained at the rate of 30 tonnes of fuelwood (or 10 tonnes of charcoal) from a plantation with 2 400 trees.

Further, it is estimated that total energy utilisation can be improved by avoiding the use of fuelwood directly (20), and encouraging the use of wood energy-products such as charcoal, methane, and distillates of wood. Charcoal is the most useful wood energy-product to date. Special portable metal kilns have been designed to produce charcoal more efficiently than the traditional method of burning wood in pits or mounds covered by earth (21). Charcoal cooking is estimated to cost only JA$0.24/day which is within the range of most poor farmers. A more efficient charcoal stove is also being tested (22), which will reduce smoke and toxicity and will be cheap enough for these farmers to buy. Heat loss can be reduced by having specially designed pots recessed into the stoves (23).

The forest fuel option appears to be the least capital-intensive of all the alternatives examined to date within both its fuel-production and end-use equipment costs. The proper husbanding of forest resources in the vicinity of subsistence farms would eventually obviate the need for long treks to obtain firewood. Since the initial and recurring cost of such energy plantations cannot be borne by subsistence farmers, government action is required. Meanwhile, it would appear feasible for farmers to exploit the energy potential of the luxurious growth in their tropical surroundings. Grass, coconut remains, and a variety of shrubs, could be cut, sun-dried, made into charcoal using small kilns (24), and then used as fuel in drought or extremely wet periods of the year. Furthermore, pelletised grass and molasses, with the effluent from biogas plants, can be used to supplement livestock feed. Energy farms of other types could also be explored, such as fresh-water and marine algae-growing which produce cell mass for energy and fertiliser.

In areas with falling water, mini-hydro installations can generate electricity or be used directly to produce mechanical energy for the operation of tools. This requires various kinds of construction and damming, special methods of conveying water, and different types and sizes of turbines. Again, this type of operation cannot be expected to be initiated by poor farmers. The cost of a kilowatt of electricity produced by this method is expected to be as high as US$1 000, therefore more work is needed to lower costs. The introduction of innovations such as wooden turbines might make this option more accessible to the poor.

The microbial generation of fuels from biomass is another possibility for satisfying the energy requirements of the rural sector. However, the raw material for this operation and the purification of the alcohols produced, have yet to be fully worked out for the Jamaican context.

Solar and wind-generated electricity still require more technological manipulation to bring the cost within acceptable limits for poor farmers. The problem of storing the energy during periods of low solar activity is not yet satisfactorily solved. It is clear, however, that the potential of decentralised energy production from solar collection cannot be written off by tropical countries like Jamaica. Foreign developments in this area must be closely followed and local research and development in well-conceived areas must be encouraged. The development of a solar cooker which can be used indoors and which can produce high temperatures would be a distinct fillip to subsistence agriculture as well as to urban households.

Cost is another significant obstacle to the deployment of alternate energy sources in the subsistence agriculture sector. The estimated cost of JA$700 for the family biogas unit mentioned above is too high for poor farmers. Likewise, the price of a better stove may appear nominal, but it is a significant investment for the poor. It appears that some form of loan scheme or cooperative strategy must be devised to assist these farmers to make more efficient use of non-commercial energy resources. Subsistence farmers will be inclined to continue with the old methods, such as cooking on open wood fires, unless they can be convinced that there are better ways, which they can afford, of accomplishing the same job.

It should also be noted that a good portion of the energy needs of subsistence farmers are met by animate energy. This is limited by the number of persons and domestic animals available and by the amount of animal food that can be obtained. Thus, while the extremely low usage of inanimate energy in this sector impedes agricultural production and prevents the transition to new industrial activities, there is not much scope for increasing it along traditional lines.

ROLE OF EXTERNAL AGENCIES

So many multilateral and bilateral aid agencies have taken an interest in the energy problems of underdeveloped countries that confusion is often created in the recipient countries as they attempt to deal with the plethora of good intentions. The small number of local professionals finds itself distracted by the constant lobbying of the various agencies. Moreover, many of the aid programmes are imprecisely defined, overlapping, or subtly tendentious. One of the first steps which external agencies could take would be to rationalise their technical assistance to avoid duplication, and ensure that all facets of the particular problem they are tackling are being attended to. This means the fullest cooperation with national planning and implementation bodies, and better coordination among local representatives of the aid agencies. A directory of the various institutions involved, together with their specific areas of expertise or altruism, would help rationalise the present position. Laying down arbitrary conditions for the receipt of aid merely to ensure the good image, or the political objectives, of the donor, should also be curtailed. A certain honesty of purpose must prevail in the delivery of technical assistance.

External agencies must also acquire an intimate knowledge of the area and the problems they wish to tackle. It is not enough to send in a team for a short period to interview the relevant national bodies, or rely on a resident diplomat to provide essential information. A conscientious understanding of the entire situation and a feel for the culture and personalities involved are absolutely necessary for success.

The rate at which so-called appropriate technologies in energy are being developed complicates their research and selection by poor countries. Accurate description and evaluation of the different types and variants of energy technologies would be of immeasurable importance to those in poor countries. Certain technologies such as photovoltaics and photobiology may be expensive at present, yet may be ideal for longer-term. External agencies could usefully provide a system where these technologies, or the rights to them, are acquired in "bulk", or bought not for one country but distributed at a nominal cost to many countries. This would allow one large payment to be made for a patent or for proprietary information, instead of each poor country having to handle these purchases on their own with limited negotiating abilities and technological competence.

Donors should also use their influence to ensure that poor countries take the dilemma of their subsistence agricultural sector seriously. Programmes funded under such a scheme should be monitored carefully, not only to ensure that targets are met but also to gather valuable information as implementation takes place. Careful documentation of successes and failures, and their causes and consequences, will be invaluable to the programmes which follow.

Although the contribution which renewable energy technologies can make to the energy needs of developing countries is not clear, the position in the poor rural areas is so desperate that these will have to be relied upon. They must, therefore, be fully supported, simply because no alternatives have yet been envisaged, and action is needed now. Funding agencies should bear in mind that intimate knowledge can make the difference between success and failure and that as far as possible

local human resources should be utilised. Collaboration
between local and foreign institutions on projects to
provide energy to the rural sector can do much to educate both sides and help focus the world's research and
development potential on the serious problems of poverty
(25). The statements of national governments should not
always be taken as the last word. Non-governmental
agencies, professional associations and other private
concerns must not be overlooked when projects are formulated and implementation is undertaken. Competition
between public and private sector bodies may highlight
obstacles in the proper use of technical assistance.

External agencies must thus become more knowledge-
able about the unique problems of this sector, and must
be prepared to act with patience, honesty and
persistence. They must make a positive effort to sensi-
tise local management to this fundamental but often
neglected problem. The governing elite in underdeveloped countries are disinclined to be bothered with
those who are not visible and who bring little
affluence to their urban base. This shortsightedness
must not be allowed to prevail.

REFERENCES

1. MacPherson, 1973, Caribbean Lands: A Geography of
    the West Indies, Longmans Caribbean Ltd., Jamaica.
2. National Planning Agency, Kingston, Jamaica, 1979,
    Economic and Social Survey: Jamaica.
3. Department of Statistics, Kingston, Jamaica, 1979,
    National Income and Products.
4. Ashby, W. R., 1980, "Energy Assessment in Jamaica -
    A Progress Report", Ministry of Mining and Natural
    Resources of Jamaica, Paper for National Academy of
    Sciences Workshop on Energy Assessment Methodolo-
    gies in Developing Countries, Jekyll Island, Geor-
    gia, U.S.A.
5. Personal Communications.
6. Coke, L.B. and Gomes, P.I., 1979, "Agriculture in
    Science and Technology Policy in the Caribbean",
    Social and Economic Studies, Vol.28, no.1, Insti-
    tute of Social and Economic Research, University of
    the West Indies, Jamaica.
7. Girvan, N., 1979, Some Economic Facts for the Eco-
    nomy: The Way Forward, National Planning Agency,
    Kingston, Jamaica.
8. Durant-Gonsalez, V. and Graham, V., 1979, The Me-
    chanical Technology of Small-Scale Agriculture in
    Jamaica, Scientific Research Council, Jamaica.
9. Ashby, W.R., 1980, A Survey of Alternative Energy
    Possibilities in Jamaica, Petroleum Corporation of
    Jamaica, Kingston.
10. Bardowell, D. and Gordon, D., 1980, Energy End Use

Surveys of Jamaica, 1: Household Energy Survey (1979-1980), Ministry of Mining and Energy and the University of the West Indies, Kingston, Jamaica.

11. Richards, J.A., 1978, Jamaica Energy Problems as They Relate Specifically to Agriculture, Ministry of Agriculture, Kingston, Jamaica.

12. Ministry of Mining and Energy, Kingston, Jamaica, 1980, National Energy Policy/Programme, Ministry Paper no.8.

13. Robinson, E., 1980, "Peat as Fuel", Jamaica Journal, no.44, pp.46-51.

14. Wright, R., 1979, "Oil and Gas Exploration in Developing Countries such as Jamaica", Jamaica Journal, no.43, pp.77-83.

15. Ventura, A.K., 1979, "A Commentary on the I.Q. of the Undeveloped Countries and the Jones' Intelligence Doctrine", Technology in Society, Vol.1, pp.255-259.

16. Personal Communications with Mr. Carlyle McKensie, Director, Canadian Universities Overseas, Kingston, Jamaica.

17. Ventura, A.K., 1980, "Cultural Impact of the Transfer of Technology on Developing Countries", Cultural Dimensions of Development, Centre for International Development, Neuilly Sur Seine, France.

18. National Academy of Sciences, Washington D.C., U.S.A., 1973, Report of Ad Hoc Panel, Ferrocement: Applications in Developing Countries.

19. Lee, K.C., 1980, A Suggestion to Solve Jamaica's Energy Problems, Scientific Research Council, Kingston, Jamaica.

20. Eckholm, E., 1975, The Other Energy Crisis - Firewood, Worldwatch Institute Paper 1, Washington D.C., U.S.A.

21. Paddon, W.R. and Harker, A.P., 1979, "The Production of Charcoal in a Portable Metal Kiln", Rep. Trop. Prod. Inst., G119, iv, 29pp., London, England.

22. Canadian Hunger Foundation and Brace Research Institute, MacDonald College of McGill University, Ontario, Canada, 1977, A Handbook on Appropriate Technology, pp.B7, 1-8.

23. Arnold, J.E.M. and Jongma, J., 1978, "Fuelwood and Charcoal in Developing Countries", Unasylva, Vol.29, no.118, pp.2-9.

24. Little, E.C.S., 1973, The Minicusab Kiln for the Rapid Small-scale Manufacture of Charcoal from Scrub, Coconut, and Coconut Shells, Report of UNDP/FAO Rhinocerous Beetle Project, Apia, Western Samoa, pp.25-34, Samoa.

25. Ventura, A.K., 1979, Contribution to the UNCSTD Debate, Scientific Research Council, Kingston, Jamaica.

7
Senegal

El Hadji Sene

Senegal is a small country on the west side of Africa. It covers 197 600 sq.km. and has a population of 5.7 million. It has common borders with Mauritania in the north, Mali in the east, Guinea and Guinea Bissau in the south. The Gambia, an English speaking country of 10 500 sq.km., stretches into Senegal for a distance of 300 km eastward along the river Gambia.

Climatic conditions and rainfall vary greatly from north to south; but the temperature differences are less marked. Rainfall, in fact, is the most decisive factor in shaping the landscape and climatic zones of the country. Three such zones can be distinguished.

The Sahelian zone covers roughly 25 percent of the country. Within it is the Sahelo-Saharan sector in which the annual rainfall is 300-500 mm and the main vegetation is the Acacia, though other species occur. The rest of this zone is the Sahelo-Sudanian sector where annual rainfall is slightly higher, in the 500-700 mm range. This zone is the principal area for cattle raising. It consists of steppes and wooded savannah. The natural annual rate of wood growth is low - far below 1 cu.m./ha ; a value of 0.3-0.5 cu.m./ha can be assumed.

The Sudanian zone covers 55 percent of the country. Rainfall is between 700 mm and 1 200 mm per annum. Some authors make a subdivision of this zone into the Sudano-Sahelian sector (annual rainfall 700-900 mm) and the Sudanian (900-1 200 mm). Here the vegetation* is much more varied, with the Combretum species being the

---

* The principal species are: Cordyla pinnata, Parkia biglobosa, Combretum species (mainly glutinosum), Anogeissus leiocarpus, Terminalia macroptera, Bombax costatum, Tamarindus indica, Sterculia setigera, Cola cordifolia, Ficus species.

132

most important source of fuelwood. In this area the rate of natural wood growth improves considerably and annual production varies between 0.5 and 1.5 cu.m./ha.

The Guinean zone covers the remaining 20 percent of the country. It has an annual rainfall of 1 200-1 500 mm. Annual wood production is over 1 cu.m./ha.* It should also be noted that despite these regional charac- teristics of vegetation and landscape, some tree spe- cies occur throughout the country. Notable among these is the Borassus aethiopium that occurs in the valley of the river Senegal along the north-east boundary of the country, in mid-Senegal, the east, and Casamance in the south. This is also so of the coastal mangroves which are found from the marshy delta of the river Senegal in the north down to the tributaries of the river Casamance in the south.

Winds are also of major importance in Senegal be- cause of their relationship with the rains, and because of the damaging effects they can have on vegetation. The most important are the southern and maritime 'alize', and the north-eastern 'harmattan'. The former are related to the summer rains, while the 'harmattan' quickens the drying of grass and the fall of leaves, and often triggers the deadly series of bush fires which destroy pastures in the Sahelian zone.

LAND USE AND CROPS

The area under forest cover (forest reserves, fauna reserves, pastoral reserves, controlled hunting areas, national parks) is about 7 million ha or 35 percent of the country. At least another 3 million ha, though under no special legal protection, are under good savan- na or forest cover.

Livestock are accepted in the forest reserves and sylvo-pastoral areas. In 1978-1979, the estimated popu- lations of the different stock were as follows:

- cattle   2 500 000
- sheep)
- goats) 2 800 000
- horses   240 000
- camels   7 000

There is considerable fluctuation in the relative areas of natural forests and cultivated lands, for the most part at the expense of the forests. The principal

* The main species are: Khaya senegalensis, Daniella olivieri, Ceiba pentandra, Afzelia africana, Pterocarpus erinaceus, Cordyla pinnata.

crops are the following:

- groundnuts (1 200 000 ha); production is unpredict-
able these years, due to erratic climatic conditions;
under normal circumstances Senegal produces 900 000
- 1 000 000 tonnes;
- millet and sorghum (1 000 000 ha); average production
800 000 tonnes;
- rice (92 000 ha in 1978); produced through a traditional sector, mainly in the Casamance area, and a
modern sector developed by intensive extension-work
through government agencies; production 145 000 tonnes
in 1978;
- niebe beans cultivated along with other crops, such as
millet, mainly in the northern half of Senegal;
- corn (57 000 ha); making considerable progress in the
Sine-Saloum, Senegal Oriental, and Casamance areas;
average production 53 000 tonnes;
- cotton (49 000 ha); making good progress in eastern
Senegal, though often hampered by irregular rainfall,
pests, and lack of competitiveness with groundnuts;
production 34 000 tonnes in 1978.

DEMOGRAPHIC AND ECONOMIC DATA

In 1980 the population of Senegal was estimated to
be 5.7 million. The average rate of increase is 2.7
percent (4 percent in urban sectors and 2.1 percent in
rural areas). The urban population is about 30 percent
of the total. Distribution is not even throughout the
country. The western areas and so-called "groundnut
bolt" have a population density of 50 inhabitants/sq.km.
or higher, while the northern and eastern areas are
nearly empty, with only 5 inhabitants/sq.km.

Table 1. Exports 1978

	Weight (tonnes)	Value ('000 000 F.CFA)
Peanuts etc.	219 000	23 539
Cotton	10 505	3 415
Fish and other marine products	46 746	17 663
Gum arabic	562	139
Leather and hides	958	514
Phosphates	1 739 000	13 713
Marine salt	128 115	3 114

Senegal imports heavily. The items with the greatest impact on the economy are food - mainly rice and wheat - oil, and wood products. The oil bill is a particularly heavy burden. Wood is imported for building purposes and furniture-making; the total wood imports in 1978 were 40 000 tonnes. Exports consist mainly of agricultural and fishery products, but a substantial contribution is made by minerals. Table 1 shows the volume and value of exports in 1978*.

The swift rise of the oil bill and the decline of the groundnut crop, as a result of climatic changes, have placed Senegal in very difficult economic circumstances. The Government has drawn up an emergency plan for financial and economic recovery as part of its Sixth Development Plan.

THE RURAL SUBSISTENCE SECTOR

Some 70 percent of the Senegalese population live in the rural areas. They engage in agriculture, animal husbandry, and fishing. An increasingly important proportion of the rural population undertake forest-based activities, including lumbering, fuelwood-gathering, charcoal-making, and the production of non-wood forest products.

Groundnut production is vitally important to the national economy as can be seen from the export statistics. It is also the main source of cash in the rural subsistence sector. In eastern Senegal, cotton is acquiring greater importance and is another source of cash in the rural sector. Substantial increases have been granted recently to farmers for their cash crops (Table 2) as a means of encouraging an increase in output but a great deal remains to be done to give food production the importance it deserves.

Table 2. Price increases for farm produce

	Old producer prices (F.CFA/kg)	New (1981-1982) producer prices (F.CFA/kg)
Groundnuts	50.0	70.0
Cotton	49.0	55.0
Millet	40.0	50.0
Rice	41.5	51.5
Maize	37.0	47.0

* $US1.00 = F.CFA 225.00 (July 1980)

Animal husbandry, because of the climatic conditions and the availability of good pasture, is particularly important in the northern half of the country. Until recently, cattle-raisers used to overstock their herds; but with the activities of the Husbandry Development Agency, coupled with the frequent failures of subsistence crops, a tendency to sell more stock has recently been noted. A better integration between agriculture and animal husbandry is well under way in the groundnut belt and the Senegal River valley and will undoubtedly give further impetus to this tendency.

At the beginning of national sovereignty Senegal nationalised 90 percent of the country's land. Before, land tenure had been under the control of the so-called 'lamanes', people from affluent families who distributed the land in return for certain material privileges. After nationalisation, the Senegalese Government created rural communities ruled by councils which deliberate on the distribution of land to farmers. Retention of tenure is decided on the basis of the actual work carried out on the land; a piece of land which is left derelict may be withdrawn by the rural council and given to a prospective better user.

Women play a role as important as men's in rural society. They participate equally in field activities; in mid and southern Senegal they used to be the sole rice growers, while men worked on groundnuts and other cereals. Women are exclusively in charge of all tasks related to cooking. Specifically, they have the day-to-day task of finding cooking fuel.

The methods of cooking in the Sahelian countries have been widely described. In Senegal two methods are used in the rural areas: the 3-stone support and the tripod. These are both very demanding in wood consumption and since 1977, the year of the Club du Sahel and CILSS report on energy in the Sahelian countries (1), efforts have been aimed at improving the situation. In cities the so-called 'fourneau malgache' is used with charcoal only. This too is susceptible to improvement in its efficiency of fuel use.

ENERGY IN SUBSISTENCE AGRICULTURE

Throughout the rural subsistence sector, the main fuel source is wood. The only other source is kerosene which is widely used in all Senegalese villages for lighting purposes. In 1977 Senegal imported 18 000 tonnes of kerosene in a total of 566 000 tonnes of all oil products.

The availability of wood varies considerably depending on which area of Senegal is considered. The Senegal River valley has been self-sufficient in fuelwood up to now. The local population has no problem and fuelwood is simply and freely gathered from forests of Acacia nilotica. Large areas of these forests have been dying as a result of the severe droughts in 1972 and 1977, and the inadequacy of the Senegal River floods. The new agricultural irrigation projects connected with the international Three State Programme for the Senegal River will also reduce the forested area and, of course, the availability of wood.

The Diery area is a strip of land 10-15 km wide south of the Senegal River valley; this zone used to be covered with mixed savanna species of Balanites aegyptiaca, Acacia senegal, and Acacia raddiana all of which have been severely decimated by the droughts; nevertheless, fuelwood for the rural population is not yet posing a serious problem.

South of the Diery, the so-called sylvo-pastoral zone has also seen its trees killed by drought. In this area, people can still just find what they need, but in many places fuelwood is scarce and even absent; farmers or herdsmen have to go 3-4 miles from their settlements to find suitable wood unless they are prepared to use the extremely light stems of Calotropis procera. The use of cowdung is not common.

In these three zones, wood for fuel is still available but it is evident that a crisis could occur if nothing is done immediately to reafforest. However, in the groundnut belt, mainly the divisions of Louga, Kebemer, Tivaouane, Bambey, Mbacke, Mbour, Fatick and Gossas, the fuelwood position has become really critical and people have to go a long way from their villages to find any wood, if at all. In these areas, agricultural residues are often used because of the fuelwood crisis. In southern Sine-Saloum, eastern Senegal, and Casamance, fuelwood is readily available and no immediate threat is in view.

It should be noted that in all those areas where wood is available, the fuel demands of the big cities compete heavily with the needs of rural subsistence. It is only because rural consumers are not very particular about the quality of the wood they use that the position remains manageable.

Only in very rare cases is wood bought in the rural areas; people simply collect it in the nearby bush or forest. This changes in larger villages of 1 500 - 2 000 people and upwards, where at least the better-off in the community buy their fuel, either as wood or charcoal. In the big cities of Dakar, Saint-Louis, Thies, and Kaolack most families use charcoal; fuelwood, however, continues to be used in the poor suburbs.

The trade in fuelwood and charcoal to meet the needs of the big cities is well organised throughout the country. The western cities, of which Dakar is by far the largest, obtain their fuelwood and charcoal from the

forests near Dakar, the forests of the Senegal River
basin 300 km away, the central and eastern forests, and
the distant Casamance area.

Fuelwood cutters and charcoal burners have to be
registered annually with the Forestry Department. They
receive a licence which allows them to apply for logging
permits, either as individuals or through cooperatives.
The creation of cooperatives is encouraged, and 80 percent of the wood permitted to be cut each year is allocated to them.

Wood and charcoal operations are efficient and a
lot of wood is taken from the upcountry areas for sale
in the cities. Every year 80 000 to 90 000 tonnes of
charcoal and 100 000 steres* of fuelwood are taken to
Dakar and the neighbouring towns of Thies and Mbour.
The intermediate cities in the country are quite often
unable to get all the fuelwood and charcoal they need.
Trade with the big cities also reduces the availability
of wood in the rural and semi-rural areas.

The development of modern agriculture has also had
some adverse effects on wood consumption. Groundnut and
cereal production have been improved by the introduction
of small-scale machinery. This introduction of small
simple machines in the rural sector has, in turn, led to
the emergence of a handicraft sector of village black-
smiths, with a consequent rise in the use of charcoal in
the villages. The quantities involved have not been
measured but there is no doubt about the tendency.

PAST AND PRESENT ENERGY POLICIES

Energy policy in the rural subsistence sector did
not exist before 1977; indeed, there was little national
energy policy either. Since 1977, however, the Senegalese Government, together with other Sahelian governments, have endeavoured to devise and implement an energy policy, following the recommendations of the CILSS
energy strategy report.

In Senegal, an attempt had been previously made to
reduce the impact of urban wood consumption on the
forests and savannas. This was based on the use of
butane gas as a substitute for charcoal. The programme
began in 1973 and went well at first but by 1974, when
the prices of petroleum products had more than doubled,
what had appeared to be a good ecological solution was
proving to be an economic disaster

The programme was called 'Blip Baneh' (Joyful Blip)
and it set itself the ambitious programme of reducing

---

* 1 stere = 1 cu.m. stacked wood = 0.6 cu.m. equivalent
  solid.

charcoal consumption by 15 000 tonnes in the first year, 35 000 tonnes in the second year, and so on up to 100 000 tonnes in the fifth year. This, it was esti- mated, would reduce total charcoal consumption by 50 percent. Gas burners specifically adapted to Senegalese cooking practices were devised and successfully adopted. But the substitution of wood and charcoal by gas did not work at all. In Table 3, the numbers of gas-fired cooking stoves, and the quantities of gas sold, are shown together with the quantities of wood and charcoal used concurrently. The operation continues, but it is not capable of replacing the use of charcoal because of the high price of the gas. The 'Blip Baneh' programme resulted in very good business for the company involved; but it failed to reduce the demands in char- coal in the big cities, particularly in Dakar for which it was mainly intended. Needless to say, this programme had no effect whatsoever on the rural subsistence sector energy balance.

Table 3. Butane gas, wood and charcoal use, 1974-1980

	'Blip Baneh' cooking stoves	Quantity of gas sold (tonnes)	Wood use (tonnes)	Charcoal use (tonnes)
1974	7 200	178 200	26 461	92 510
1975	9 000	453 600	50 187	93 081
1976	13 600	955 800	58 195	85 091
1977	25 100	1 863 000	37 602	93 519
1978	34 400	3 083 400	31 952	90 083
1979	53 500	5 124 600	-	-
1980	59 000	5 761 800	-	-

Now, however, energy policy for the rural sub- sistence sector is recognised as important, and some basic principles have been established around which it can be built. These include the following important guidelines:

- the solutions to energy problems, particularly in the rural sector, will only come from a multi-pronged approach;
- the so-called new energy resources, such as solar energy, offer no immediate solutions to rural families and need more research;
- wood will remain for many years to come the main source of energy in the rural areas;

- development of indigenous energy resources such as the deposits of peat in western Senegal would solve some of the country's energy problems;
- agricultural residues such as groundnut shells could be used for fuel, and improved methods of utilisation could be devised.

In the crucial area of wood policy, the following approaches are being used:

- stopping the misuse of wood and developing methods of economising the resource, both at the level of processing and that of the consumer;
- devising improved cookstoves and distributing them widely among rural households;
- improving natural forest management;
- establishing new woodfuel plantations, either through government projects, or through rural community and individual projects.

It might be noted here that women, in the Senegalese rural sector, are very receptive to new ideas, and often far more so than men. The education programmes aimed at improving the use of energy and devising new cookstoves have been directed towards women as their main targets in order to achieve the most rapid results.

RECENT INITIATIVES

Community forestry is given a prominent place in the Sixth National Plan starting in July 1981. In the Fifth Plan a start was made on rural community plantations oriented mainly to solving fuelwood supply problems. In the 1980 planting season 1 000 ha of fuelwood plantations were established by rural communities and individuals. Some 500 000 seedlings were also distributed on an individual basis to be planted in compounds for later pollarding.

Research has successfully devised an improved charcoal kiln in the Casamance area. This raises the average yield of charcoal from under 20 percent to over 25 percent. This new kiln is being promoted through a "Renewable Energies Project" being implemented by the Forestry Department.

Much effort is going into devising and popularising new and more efficient cookstoves. A very interesting project called the 'Ban ak Souf'* (clay and sand) cook-

---

*The Ban ak Souf programme is funded by USAID and is implemented by the Centre d'Etude et de Recherche sur les Energies Renouvelables (CERER).

stove is under way.   It started in March 1980 and   aims
at a significant reduction in the quantity of wood used.
The design is still under development but its principles
are to insulate the burning material within a combustion
chamber and control the intake of air.

The programme started by building stoves for demonstration.   Later,   masons were trained in stove-making.
Then an intensive media campaign was launched, sponsored
by   the Ministry of Industry.   Many intensive   training
sessions   have   been   undertaken   in   the   first   year.
Assessing the first results of the project,   the "Ban ak
Souf   Cookstoves in   Senegal" report   (Gern, E., et.al.)
says: "The achievements are impressive: nearly a thousand stoves built, of a wide range of designs. They save
between 30 percent and 60 percent of the fuel previously
needed.   The majority are in daily use.   The owners are
often wildly enthusiastic about them."

FUTURE POLICIES

The   position   of   subsistence agriculture   in   the
country is economically very weak.   Farmers and cattle-
raisers   alike   have   suffered   tremendously   from   the
drought   years;   they   need time and a lot of rain   for
rehabilitation.   In the meantime, their energy supplies
should be, if not free,   available at a very low cost.

It   is important for policy-makers to realise that,
up to   now,   households   in the   rural   sector   have   not
counted   fuel   for   cooking,   lighting,   or   produce-pro-
cessing   as an item of cost. They have used   wood,   and
collected it free from where it was growing.   Education
will be needed to make rural people aware of the changes
that   are   occurring   in the availability   and   cost   of
energy supplies.   The most urgent areas for action are,
in fact, in education, training, and planning.

Education   will   have   to be used   to   counter   the
belief   that natural forests are a gift of God and   will
regenerate with no need for man to interfere.   This is a
basic   hindrance   to any policy aimed at   improving   the
present fuelwood supply position.   Education will   also
have   to   be used to make people aware of the   need   for
restraint   in   the   use of forests and of   the   need   to
protect and expand fuel sources.   An open-mindedness to
new   methods,   new sources of energy,   new utensils   and
cooking methods will have to be inculcated.

Training   will   have to address such issues as   the
improved   use   of local   resources,   better   methods   of
felling   so   as   to promote coppicing,   new   methods   of
charcoal-making and improvement of kilns, new methods of
cooking, the making of improved stoves, and new uses for
wood   and   agricultural residues   such   as   briquetting.
Training   is also needed in plantation and nursery techniques   at village level,   and for combined   methods   of

farming and tree-growing, using foliage for fodder and wood for fuel.

Planning must be seen to address itself to solving the problems of the many rather than the few; it must be based on a knowledge of the full range of energy technologies available, including sources such as peat. It must allocate funds to the areas for priority action; and it must combine local community initiatives with those of the state.

ROLE OF EXTERNAL AGENCIES

External agencies have often worked successfully with the Senegalese Government on important projects. Their role will become even more significant during the Sixth Development Plan. Energy problems are being fully recognised in this Plan, but the country does not have the resources in finance or manpower to solve them.

In order to solve the energy problems of the sub-sistence sector, not only financial support is required, but also a broad knowledge of the methods which have been used elsewhere to deal with such problems, and which can be adapted to Senegalese social and economic conditions. Bilateral and international cooperation can be very efficient in this.

Table 4 shows some of the projects in which external agencies have collaborated with the Senegalese Government in programmes related to the energy problems of the subsistence agricultural sector. This illustrates the important role these agencies have, both in policy-framing and the implementation of relevant projects.

Table 4. Collaborative rural energy projects between external agencies and the Senegalese Government

Project title	External agency	Senegalese counterpart	Objectives of project
Renewable energy resources	USAID Peace Corps	CERER Forestry Dept.	.better use of resources .design and dissemination of improved charcoal kilns and cookstoves
Village & community wood lots	USAID AFRICARE Peace Corps	Forestry Dept.	.establishment of 50 village & community wood lots (100 to 200 ha)

Table 4 (ctd')

Project title	External agency	Senegalese counterpart	Objectives of project
			.dissemination of cookstoves
Bandia fuel-wood project	USAID	Forestry Dept.	.establishment of 6 000 ha plantation to provide fuelwood for cities and villages around Dakar
Fuelwood project	World Bank France FAO	Forestry Dept.	.management of natural forests (10 000 ha) .state plantations (2 000 ha) .village & community wood lots (3 000 ha)
Long-term forest master-plan	France	Forestry Dept.	.study & design of a long-term policy in forestry & particularly fuelwood
Other projects related to fuelwood under design	Netherlands Sweden USAID ADB ...etc	Forestry Dept.	

REFERENCES

1. CILSS, Club du Sahel, 1978, Energy in the Development Strategy of the Sahel: Situation, Perspectives, Recommendations.

8
Nigeria

G. J. Afolabi-Ojo

GEOGRAPHICAL AND ECONOMIC BACKGROUND

Nigeria has an area of 941 849 sq.km., with a
north-south extension of 1 046 km, and an east-west
extension of 1 127 km. The coastline runs more or less
east-west for most of its 960 km length, and is marked
by lagoons, creeks, and the extensive Niger delta
consisting of sand and silty mud deposits. The country
rises steadily northwards, from the coastal creeks and
lagoons, through plains and rock ranges of sandstone and
granite with an average height of around 600 m above sea
level, to a hinterland plateau which rises to 1 830 m,
and finally to a region of undulating sandy plains in
the extreme north.

The country lies between latitudes 4-14 N, and
has a hot, wet, humid, tropical climate. The mean maximum temperatures are 32.2 C in the south, and 40.6 C in
the north; the mean minimum temperatures, on the other
hand, are 12.8 C in the north and 21.1 C in the south.
The range of temperature through the year is generally
low; for example, in Port Harcourt it is 7.7 C, Lagos
8.9 C, Ilorin 11.5 C, Kaduna 13.5 C, Sokoto 14.4 C, and
Maiduguri 15.1 C.

The relative humidity varies considerably from the
wet season to the dry season, and also from the coast to
the hinterland. The lowest mean values, of about 20
percent, are recorded during the dry season, especially
from January to April, in the north; and the highest,
of over 90 percent, during the wet season, especially
from June to October, in the south. Two dominant air
masses shift over Nigeria, the dry north-easterly continental air mass from the Sahara, and the humid south-
westerly maritime air mass from the Atlantic, coming
into contact with each other in the Inter-Tropical Dis-
continuity (ITD) zone. The seasonal migration of the
ITD to the north, in July, brings the wet season; while
the move to the south, in January, brings the dry sea-

son. This causes a double peak in the rainfall in the southern parts of the country, and a single peak in the north. As much as 400 cm of rain falls during about eleven months of the year in the southern parts; but it is less over the rest of the country reducing gradually, but with some irregularity, to around 50 cm, during about three months, in the northern parts.

Broadly reflecting the amount and distribution of the rainfall, the vegetation of the country varies from mangrove swamps along the coast in the south, through a zone of rainforest characterised by luxuriant trees laced with lianes and epiphytes, to the Guinea savanna zone with its deciduous trees interspersed with grassland, and finally to the Sudan savanna of tall grassland dotted with sparse trees, especially the acacia species, in the north.

The soils, which derive their main characteristics from the parent geological rocks as well as from the climatic conditions of the country, show considerable diversity. In general, four main groups of soils can be recognised:

- hydromorphic and organic soils developed on alluvial, marine, and fluvio-marine deposits of variable texture, notably along the coast and river flood-plains;
- the regosols and brown soils developed on drift and continental sedimentary deposits in the northeastern parts of the country;
- the ferralsols, some (the achrosols) with iron concretions and some (the oxysols) without, developed essentially on sedimentary rocks;
- the highly ferruginous tropical red and brown soils of the basement-complex rock areas (1).

From the geographical parameters of location, size, topography, temperature, wind, rainfall, vegetation, and soils, briefly outlined above, it can be seen that the ecological background of subsistence agriculture is indeed varied and complex. The economic setting of the country is also a reflection, to a considerable extent, of these geographical resource endowments, but transformed by the effects of a varied and dynamically changing series of human inputs. Agriculture, for example, is carried out in all parts of the country and has dominated the national economy for many decades, if not centuries.

Until the oil boom of the 1970s, more than half the total national revenue, in fact, was derived from agriculture and the vast majority of the population was engaged in agricultural activities. Although the contribution of agriculture, including livestock, forestry, and fishing, to the gross domestic product is now down to about 19 percent, as can be seen in Table 1, the pro-

portion of the inhabitants engaged in agriculture has
not fallen as drastically. In 1952-1953, agriculture,
forestry, and fishing were the primary occupations of 78
percent of the adult male population; by 1966-1967
this had fallen to 71.1 percent; and in 1970 it was
62.2 percent (2).

Table 1. Projected Gross Domestic Product at 1977
factor cost: 1980-1985

(% distribution)

Sector	1980	1981	1982	1983	1984	1985
Agriculture	12.1	11.8	11.5	11.1	10.8	10.4
Livestock, forestry & fishing	8.7	8.4	8.2	8.0	7.7	7.5
Mining & quarrying	23.5	22.4	21.4	20.3	19.3	18.3
Manufacturing	7.4	7.9	8.5	9.1	9.8	10.5
Utilities	0.3	0.4	0.4	0.4	0.4	0.4
Construction	10.5	10.3	10.1	9.9	9.7	9.4
Transport	3.5	3.7	3.9	4.1	4.2	4.4
Communication	0.3	0.3	0.3	0.4	0.4	0.4
Wholesale and retail trade	20.0	20.6	21.1	21.7	22.2	22.8
Housing	4.1	4.2	4.2	4.2	4.3	4.3
Govt. services	6.3	6.6	6.9	7.2	7.5	7.8
Other services	3.3	3.4	3.5	3.6	3.7	3.8
Total	100.0	100.0	100.0	100.0	100.0	100.0

Source: Federal Ministry of Planning, Lagos, Outline of
the Fourth National Development Plan, 1981-
1985.

The recent importance of sectors such as mining and
quarrying, and wholesale and retail trade, is partly
responsible for the relegation of agriculture to third
position in contribution to the Gross Domestic Product.
Nonetheless, the population of agricultural workers is
still by far the largest in the country. Over 80 percent of the adult male population in the rural areas are
farmers. The vast majority of these farmers are small-
holders, more appropriately known as small-scale or
subsistence farmers "who account for 90 percent of the
total agricultural output" (3).

THE RURAL SUBSISTENCE SECTOR

In most parts of Nigeria, the rural subsistence
sector is still the region least transformed by man.
Most of the infrastructural facilities of development,
change, and modernisation are not yet available there.
Many areas are not connected with the adjoining urban
centres by motorable roads, but only by bush paths and
unpaved dry-season roads. However, during the period of
light work on the farms and also during major festivals
and ceremonies in the urban centres, many of the inhabitants of the rural areas, especially in Yorubaland, make
it a point of duty to travel to adjoining parent towns
where they have their permanent homes.

The rural subsistence sector is characterised by its
dependence on the nearby towns and cities with which it
has historical, cultural, and economic linkages. More
often than not, these urban areas tend to sap the economy of the rural sectors associated with them. Many of
the recently established industrial projects designed to
boost the economy of the nation have been located in or
near towns where they can be assured of the infrastructural facilities which cannot be found further away.
Such projects further tilt the balance against the rural
areas which become more and more impoverished. As a
result, the young and adventurous drift to the urban
areas in search of support and sustenance. There is,
therefore, a growth of the cities and a steady dwindling
of the rural population in which only the aged are left
behind.

Another characteristic of the rural subsistence
sector is the generally low level of productivity of
both labour and land. In fact, the human labour input
is at such a low level that the productivity of labour
is generally reckoned to be zero, or even negative.
Similarly, the productivity of the land is so low that
the nutrient yield per hectare does not even rise to
that of per capita nutrient requirements. These low
levels of productive efficiency are the result of the
inadequate use of farm machinery, fertilisers, chemicals, and improved seeds.

Although inhabitants in the rural communities are
primarily farmers, they also engage in complementary and
supplementary occupations such as crafts and petty
trading. They also take part in various village industries, most of which are small-scale, with products
destined for domestic markets only. Incomes in rural
subsistence are low and difficult to compute since they
are partly in kind rather than cash. Even in the buoy-
ant days of export crop production - cocoa, rubber, palm
products, cotton, and groundnuts - much of the income,
especially that in foreign exchange, did not reach the
hands of the rural farmers but was siphoned off by

middlemen and Commodity Marketing Boards. Only an insignificant proportion of the capital derived from agriculture was invested in modernising subsistence production. The subsistence sector lacked the capacity for capital formation by itself and therefore remained impoverished.

Most subsistence farmers produce food only for themselves and the extended family dependent on them. The food grown includes root crops such as yam, cassava, and cocoyam in southern Nigeria; grain, especially guinea corn and millet, in northern Nigeria; and a mixture of root and grain crops in the middle belt. In recent decades some traditional export crops have been cultivated by small-scale farmers attempting to produce beyond the subsistence level. Cocoa, kola, rubber, and oil palm were grown in the south, rice and beniseed in the middle belt, and cotton and groundnuts in the north. As a result of many adverse conditions including labour shortage, a drop in commodity prices in the world market, and competition for land by non-agricultural claimants, export crop production has now dwindled to the extent that some of the commodities, for instance groundnuts, previously grown and exported in large quantities are now being imported.

Most subsistence or small-scale farmers normally operate small-holdings. The plots vary from an average of about 0.4 ha per farmer in Imo and Anambra States where there is considerable pressure of population on limited land resources, to about 1.0 ha in places representing the average conditions in the country, up to about 1.6 ha in the northern states. From a variety of sources it has been estimated that the average size of the farm holding is 1.3 ha in Kano State and 3 ha in Sokoto State, that about 56 percent of the cultivated area in the country consists of farms smaller in size than 2.02 ha, and that farm sizes of more than 4.05 ha account for 27 percent of the total cultivated area (4). There are as many as 5 million small-scale farmers in the country (5).

The generally small size of farm holding is related to the limited production required by the subsistence farmers to meet their needs; the simple and rather ineffective tools used for farming; the land tenurial system which accords to individuals control of the plots being cultivated by them even though the ownership may be vested in the community; and the rights of individual holdings conferred on members of mutual assistance groups who may find it necessary to engage in some cooperative endeavours to exploit the advantages of economies of scale. Moreover, the necessity to keep some plots fallow for a number of years reduces the amount of land available for cultivation and makes the size, per farm holding actually under cultivation, much smaller. Most of these small-sized plots are scattered and fragmented. In some parts of the country each household has at least two farm plots, one close to the settlement (known as the nearby farm, 'oko etile') and another further away (known as the distant farm, 'oko egan') in areas of prolonged bush fallow.

The agricultural output from small-sized farms, operated mainly with human labour provided by the family and using no labour-saving devices and little or no chemicals for regenerating the soil, is low when related to the potential of the land. The traditional strategy of increasing productivity, through mixed cropping, goes some way to augment the gross return per hectare, but does not increase the actual yield of each crop. It is therefore not unusual to find side by side, or at close quarters, two contrasting patterns of farming, the traditional which is essentially subsistence, and the modern which is cash or export oriented. By and large, the former still dominates the agricultural landscape of Nigeria.

A major feature of the traditional economy has been that of real, or disguised, full employment in the farming sector. Every able-bodied male adult takes part in farming, either full or part-time. A few privileged farmers with a large dependent labour force and relatively large farms are able to produce some surplus. All the rest manage only to provide enough for their basic consumption. It is these who were invariably hit by food scarcity at the peak of the dry season, more aptly described as the hungry season.

ENERGY USE IN THE RURAL SUBSISTENCE SECTOR

Other than for domestic purposes, there is practically no use of fuels in the rural subsistence sector of Nigeria. Agriculture, which is the major economic activity, depends almost totally on human labour. For clearing and tilling the land, simple implements such as cutlasses and hoes are still being used. Electricity, which has been provided for most urban centres, has yet to reach the majority of villages though, in recent years, efforts have been made by the Government to extend the rural electricity supply. Even when this objective has been attained, additional efforts are required to take the supply beyond domestic use and into meeting agricultural and rural industrial needs. This requires adaptations to farming methods and devices. The farming sector will continue to pose intractable problems for power supply as long as the type of machinery using such power is not available on farms.

The non-use of energy for agricultural purposes in the rural subsistence sector is indeed remarkable. Throughout the preceding three or four decades of con-

tact with Western agricultural practices, during which
mechanisation has been assuming increasing importance,
traditional subsistence agriculture has not been dis-
posed to adopt the methods of modern agriculture. Just
as the same crops have been grown over many years, so
too have the methods and tools in use remained more or
less constant. Farming models which the Ministries of
Agriculture and Natural Resources were anxious to introduce and which would have been accompanied by the use of
energy were either still-born or short-lived. The failure of these models has meant that introducing energy
sources for agriculture has, for all practical purposes,
been a non-event in the history of agricultural development in Nigeria.

It may be argued that the use of energy in subsistence agriculture has been absent over the centuries
mainly because of the relatively cheap and abundant
availability of human labour. As has been pointed out
elsewhere,

> the population estimate for Nigeria indicates that
> the country possesses an ample supply of human
> labour. About 80 percent of the adult working
> force of Nigeria are employed in primary production
> and related activities, and the proportion living
> in rural communities lies between 72-82 percent.
> Labour supply is, however, critical at certain
> times of the year and could be worse with large-
> scale mechanisation (6).

In other words, as long as the level of agriculture
is still subsistence, human labour will be more than
adequate to sustain it. But whenever agriculture
reaches a modernised level, for instance through the
introduction of mechanisation, the labour supply will
become critical. It has been noted that

> the supply of labour to primary production is like-
> ly to follow a downward trend in Nigeria, unless
> concerted efforts are exerted to reverse it. In
> this connection it should be pointed out that the
> costs of hired labour have been rising, based on
> minimum wages for urban labour-use. In addition,
> young men are unwilling to undertake the heavy
> chores of weeding with simple tools which magnify
> the drudgery of primary production. These situa-
> tions pose serious problems for the supply of farm
> labour in the decades ahead (7).

That energy is not used for agricultural purposes
in the rural subsistence sector does not mean that some
forms of energy resources are not available there.
There are indeed various forms of energy which have

been, and are being, tapped in the rural areas for domestic purposes especially cooking, heating and lighting. These energy resources are mainly of the biofuel category and include woodfuels and animal dung. In recent years, kerosene is becoming a popular fuel, especially for lighting, using bush-lamps, lanterns, and pressure or tilley lamps. Recent research findings indicate that, in most parts of Nigeria, fuelwood is the leading source of energy for cooking and heating, and that kerosene is by far the most used for lighting purposes (8).

PAST AND PRESENT POLICIES IN SUBSISTENCE AGRICULTURE

From the time when Nigeria began to show interest in planning the whole of its economy, considerable importance has been attached to upgrading agriculture. Many policies and strategies were proposed at various stages in the country's successive Economic Development Plans. In the First National Development Plan of 1962-1968, concern for agricultural development was included as one of the five major priorities which sought "to achieve a modernised economy consistent with the demo-cratic, political, and social aspirations of the people". The reference to agricultural developments was unambiguous in its target,

> an increase in the production of export crops through better seed distribution and more modern methods of cultivation, as well as through the increase in the area under cultivation, the intro-duction of more modern agricultural methods through farm settlements, co-operative (nucleus) planta-tions, improved farm implements such as hydraulic hand presses for the expression of palm oil, and a greatly expanded agricultural extension service (9).

This is the least any government with an awareness of the country's almost total dependence on agriculture might have done, and, in retrospect, it is easy to condemn it for not having done more. In the opinion of the Federal Ministry of Agriculture and Natural Resour-ces,

> the Plan accorded no more than peripheral atten-tion to agriculture, a sector which is the largest in terms of contributions to the GDP and employment capacity. The little attention that was paid to agriculture was directed to export crops, a point that belies the objective of balanced growth (10).

Beyond planning to provide improved farm implements such as the palm oil hand presses, no attempt was made to introduce any worthwhile labour-saving devices into agricultural operations. In short, the energy input proposed for the period 1962-1968 was virtually nil.

The energy input implied in the 1970-1974 Development Plan was not much of an improvement. It went as far as providing for the development of "crop production, irrigation and research, credit, mechanisation, manpower and agricultural extension services" but, apart from the broad consideration given to mechanisation, no specific attention was directed to improving the quantity or quality of energy inputs for agriculture.

The 1975-1980 Third Development Plan and the 1981-1985 Fourth Development Plan share common views in large measure on agricultural modernisation. As stated in the 1981-1985 Plan,

> government policy is expected to emphasise promotional activities aimed at increasing the output of smallholders who currently account for more than 90 percent of domestic food supply. The bulk of the targeted incremental production is expected to come from these smallholders through increased productivity and multiple cropping (11).

As can be seen from the various policy measures in successive Development Plans, the Government has persistently spearheaded the drive for agricultural transformation in Nigeria. The policies enunciated have been translated into concrete programmes, some of which have been adopted or, in fact, already implemented, and a few of which are still in the pipeline. In general, all the policies so far considered for the "modernisation and development of the agricultural sector may be grouped into eight classes of farm policies, namely: developmental, compensatory, regulatory, permissive, remedial, educational, punitive and adaptive" (12). These groups are neither water-tight nor mutually exclusive, but they are convenient for use as a theoretical typology of farm policies.

Developmental farm policy is concerned with the broad issues of the development process. It includes various programmes and projects undertaken by government to ensure the involvement of farmers in agricultural development. Examples include the introduction of farm machinery, food processing and fertiliser plants, irrigation projects, facilities for transportation, and marketing networks. More often than not, the inputs provided by the Government are so beyond the reach of small-scale farmers that they hardly benefit from them.

Compensatory farm policy tends to make up for losses sustained by farmers in developing the technology and practice of agriculture. Subsidies are used to guarantee minimum selling prices for export cash crops and thus act as a means of encouraging farmers to step up production. Although price inducements for agriculture have long been applied in Nigeria, the policy has not had its full impact on subsistence farmers who frequently have to operate through buying agents or other middlemen. It has been consistently asserted that the former Marketing Boards and their modern counterparts have tended to benefit everyone except the actual small-scale farmers whose interests they were meant to protect in the first place.

Regulatory farm policy attempts to control and monitor the development of modern agriculture through laws on land use, such as the 1976 Land Use Decree, and through enforcement of laws on standard weights, measurements, and gradings of crops and livestock. In particular, the Land Use Decree made generous provisions of land for agricultural purposes.

Permissive farm policy is designed to enable the Government to assume advisory and supervisory responsibilities for the implementation of agricultural modernisation processes, particularly co-operatives, farmers' unions, credit groups, and market associations. It is noteworthy that in spite of the best intentions, and although the Government has employed various forms of credit policy, credit has not been available to the average farmers, because they are unable to provide the mandatory collaterals and are constrained by the low productive capacity of the traditional agricultural system. Recent attempts to institute Agricultural Co-operative Banks and other Agricultural Credit Guarantee Schemes have been to the advantage of a few large-scale corporate farmers rather than the numerous subsistence farmers. The Government has also sponsored various farmers' co-operatives, through its institutional development policy, in order to mobilise small-scale producers. The Government is also setting up a National Agricultural Co-operative Management Centre to train agricultural co-operative managers and leaders of co-operative organisations. It remains to be seen whether subsistence farmers can fit into the structure of these organisations.

Through its remedial farm policy, the Government has sought to deal with the problems brought about by the process of modernising agriculture. For instance, there is an active programme for pest eradication, and institutes have been set up to focus on the problems of tsetse fly and locusts, among others. Similar steps have been taken to establish packages of improved farm practices, public and corporate farms, and credit for insurance schemes (13).

The educational farm policy of the Government is

executed mainly through agricultural extension services.
Farm institutes and farm settlements which have been
established in some parts of the country offer special
training opportunities for farmers. The impact of these
schemes on small-scale farmers seems to be of little
significance so far, because of the gap between the
extension agents and the farmers, and because of the
remoteness from the experience of the average small-
scale farmer of the models being provided. With an
estimated 1:2 500 ratio of extension workers to farmers
in Nigeria, as contrasted with 1:250 in Kenya, it is obvious that the demonstration effect of experimental
farms may not have the same impact on the average subsistence farmer in Nigeria as in Kenya.

Punitive farm policy is not yet developed to any
noticeable extent in Nigeria. Such policy operates to
draw attention to the negative consequences of flouting
any of the other policies. For instance, it is a well-
known practice to destroy cocoa beans which do not
measure up to the gradings approved by government. Similarly, livestock infested with disease, as ascertained
by veterinary officers, are discarded and kept away from
sales. But it is inconceivable that any serious punitive measures would be extended to small-scale farmers
who are, for practical purposes, outside the jurisdic-
tion of the Government when it comes to enforcing agricultural regulations.

Adaptive farming policy focuses on what may be
described as technology transfer in agriculture. The
Government has attached considerable importance to mechanisation as a "means of reducing the tedium of farm
operations and the unattractiveness of farming as an
occupation" (14). Furthermore, the Government proposes
to make mechanisation more productive and profitable "by
the use of better and adaptable simple implements, and
the introduction of intensification of animal power
through a properly co-ordinated intensive scheme". It
is, however, realised that the adaptive farm policies
adopted so far are more relevant to large-scale farmers
with operations which can benefit from economies of
scale than to the small farmers. Neither the National
Mechanisation Centre nor the Farm Service Centres can
guarantee that subsistence farmers will be able to me-
chanise their production in the immediate future.

The typology of farm policies described above is
not exhaustive. As has been pointed out, some of the
programmes or projects cited belong to more than one
type of farm policy. Three such policies deserve some
mention, because of their importance. They are: integrated agricultural and rural development projects; the
"Operation Feed the Nation" programme; and the Green
Revolution programme.

It was partly to establish farming as a modern way

of life and partly to ensure that the country approaches
self-reliance in food production that the Federal Military Government in 1976 established the "Operation Feed
the Nation" programme. Considerable awareness of modern
agriculture was generated among practically all the
inhabitants of the country, irrespective of their status
in life. Emphasis was placed on involving university
students, and students in other institutions of higher
learning in the project. Eventually the scheme succeeded in benefiting non-farmers many more times than
the real farmers who were operating at the subsistence
level, where the project was hardly applicable.

In order to derive maximum benefit from the scheme,
the succeeding civilian Federal Government modified the
"Operation Feed the Nation" programme in 1980 to produce
the Green Revolution programme. Like "Operation Feed
the Nation", the Green Revolution programme was designed to cover all sectors of agricultural development
including crops, livestock, fishing, and forestry, and
to cater for supporting services, as well as infrastructural and institutional research. The scope of the
Green Revolution programme is vast, but it is likely it
will overlook the needs and conditions of small-scale
farmers. However, it is, at this stage, too early to
make a thorough critique, and it is sufficient to note
that the attention it gives to energy inputs in agriculture leaves much to be desired.

FUTURE POLICIES AND THEIR BASIS

The objectives of the agricultural sector in the
Fourth Development Plan 1981-1985 more or less specify
the basis of future government policies in Nigeria.
These objectives are:-

- the attainment of self-sufficiency in food in about
  five years, and increased production of other raw
  materials, to meet the needs of a growing nation;
- increased production of livestock and fish to meet
  domestic needs and create a surplus for export;
- increased production and processing of export crops
  with a view to expanding and diversifying the country's foreign exchange earnings; in this respect a
  target of seven years is being set for the revival of
  our cash crops;
- the expansion of employment opportunities to absorb
  the increasing labour force of the nation;
- the evolution of appropriate institutional and administrative apparatus to facilitate the rapid development of the country's agricultural potential (15).

For too long, the transformation of the rural
subsistence sector has been pursued without adequate

attention being given to energy. It is now apparent
that rural development and modernisation will remain a
dream for as long as nothing concrete is done to improve
the energy supply. Subsistence agriculture which continues to develop almost entirely on human labour will not
be able to attain its level of potential productivity.

It is reasonable to expect that some renewable
energy sources such as biomass, flowing water, wind, and
solar can be tapped in the near future, in the rural
environments of Nigeria. These sources seem to be
available in unlimited quantities if the appropriate
technology to harness them can be provided. Suitable
non-human energy is required for operating small-sized
mechanical devices for clearing and tilling the land,
and for weeding and harvesting. Power from readily
available sources is also required for processing and
storing agricultural crops. Already there are samples
of solar drying bins, power grinders, and decorticators
being used in farm institutes and settlements, in agricultural extension services, and on research farms.
Such devices should be made of local materials, as far
as practicable, and must be simple, cheap, and easy to
use and repair before they can find their way to subsistence farmers. To attain this goal there is need for
intensive research into rural energy inputs, as has been
done by the Government in other sectors of agricultural
development. Findings such as those of the Rural Energy
Systems in Nigeria project at the University of Ife on
renewable energy for rural development should be considered for implementation if the transformation of
subsistence agriculture is to be guaranteed (16).

But, above all, there is a dawning awareness that
agriculture and general rural living conditions cannot
be separated; both are sides of the same coin. Any
attempt to change or improve one must take into account
the need for corresponding changes in the other. This
is not a new idea for the Federal and States' Governments in Nigeria and, in fact, some steps were taken
back in 1970-1974 to experiment with Integrated Rural
Development pilot programmes in Bauchi, Benue, Kaduna,
Kwara, Niger, Plateau, and Sokoto States. "The scheme
aims at providing improved services, in the form of an
integrated package, to existing smallholder farming
communities with the objective of increasing productivity, raising farmers' incomes, and bringing overall socio-economic development to the rural areas" (17). It
is expected that the present concern for an integrated
approach to rural development will be further intensified in the future in order to ensure the creation and
stimulation of all the necessary ingredients and sub-
systems for rural development.

THE ROLE OF EXTERNAL AGENCIES

Much of what has been described above pertains to the role of the Federal and States' Governments across the country. It is important to stress that such policies were not evolved in isolation. Indeed, agricultural development has benefited now and then from interventions by external agencies such as aid from the World Bank, agricultural machinery from the world market, and the fruits of research work in agriculture, especially in the tropical world, as represented by the presence of the International Institute of Tropical Agriculture based in Ibadan. In spite of the obvious benefits accruing from these external agencies, the time has come for a more rigorous assessment of their role in view of the incontrovertible fact that the benefits are not without their associated costs. Two pertinent observations need to be made.

First, Nigeria has, for too long, depended on the outside world, especially the First World, in the structuring of its agricultural transformation. For example, subsistence agriculture was made to go out of its way to produce agricultural raw materials for the factories of Western Europe. Export cash crops such as cocoa, oil-palm products, groundnuts, and cotton then out-competed food crops in the bid for land, research support and funding. Nigeria was manoeuvred into producing not what it could best produce but what the outside world wanted.

Secondly, most external agencies made it a habit to dump the machinery and agricultural practices of the outside world into Nigeria, whether or not they were appropriate for the country. There was a basic assumption that the machinery and ideas suitable in overseas countries were automatically suitable for Nigeria. Agriculture has suffered a serious setback as a result of action based on this assumption. Up to now, materials, ranging from machinery to fertilisers have been shipped into the country without checking adequately whether local circumstances will permit an effective absorption or integration of such inputs. Similarly, innovative ideas on agriculture are being transmitted along wavelengths which are different from those listened to by local farmers. In short, institutions like the International Institute of Tropical Agriculture exist in a world of their own, watching from the side-lines the persistence of the traditional features of the agricultural scenario of the country.

These two characteristics of contact with external agencies should not necessarily imply that the external role is bound to be negative. Rather they should be seen as pointers to two important issues of development. First, that strenuous efforts must be made to know and understand the local environment (physical, economic, and socio-cultural) of subsistence agriculture if it is to be transformed through inputs from external sources. Second, that the low level of agricultural energy-use has been a chronic barrier to agricultural transformation in Nigeria. Attempts which have been made to overcome the barrier have not been properly adapted to the socio-economic and technological circumstances of the country and of the farmers. More than for any other policy or strategy, there is still a crying need for a bold and imaginative rural energy policy which will ensure the availability of power for transforming and sustaining subsistence agriculture.

REFERENCES

1. Areola, O., 1978, "Soil and Vegetal Resources", in Oguntoyinbo, J.S., et.al. (ed.), 1978, A Geography of Nigerian Development, Heinemann, pp.74-75.
2. Agboola, S.A., 1979, An Agricultural Atlas of Nigeria, Oxford University Press, p.11.
3. Federal Ministry of Planning (FMP), Lagos, 1980, Outline of the Fourth National Development Plan, p.19.
4. Agboola, 1979, p.21.
5. Agboola, 1979, p.24.
6. Federal Ministry of Agriculture and Natural Resources, Joint Planning Committee (FMANR, JPC), 1974, Agricultural Development in Nigeria, 1973 - 1985, p.29.
7. FMANR, JPC, 1974, pp.29-30.
8. Morgan, W., Moss, R.P., Ojo, C.J.A., 1979, Rural Energy Systems in Nigeria, United Nations University and University of Ife.
9. FMANR, JPC, 1974, p.353.
10. FMANR, JPC, 1974, p.355.
11. FMP, 1980, p.20.
12. FMANR, JPC, 1974, pp.363-4.
13. FMANR, JPC, 1974, p.364.
14. FMP, 1980, p.22.
15. FMP, 1980, pp.19-20.
16. Morgan, et.al., 1979.
17. FMP, 1980, p.23.

9
Korea

Yoon Hyung Kim

GEOGRAPHIC AND ECONOMIC DESCRIPTION

The Republic of Korea is a rather small and compact peninsula covering 98 799 sq.km. The greatest distance from one end to the other is only 400 km. About 23 percent of this area, or 2 207 000 ha, is cultivable; 67 percent (6 593 000 ha) is forest land area, and the remaining 10 percent is taken up with urban areas, industrial estates, and roads.

Korea's* population was 38.2 million in 1980. With 387 people/sq.km., the density is higher than any other country with more than 4 million people, with the exception of Taiwan. The annual rate of population growth, however, has substantially declined, from almost 3 percent in 1961 to 1.57 percent in 1980 (Table 1).

Table 1. Population of Korea, 1961-1980

	Mid-year population ('000)	Annual growth rate (%)
1961	25 766	2.97
1966	29 436	2.51
1971	32 883	1.97
1976	36 436	1.64
1980	38 197	1.57

Source: Economic Planning Board, 1980, Handbook of the Korean Economy.

*Korea is used henceforth as an abbreviation for the Republic of Korea.

159

Korea lies in the temperate zone and has long cold winters and warm summers. The summer monsoon brings abundant moisture from the ocean, and produces heavy rainfall. About 70 percent of the rain falls during four months, June to September. The winter is long, lasting about six months in the northern interior, and four months in central and southern areas. The mean temperature during winter is generally below freezing point, due to the influence of the cold, dry air mass of the Siberian high pressure cell, and this has a great bearing on agriculture. Where the cold is not overly severe, two crops, usually rice and barley, may be grown.

Table 2. Macroeconomic indicators, 1961-1979

	GNP (in 1975 billion won*)	Value-added in manufac-tng.(in 1975 billion won)	Exports (in current million US$)	Total energy consumption ('000 toe)	Oil imports as % of exports
1961	3 004.6	249.8	40.9	9 862	1.0
1966	4 378.5	503.2	250.3	13 100	12.1
1971	6 962.5	1 349.4	1 132.2	21 273	15.4
1976	11 275.5	3 176.6	7 814.5	29 805	20.6
1979	14 759.1	4 818.0	14 704.6	40 503	21.1
		Annual growth rate (%)			
1962-66	7.8	15.0	38.6	5.8	
1967-71	9.7	21.8	33.8	10.2	
1972-76	10.1	18.7	32.7	7.0	
1962-79	9.2	17.9	30.3	8.2	

Source: Economic Planning Board, 1980, Handbook of the Korean Economy.

The GNP of the Korean economy, measured in current US dollars, increased five-fold from $6.2 billion in 1961 to $30.5 billion in 1979, an annual real growth

*US$1.00 = 485.99 won (1979)

rate of 9.2 percent. Per capita GNP rose from $82 to $1
597. This remarkable economic development brought Korea
from being one of the poorest developing countries in
1961 to a semi-industrial, middle-income nation by 1979.
The most extraordinary part of this success story is
that Korea is poorly endowed with energy resources or
any mineral base for heavy industry.

This rapid economic development is mainly attribut-
able to an outward-looking strategy of industrialisation. Korean exports, which had been stagnant at a low
level in the fifties, started to grow, at an average
real annual rate of 30 percent. This increase, stemming
from the manufacturing sector, pulled the whole economy
forward. As Table 2 shows, during 1961-1979 exports
rose from US$41 million to well over US$14.7 billion.

In the same period, manufactured goods increased
from 27 percent of total exports to over 90 percent. The
manufacturing sector expanded at a particularly high
rate of 17.9 percent, and increased its share in GNP
from 8.3 percent to 32.6 percent; meanwhile, on the
other hand, the share of agriculture declined from 47
percent to less than 20 percent. During 1963-1979, the
overall growth rate for employment was 3.7 percent per
year, substantially higher than the 3 percent growth of
the labour force, so that unemployment fell from 8.2
percent to 3.8 percent.

Significant changes in the energy sector accompanied this rapid economic progress and energy supply
increased at an average annual rate of 8.2 percent or,
if non-commercial energy is excluded, by about 13 percent a year. In particular, as oil prices rose after
the crisis of 1973-1974, the cost of oil imports increased from 1 percent of total exports in 1961 to 15.4
percent in 1971 and then to 21.1 percent in 1979 (Table
2). Korea's balance of payments deteriorated accordingly.

THE RURAL SUBSISTENCE SECTOR

The agricultural sector was greatly affected by
this rapid industrial growth. Approximately 10 million
people (more than 40 percent of the urban population in
1979) moved into the cities between 1961 and 1979 to
take advantage of better employment and income opportunities. The proportion of Koreans living in villages
fell steadily from 56 percent in 1961 to 29 percent in
1979, and the farm population, after peaking at 16.1
million in 1967, declined to 10.9 million by 1979 (Table
3).

As Table 3 indicates, agricultural employment
hardly changed between 1963 and 1979, despite a rise in
the early 1970s, because of deliberate efforts by the
Government to discourage rural-urban migration, and

because of a sharp improvement in rural incomes after
1969. Nevertheless, the share of agriculture in total
employment dropped from 67 percent in 1961 to 36 percent
in 1979. The sector's real growth rate of 3.9 percent
per year during 1961-1979 was much below that of the
entire economy so that its share of GNP dropped from
47.1 to 19.2 percent (Table 4). In the late 1960s and
early 1970s, Korea ceased being a predominantly agrarian
and rural nation.

Table 3. Distribution of population and employed labour, 1961-1979

('000)

	Population			Employed labour	
	Total	Farm		Total	Agriculture, forest & fish.
1961	25 766	14 509	(56.3)	–	–	–
1963	27 262	15 266	(56.0)	7 662	4 837	(63.1)
1967	30 131	16 078	(53.4)	8 717	4 811	(55.2)
1971	32 883	14 712	(44.7)	10 066	4 876	(48.4)
1976	35 860	12 785	(35.7)	12 556	5 601	(44.6)
1979	37 605	10 883	(28.9)	13 664	4 887	(35.8)

Note: numbers in parentheses are percentages.
Source: Economic Planning Board, 1980, Handbook of the
Korean Economy.

Although largely overshadowed by the spectacular
growth of the industrial sector, the performance of the
agricultural sector has been satisfactory considering
Korea's limited land resources and adverse natural circumstances. Growth at almost 4 percent per year has
been accompanied by diversification, with a considerable
increase in livestock production, but, in that case,
starting from a small base. In 1979 crops were 80.3
percent of the value of total agricultural production,
compared with 87.0 percent in 1962.

Crop production grew by 4.8 percent a year, mainly
because of increased production of the higher-value non-
grain crops, especially fruits, vegetables, and raw
silk. Total food-grain, in physical units, grew from
5.0 million tonnes in 1962 to 8.1 million tonnes in
1979, or by only 2.9 percent a year. Grain imports,
accordingly, rose from less than half a million tonnes

in 1962 to over 5.5 million tonnes in 1979, increasing dependence on these imports from 9 percent to 40 percent of grain supplies. The cost of imported grains, in 1979, was $945 million.

Table 4. Composition and growth of GNP, 1971-1979 (1975 prices)

	Composition					Annual growth rate(%)
	1961	1966	1971	1976	1979	1961-79
Agriculture, forestry & fisheries	47.1	42.5	28.8	24.0	19.2	3.9
Mining & manufacturing	10.0	13.4	20.9	29.5	33.8	16.9
Social o'head & other services	42.9	44.1	50.3	46.5	47.0	9.8
Total	100.0	100.0	100.0	100.0	100.0	9.2

Source: Economic Planning Board, 1980, Handbook of the Korean Economy.

Limited arable land resources are a significant constraint on agricultural production. Korea has one of the highest population-to-arable-land ratios of any country - only 0.06 ha of cultivated land per capita - about the same as in Japan and Taiwan. The cultivated area increased from 2 033 000 ha in 1961 to only 2 207 000 ha in 1979 (Table 5). Little land that can be cultivated is left unused; yet only 23 percent of the total area is under cultivation, and much of the 67 percent officially classified as forest is hills left bare by years of cutting for firewood. The Government has tried to extend the area under rice paddy by developing tideland in the coastal region, but the costs are very high. About 59 percent of the land now under cultivation is paddy land and the remainder is upland field.

The agricultural sector consists almost entirely of small owner-operated family farms with an average size of 0.61 ha for paddy and 0.41 ha for upland fields. The most notable feature, indeed, of Korean agriculture is the small size of farms. Cultivated land per farm

population was 0.203 ha in 1979, or less than 1 percent
of the comparable figure for the US. Average farm size,
however, has increased slightly from 0.893 ha in 1961 to
1.021 ha in 1979 and is expected to continue to rise in
spite of a predicted decrease in total farmland, because
of the rapid reduction in the number of farm households.

Table 5. Cultivated area, 1961-1979

	('000 ha)			Cultivated area per farm house-hold (ha)
	Paddy	Fields	Total	
1961	1 211	822	2 033	0.873
1966	1 287	1 006	2 293	0.902
1971	1 265	1 006	2 271	0.915
1976	1 290	948	2 238	0.958
1979	1 311	896	2 207	1.021

Source: Economic Planning Board, 1980, Handbook of
Korean Economy.

Table 6 shows the distribution of farms by size.
During the last decade the proportion of farm households
owning less than 0.5 ha and that within the range 1.5-
3.0 ha of arable land have declined, while those with
0.5-1.5 ha or over 3 ha have increased, as has the
average size of non-crop-producing commercial farms.
There are several reasons for these changes. Farm
households holding less than 0.5 ha of arable land are
leaving agriculture because they are underemployed and
their agricultural income is low. Farms of 1.5-3.0 ha
are too large for family farming but too small for
mechanisation and since they have to depend largely on
hired labour, they are unprofitable. Farmers on such
land are either moving out of agriculture or increasing
their acreage. In the future it is likely that the
number of farms of less than one hectare will be reduced
substantially by increasing mechanisation, but the number of those of more than three hectares and those
specialising in commercial agriculture will significantly increase.

Table 6. Distribution of farms by size

(%)

	1965	1975
Less than 0.5 ha	35.9	29.0
0.5 - 1.5 ha	48.2	52.9
1.5 - 3.0 ha	14.7	12.6
Over 3 ha	1.2	1.5
Other than cropping farms	0.0	4.0
Total	100.0	100.0

Source: Ministry of Agriculture and Fisheries, 1978, Yearbook of Agriculture and Forestry Statistics.

Korea had a land reform in 1949, from which about 62 percent of farm families benefited. There were some complaints that the fragmenting of larger farms reduced total production, but any such losses were minor and temporary. The political and social advantages of farmer-ownership were enormous and, as literacy increased, the farm population was quick to learn and adopt new practices. A high level of rural literacy is probably one major factor behind the high use of fertiliser and consequent high yield of rice.

Table 7. Owner-tenant distribution of farm households, 1945-1965

	1945	1964	1965
Full owners	13.8	71.6	69.5
Part-owners	34.6	23.2	23.5
Tenants	48.9	5.2	7.0
Farm labourers and burnt-field farmers	2.7	-	-
Total	100.0	100.0	100.0

Source: Sung Hwan Ban, Pal Yong Moon, and Perkins, Dwight H., 1980, Rural Development, Harvard East Asian Monographs 89.

During the Japanese colonial period, the rate of rural tenancy had risen from a high to a still higher level so that landlords were the main beneficiaries of agricultural growth in that period. As beneficiaries of the hated Japanese rule, however, they became politically vulnerable when it ended, and that more than anything else, even the Korean War, made possible a thorough transfer of land on near-confiscatory terms. This land reform succeeded in turning over most of the cultivated area to the families who cultivated it. Their number rose dramatically and that of tenants fell to a miniscule 5-7 percent of the total during 1964-1965, as against 48.9 percent in 1945 (Table 7). By the mid-1950s, 85 percent of Korea's land was being farmed by its owners, as contrasted with less than 40 percent in the 1930s, and their incomes had increased by 20 to 30 percent.

Unlike the situation in many less-developed countries, where landlords dominate the rural political scene, their political power was greatly weakened in Korea by the taint of collaboration with the Japanese. It is not surprising, therefore, that land reform involved far more expropriation than compensation. Much of the expropriated income went to the farmer-tenant, and another part was used to finance the Government's war effort.

ENERGY USE IN AGRICULTURAL PRODUCTION

Irrigation pumping and farm mechanisation, principally tilling and threshing, are the most important end-uses for commercial energy in Korean agricultural production. The total paddy area has increased by 7.2 percent from 1 233 000 ha in 1962 to 1 311 000 ha in 1979, and irrigation using groundwater is becoming more prominent. The most common system uses reservoirs and pumping with both electrical motors and remote diesel generators. A local association is often established to acquire and operate such a system. More than 90 percent of irrigable paddy land is already irrigated.

As Table 8 shows, electric power consumption for agricultural purposes has greatly increased since 1971. During the third Five-Year Economic Development Plan (1972-1976), the average annual growth rate of electricity consumption for agriculture was 24.9 percent, compared with 17.2 percent for total electric consumption; growth rates for 1977-1979 were 18.8 percent and 16.7 percent, respectively. Power for irrigation has remained the lowest priced use of electricity, even though the costs of distribution and the transmission losses are greater than in other uses. Another important electricity use is in livestock production. As subsistence agriculture has diversified, livestock production has increased at an annual rate of 8 percent, trebling between 1962 and 1979. Electricity came into use for heating fowl and livestock enclosures and grew significantly, though starting from a small base.

Since 1962, Korean agriculture has become increasingly mechanised, and this has continued even after the rapid rise in the price of petroleum. The main type of fuel-powered equipment used in food crop production is the power-tiller or hand-tractor. These generally are between five and ten horsepower and, unlike regular tractors, can be efficiently used on small plots.

Table 8. Consumption of electric power for agricultural purposes

(' OOO kWh)

	Total sales	Agricultural purposes
1961	1 189 386	20 851
1966	3 OO8 482	29 982
1971	8 883 592	38 402
1976	19 620 296	116 823
1979	31 144 712	195 848
	Average growth rate (%)	
1962-1966	20.4	7.5
1967-1971	24.2	5.1
1972-1976	17.2	24.9
1977-1979	16.7	18.8

Source: Economic Planning Board, 1980, Handbook of Korean Economy.

In 1966, there were only 1 555 power-tillers in use (Table 9), equivalent to one per 1 475 ha of cultivated land or one per 1 633 farms. There were then only 20 tractors in the whole country and agriculture depended primarily on simple tools propelled by human or animal energy rather than fossil fuels.

By 1971, the number of power-tillers in use had increased to 16 842. However, this was still equivalent to only one per 135 ha of cultivated land. The main means of tilling was still the animal plough of which there were then over one million. Use of larger power

machinery was still very limited, and the total stock of
tractors numbered only 183.

A programme aimed at substantially increasing agricultural mechanisation,   partially supplied by increased
domestic output of small power machinery, began in 1972.
The major factor limiting the use of agricultural machinery had been the high cost of purchasing it.   The
new programme included a promotion effort as well as
financial assistance to farmers;   at the same time, a
continuing programme for the rearrangement of paddy land
improved the efficiency of power machinery use.   The use
of agricultural machinery, power-tillers in particular,
thus grew very rapidly between 1971 and 1979 (Table 9).

Table 9. Farm machinery in Korea

	Plowing and levelling machinery			
	Power-tiller	Farm tractor	Power pump	Threshing machine
1962	–	–	12 292	8 022
1965	1 111	–	26 029	18 909
1966	1 555	20	29 929	22 333
1971	16 842	183	57 896	63 350
1976	122 079	790	85 704	144 480
1979	235 909	2 035	187 608	203 081

Source: Economic Planning Board, 1980, Major Statistics of
          Korean Economy.

By 1979,   there was one power-tiller for every 9 ha
of cultivated land,   or one power-tiller for every nine
farms and,   because the owner of a power-tiller or tractor frequently rents his equipment to other farmers, the
total   number of farms using such equipment is greater
than its stock might imply.   Moreover, the power-tiller
has   become a very popular means of transporting freight
and passengers over short distances.

Use of fertilisers and pesticides is now at a very
high level,   and Korea is one of the most intense users
in the world.   The application of fertiliser almost
tripled from 1962 to 1979 (Table 10),   to bring its use
per hectare of cultivated land up to 391 kg in 1979.

Table 10. Consumption of fertiliser

	Nitrogen	Phosphorus	Potash	Total
1962	191	90	16	297
1966	240	125	58	423
1971	347	165	93	605
1972	393	171	104	648
1973	411	232	150	793
1974	449	232	155	837
1975	481	238	167	886
1976	361	142	140	843
1979	444	226	191	862

Source: Economic Planning Board, 1980 Handbook of the
Korean Economy.

Table 11. Index of prices received by farmers for rice
and paid by farmers for fertiliser (1975=100)

	Index of rice price/ fertiliser price	Fertiliser wholesale price index	Rice procurement price index	Total subsidy (billion won)
1966	44.4	41.7	18.5	-
1967	57.2	35.5	20.3	-
1968	67.3	35.5	23.9	-
1969	75.0	39.6	29.7	-
1970	79.2	41.4	32.8	-
1971	99.3	41.4	41.1	-
1972	125.2	41.7	52.2	3.5
1973	117.6	46.7	54.9	14.7
1974	131.5	60.4	79.4	11.2
1975	100.0	100.0	100.0	120.3
1976	67.7	179.7	121.6	41.8
1977	73.6	179.7	132.2	31.1
1978	86.1	179.7	154.8	-
1979	111.2	180.7	201.0	-

Source: Economic Planning Board, 1980, Handbook of
Korean Economy.

Fertiliser sales have been a legal monopoly of the National Agricultural Cooperation Federation (NACF) since 1962. Most farmers are members of a local unit of the NACF and buy from it all their fertilisers, pesticides, seeds, as well as most of their other inputs. Credit is available through the NACF at rates below those in the private money market. The NACF imported fertiliser at international prices until 1968 when Korea became self-sufficient in nitrogenous fertilisers, produced from naptha as feedstock. Up to 1972, the NACF sales price usually covered the full cost of buying, storing, and distributing domestic and imported fertiliser. After that, however, government subsidy was required and this rose sharply in 1975 when the increased cost of domestic production had not yet been fully passed to farmers. In 1975 the Government increased the selling price of fertiliser by 80 percent, which eliminated the deficit in the Fertiliser Fund. The current policy is to adjust selling prices to reflect changes in costs. Table 11 shows the movement in relative rice and fertiliser prices over the 1966-1979 period, together with the amounts of government subsidy in the years 1972-1977.

Table 12. Energy intensity by sector, 1970-1978 (excluding non-commercial energy)

(toe/million won)

	1970	1975	1978
Agriculture	0.067	0.102	0.128
Fishery products	3.248	2.944	4.813
Mining	1.373	1.235	1.211
Manufacturing	1.280	1.020	0.824
Electricity	15.252	14.544	13.831
Construction & other utilities	0.829	0.554	0.449
Transport and storage	5.240	4.237	3.826
Commerce and services	0.616	0.460	0.553
Total	1.226	1.152	1.065

Source: Bank of Korea, Input-Output Tables of 1970, 1975, 1978.

In summary, Korean farmers have made substantial efforts to adjust their production methods to a land-short, and in later years an increasingly labour-short, factor endowment by diversifying production towards non-grain crops and livestock, by large-scale investments in irrigation, by rapid mechanisation and by heavy dressings of chemical fertilisers. One important consequence has been that Korean agricultural production has become more energy-intensive.

As Table 12 shows, direct energy-use coefficients in agriculture, expressed in tonnes of oil equivalent (toe) per 1975 million won of gross output, increased sharply from 0.067 in 1970 to 0.102 in 1975 and then further to 0.128 in 1978. Other industries, by contrast, achieved substantial energy economies after the oil crisis; in the manufacturing sector, direct energy-use coefficients fell from 1.28 in 1970 to 0.824 in 1978 (Table 12).

ENERGY USE IN RURAL HOUSEHOLDS

Farm households use energy for cooking, home heating, lighting, and operating electric appliances. According to a recent survey, 82 percent of the fuel used in rural areas is firewood and 18 percent coal briquettes. In urban areas, on the other hand, 16 percent of the fuel used is oil, 82 percent briquettes and only 2 percent firewood. The same survey indicates that rural households use 25 percent of the total energy they consume for space-heating, 8 percent for lighting or electrical appliances, and 67 percent for cooking or water-heating.

In Korean residences it is common for energy to have simultaneous uses for space-heating, cooking, and water-heating, particularly during the winter. Almost all homes are built with an 'ondol', a space between the ground and the floor of the house so designed that large coal briquettes can be inserted at the sides. As the briquettes burn, they heat the air below and the floor itself, and heat also radiates into the rooms. At the same time the briquettes provide heat for cooking. The system is fairly efficient since heat rises through the entire house, and also requires little capital investment. It has the disadvantage that briquettes are messy and cumbersome to use, somewhat bulky to store and, more importantly, give off carbon monoxide. Kerosene and propane space-heaters and stoves are an attractive alternative but their purchase requires a capital outlay, and petroleum fuels have generally been more costly per unit of energy than coal. Electricity, as late as 1964, had reached only 12 percent of Korea's villages, and the big push for their electrification did not begin until the early 1970s. By 1979, however, 98 percent of villages had electricity, and in most it was available for home as well as productive uses.

THE TRANSITION FROM FUELWOOD

Korea's energy resources are limited to anthracite coal, hydropower, and fuelwood. Some other sources of energy (solar, tidal power, wind, and geothermal power), of course, do exist but are largely untapped due to the limitations of present technology. Anthracite coal is the main resource and some 545 million tonnes are recoverable (about 30 years at the 1979 production rate). Deposits are located in mountainous areas and require labour-intensive mining with a relatively low productivity. The quality of this coal, moreover, is relatively poor (about 3 500 to 5 000 kcal/kg). Korea's hydroelectric potential is estimated at about 2 000 MW and is concentrated on four main river systems (Han, Noktong, Kum, and Sumjin); most sites are small and have a low head so that relatively costly dams are needed for power production.

Table 13. Structure of primary energy supply, 1961-1980 (coking coal excluded)

	Domestic			Imports			Total
	Coal	Hydro	Fw*	Oil	Coal	Nuc*	
1961							
(ttoe*)	3 226	163	5 636	790	0	0	9 815
(%)	32.9	1.7	57.4	8.0	0	0	100.0
1965							
(ttoe)	5 291	178	5 142	1 439	0	0	12 050
(%)	43.9	1.5	42.7	11.9	0	0	100.0
1969							
(ttoe)	5 649	359	4 355	6 981	0	0	17 342
(%)	32.5	2.1	25.1	40.3	0	0	100.0
1973							
(ttoe)	7 244	306	3 672	13 624	0	0	24 846
(%)	29.2	1.2	14.8	54.8	0	0	100.0
1979							
(ttoe)	7 887	582	2 892	24 590	954	788	37 793
(%)	20.9	1.5	7.7	65.3	2.5	2.1	100.0
1980							
(ttoe)	8 602	496	2 517	24 024	1 475	869	37 983
(%)	22.7	1.3	6.6	63.2	3.9	2.3	100.0

Note: *ttoe = thousand tons oil equivalent
*Fw = fuelwood   *Nuc = Nuclear
Source: Ministry of Energy and Resources, 1981.

At the beginning of the industrialisation drive of
the first Five-Year Plan, Korea's main energy supply was
fuelwood, but this could not furnish sufficient energy
for industrial production and power generation which
were growing at average annual rates of 15-17 percent.
The Government, therefore, decided to substitute anthracite coal for fuelwood as the dominant source of primary
energy.

A number of steps were taken to encourage national
coal production. As a result, the output of anthracite
increased two-fold from less than six million tonnes in
1961 to about twelve million tonnes in 1966, and the
share of coal in total primary energy consumption rose
from 33 percent to 44 percent while that of fuelwood
declined from 57 to 43 percent (Table 13). At the same
time, there was steady progress in reforestation of
mountains which had become denuded through half a century of reckless exploitation. Concerted efforts at
reforestation were pursued from the early 1960s, and
laws were passed to preserve the remaining forests. The
reforestation programme was aimed at controlling erosion
and protecting watersheds, so that wood supplies became
limited to those available from thinning and removal of
excess trees. Cutting was allowed only by permit.
There were mutual financing associations for reforesting
mountains in every village, and forestry cooperatives
were established in every city and county.

Concurrently, the Government actively encouraged
the industrial sector, and even the urban residential
and commercial sector, to replace firewood by domestic
anthracite coal. Most of the limited firewood was then
available to the rural sector. The result was that
firewood's share in the industrial demand for energy
declined from 71 percent in 1961 to 16 percent in 1966,
but its share in the residential and commercial sector
fell much less, from 58 to 52 percent. The absolute
amount of firewood consumption fell from 5 636 thousand
toe in 1961 to 5 142 thousand toe in 1965 (Table 13).

It should also be pointed out that the transition
from fuelwood to coal briquettes in the urban sector was
successful partly because of a technological break-
through in using briquettes simultaneously for both
cooking and space-heating. In the past, briquettes had,
for the most part, only been used in special briquette
cooking stoves. The technique of using them for cooking
and space-heating was developed in Pusan where big
numbers of refugees were crowded during the Korean war.

THE SECOND ENERGY TRANSITION

As the economy expanded rapidly in the early 1960s,
the pace of urbanisation was accelerated and the population in the largest cities nearly doubled between 1961

and 1966, to reach 23 percent of the national total. This was accompanied by a virtual explosion in the demand for coal in household cooking and heating, coupled with an extraordinary growth in demand in the industrial and power sectors. Severe shortages of coal briquettes late in 1966 caused the Government to adopt a new energy transition policy of replacing anthracite coal by oil as the major fuel. Measures to achieve this ranged from administrative orders and guidelines to publicity campaigns which stressed the greater convenience and cleanliness of oil.

The Government began by restricting coal consumption in non-residential uses, rather than in the residential sector where it was essential. The power company was ordered to use oil instead of coal in all generating plants capable of burning either fuel. This restrictive policy, of course, led to inefficiencies and to maintenance problems in coal-fired plants.

The Government also strongly encouraged industrial plants to replace coal by oil and to install oil-burning equipment. Large numbers of kerosene space heaters were imported duty-free from Japan; the use of other oil-heating appliances was encouraged; large quantities of heating oil to meet immediate needs were imported; and plans were drawn up to meet future growth in fuel needs from an expanded domestic refinery capacity as well as from direct imports. Substitution of petroleum for coal was successful because the necessary expertise in the field of petroleum was acquired (by joint ventures with foreign oil companies), because petroleum has comparative technical advantages in power generation and industrial uses, and because oil-heating for middle and upper-income households and for commercial uses was cleaner and more convenient. As a result of increased competition from petroleum fuels and imposed price ceilings on coal, coal production fell by 17 percent in 1968, remained at this lower level through 1969, and then regained its 1967 level.

Much unemployment and hardship were created in coal regions. Briquette prices continued to decrease in real terms from 58.62 won in 1961 to 34.27 won in 1973, well below production costs. Only in 1974 did the price of coal again cover its production cost. The Government's policy has been to subsidise briquettes because of their importance to the middle and lower segments of the population.

During the second Five-Year Plan (1967-1971), coal's relative contribution to industry and power generation declined considerably. In 1966, it had accounted for 78 percent of thermal power generation and for 40 percent of industrial requirements; in 1971, its respective shares were only 5 and 6 percent. This significant shift in Korea's energy policy can be better seen

in the sharply increased share of oil in total primary
energy supplies from 8 percent in 1961 to 55 percent in
1973 (Table 13).

Concurrently, there was steady progress in reforestation. In 1967, the Office of Forestry was formed to
strengthen forest administration by consolidating previous random assistance for reforestation and erosion
control. It designated all forest lands as absolute or
relative on the basis of a forest land classification
survey of 1969, and this encouraged collective reforestation. Reflecting the nation's fervent wish for unification, the Unification Garden Movement was launched in
1971; under this, trees were planted on denuded mountains around villages, with the voluntary participation
of various social groups.

Reforestation was further promoted by a Green Belt
policy, also begun in 1971. The Government designated
Green Belts within which development was to be restricted, in order to discourage expansion of cities and
to preserve farmland and natural amenities. The first
Green Belt, of 469 sq.km., was prescribed around Seoul
in July 1971, and over the next seven years other Green
Belts were prescribed for a further ten major cities and
for fourteen regions. Altogether, these Green Belts
comprise 5 397 sq.km. or 5.5 percent of Korea's land
area.

The New Community Movement, also launched in 1971,
was an attempt to mobilise farmers, on a national scale,
to raise the standards of living in rural areas. It had
three major objectives: transforming conservative rural
attitudes, promoting agricultural productivity and incomes, and improving physical and environmental conditions in villages. These objectives were in conformity
with the Government's reforestation programme and, by
1981, co-operative rural efforts had led to the reforestation of nearly one million hectares of farm area.

THE THIRD ENERGY TRANSITION

The oil crisis of 1973, the steep rises in oil
prices in 1974, the prospect of further price increases,
and the possibility of future shortages led the Government to a third energy transition involving strict conservation, greater use of domestic energy resources, and
a different mix of imported fuels. In the past, the
main concern of energy policy had been to ensure that
energy did not become an obstacle to economic growth.
Since the overall development strategy was to build a
strong export-oriented industrial base, most efforts
were directed towards supplying cheap energy to critical
sectors (power and industry), generally at subsidised
prices. Development of domestic resources, particularly
coal, was limited to what was necessary for supplying

the residential and commercial sectors.

The continuous availability of relatively inexpensive imports of energy allowed economic growth to proceed with minimal energy constraints until world prices of fuels rose in 1973-1974. Up to then the range of choices had been narrow and energy planning was limited to adjusting supply to demand; sophisticated analysis was not required in a dynamic economy where temporary excess capacity could be rapidly absorbed. However, the increase of world oil prices drastically changed this.

The Government reacted promptly and launched an interim programme for increased development of domestic energy resources and a nationwide campaign to conserve energy. It also began preparing long-term plans for rationalising energy supplies and minimising their cost. A main objective was to increase production of domestic coal, the price of which was raised by 51 percent in 1974 and by another 26 percent in 1975.

Coal is now mainly used in the commercial-residential sector where traditional systems of heating prevent its substitution by other fuels. It is regarded as an essential commodity, like rice, and the Government has taken measures to ensure that its price remains at an acceptable level for low-income groups and that sufficient resources are available to finance modernisation of existing mines and development of new ones. Subsidies to the coal industry are mainly financed by the proceeds of a special tax levied on Bunker-C fuel oil. This tax, which is now levied at a rate of 6 percent and yielded 118 000 million won in 1980, has both discouraged consumption of refined oil products and provided resources for developing domestic coal as a substitute for imported oil in the residential sector.

These measures led to an increase of coal production from about 14 million tonnes in 1973 to over 17 million tonnes in 1975. Although the Government had also promoted maximum exploitation of hydroelectric resources, neither hydropower nor domestic coal could meet the increases in energy demand arising from rapid economic development and industrialisation. Consequently, the Government looked to other imported fuels and, in particular, to nuclear power and coal. Since the oil crisis, the central feature of the Korean programme of electric power expansion has been a massive shift towards nuclear power and coal-fired thermal power. As Table 12 shows, the share of nuclear fuel in total primary energy supplies reached 2.3 percent in 1980.

As domestic coal approached its maximum rate of production, the Government also began to import anthracite in order to slow down substitution of petroleum products for coal in the residential and commercial sectors. This import of anthracite is desirable for two

main reasons. First, the current supply-demand mix of
petroleum products is so well balanced that an increase
in demand for middle distillates, such as kerosene and
light fuel oil, could create an imbalance which would
require additional refinery investment, or else large
imports of high-priced petroleum products. Secondly,
there are, in the short-term, no practical alternatives
to the use of coal by the residential sector.

Simultaneously, the Government encouraged the cement industry to replace oil by imported bituminous
coal, so that the share of imported coal in total primary energy supplies increased from 2.5 percent in 1979 to
3.9 percent in 1980 (Table 13), and that of oil declined
from 65.3 to 63.2 percent. Although the main results
are expected to come over the next five to ten years,
some of the decisions taken since 1974 have already
brought significant changes in energy supply.

Table 14. Income of farm and non-farm households

(1975 '000 won)

	Farm households		Non-farm households		
	Real income (A)	Index (1975=100)	Real income (B)	Index (1975=100)	Terms of trade (A/B)
1962	416	47.7	593	69.0	0.70
1966	403	46.2	500	58.2	0.81
1971	642	73.6	814	94.8	0.79
1976	1 002	114.8	998	115.0	1.02
1977	1 126	129.0	1 105	128.5	1.02
1978	1 295	148.3	1 317	153.3	0.98
1979	n.a.	n.a.	1 532	178.1	n.a.

Source: Economic Planning Board, 1980, Major Statistics
of Korean Economy.

The Government has also consistently sought to
improve rural living conditions by policy measures which
range from land reform, price support for grains, subsidies for agricultural inputs (electricity, fertilisers,
pesticides) to the New Community Movement. Rural living
standards improved significantly during 1962-1979 and
rural incomes have been able to keep pace with those in
urban areas (Table 14). Although the farm population

has declined from 14.5 million to less than 10.9 million, the rural demand for briquettes has substantially increased.

Although demands for firewood have continued to decline, reforestation has been vigorously promoted. It was given a major impetus by the Forestry Development Law and the launching of the first Ten-Year National Forest Plan in 1973. Subsidies and loans have been provided for forest development and owners of forests are obliged to develop them in an efficient manner. Administration has been strengthened by establishing a forestry bureau in each province and a forestry division in every city and county. Consequently, as is shown in Table 15, the proportion of denuded to total forest land fell from 37 to below 7 percent in 1979. The total growing forest stocks had reached almost 120 million cu.m., and the quantity of wood was 17.9 cu.m. per hectare.

Table 15. Forestry achievements, 1961-1979

	Forest land area ('000 ha) (A)	Denuded forest land		Forest growing stock	
		Area ('000 ha) (B)	B/A(%)	Cumulative stock 1 000 cu.m. (C)	C/A (cu.m/ ha)
1961	6 701	2 484	37.1	n.a.	n.a.
1965	6 687	1 254	18.8	59 716	9.0
1969	6 627	835	12.6	66 750	10.1
1973	6 586	799	12.1	74 466	11.3
1979	6 571	446	6.8	117 281	17.9

Source: Economic Planning Board, 1980, Major Statistics of the Korean Economy.

10
India

T. L. Sankar

The single most significant statistic in India's
agricultural system is the dominance of subsistence
farming. A recent survey (1976-1977) indicates that over
40 percent of rural farming households have less than 1
ha; these are officially labelled "marginal farmers".
Another 25 percent have farms of 1-2 ha, and are known
as "small farmers".

It is difficult to identify subsistence farmers,
who can be defined as those striving to fulfill the
current consumption needs of their families by their
efforts on land they own, or lease from other owners,
solely by the size of their landholdings. The average
income of farm households depends on the nature of the
soil, the crop cultivated, and the technology used. For
the purpose of this paper, however, we will treat "subsistence farmers" as all those owning or cultivating
less than 2 ha, thus including in the definition both
marginal and small farmers together. The predominance of
subsistence farming is not confined to a single state or
a region in India but occurs in all states, except
Haryana and Punjab where capitalist methods of farming
have already taken deep roots.

The annual income from a hectare of farmland cultivated by a relatively small farmer (without allowing any
payment for family labour) is around $250-375*, which
means a per capita monthly income of $4.2-6.3 for a
family of five. Farmers with one hectare of land are
therefore classified as below the poverty line, and
those with two hectares hover dangerously around it.

The expression "subsistence farmer" conjures up
visions of a poor farmer, steeped in tradition, ignorant
of new farming technologies, and toiling endlessly to
eke out a meagre living. But recent surveys in India

---

*Rs8.00 = US$1.00 (1980)

indicate that when compared to farmers in the country as a whole, subsistence farmers, as a class, are as capable of adopting modern technologies and improving returns from the land as the rest.

FACTORS DETERMINING ENERGY USE IN SUBSISTENCE PRODUCTION

Farm management studies in the 1950s in India revealed that investment in implements, wells, draught animals, and other equipment per unit of land was inversely proportional to farm size. The small farms operated by subsistence farmers had investments per hectare almost twice that of the investment in the larger farms (Table 1). Later studies, however, show that investment on the farm is related to the nature of the crops cultivated and the agro-climatic environment. A study in three different sub-regions of the state of Punjab for the year 1969-1970 revealed that in the areas where the joint use of canal and sub-soil water was possible and the intensity of the cultivation was high, the investment in equipment was much higher per hectare in larger farms than in smaller farms. The quality and the modernity of the implements and machinery also increased with farm size. In other words, richer farmers seemed to invest more in modern labour-saving equipment, while small farms used traditional labour-intensive equipment.

Table 1. Investment   per   acre   in   various   items   on
          holdings of different sizes

(US$/ha)

Items	Farm size group (ha)				
	0-2	2-4	4-8	8-20	20+
Implements & machinery	11.7	6.9	8.5	7.1	3.0
Wells	7.4	6.9	5.9	3.1	0.5
Draught animals	20.0	12.2	13.6	10.4	5.0
Milch animals	18.2	14.8	11.7	8.4	5.2
Cattle sheds	21.7	15.0	12.8	7.8	9.2
Total	79.0	55.8	52.5	36.8	23.0

Source: Farm management studies data (1956-1957), in
         Chadha, G.K., "Farm Size and Productivity Revi-
         sited", 30 September 1978, Economic and Politi-
         cal Weekly.

On the other hand, recent surveys indicate that, in most states, the percentage of subsistence farmers adopting high-yielding and improved varieties is higher than the percentage for farms of all sizes. This is particularly so in the case of the smaller subsistence farm with less than 1 ha (Table 2).

Table 2. Percentage of area under high-yielding and improved varieties by size of farm, 1976-1977

(%)

State	Size of farm (ha)					
	Below 1		1-2		All farms	
	Khariff	Rabi	Khariff	Rabi	Khariff	Rabi
Andhra Pradesh	20.1	25.3	17.9	27.2	14.8	25.4
Haryana	33.6	18.8	42.9	50.5	41.1	55.8
Karnataka	5.8	16.8	7.7	10.4	5.4	9.9
Kerala	22.6	80.6	19.8	97.0	22.3	30.5
Punjab	39.0	68.8	52.8	79.7	59.0	80.6
Tamil Nadu	36.1	34.5	32.7	34.2	32.1	36.9
Uttar Pradesh	25.4	40.9	24.4	46.6	21.7	45.1
West Bengal	9.4	27.9	6.7	22.2	8.4	23.2

Note: Khariff is a long-term summer crop.
        Rabi is a short-term winter crop.
Source: Roy, T.K. and Siddique H.Y., July 1980, "Fertiliser Use in India", MARGIN.

As can be seen from the table, 20-30 percent of the subsistence farmers have adopted HYV crops. While time-series data are not available, it appears reasonable to assume that the percentage of subsistence farmers adopting HYV has been increasing throughout the seventies.
In view of the use of HYV by a significant, and increasing, segment of subsistence households, adoption of chemical fertilisers by these households can also be expected. Table 3 shows that the percentage of subsistence households using fertilisers is very close to the national average.

Table 3.   Households using fertilisers, by size of farm,
           1976-1977

(%)

State	Size of farm (ha)		
	Below 1	1-2	All households
Andhra Pradesh	44.9	66.9	62.2
Haryana	44.1	57.0	68.6
Karnataka	34.4	39.7	38.5
Kerala	77.8	96.4	80.1
Punjab	71.8	94.4	95.3
Tamil Nadu	67.0	75.1	73.7
Uttar Pradesh	30.0	44.4	44.6
West Bengal	61.1	64.8	65.7
All India	36.8	44.8	45.2

Source: Chadha, G.K., 30 September 1978, Economic & Political Weekly, Vol.XIII, No.39.

Table 4.   Fertiliser   input per fertilised   hectare,   by
           size of farm, 1976-1977

(kgs)

State	Size of farm (ha)		
	Below 1	1-2	All households
Andhra Pradesh	124.3	113.8	104.4
Haryana	69.1	72.6	74.1
Karnataka	213.0	184.3	159.3
Kerala	94.5	77.1	88.7
Punjab	87.3	80.7	92.6
Tamil Nadu	128.3	124.4	127.6
Uttar Pradesh	69.2	62.8	61.7
West Bengal	83.9	85.8	76.4
All India	92.3	85.8	76.4

Source: Chadha, G K., 30 September 1978, Economic & Political Weekly, Vol.XIII, No.39.

Fertiliser use, per hectare of land, is found to be higher in subsistence farms than for all farms in most of the states. As would be expected, in the two states of Haryana and Punjab, which have a highly capitalist form of agriculture, it is found that fertiliser consumption per hectare in the state as a whole is higher than that of the subsistence farms (Table 4).

Table 5. Energy use in agriculture in India

Fuel	Total (in mtoe)	per hectare (kgoe)	per capita (kgoe)
Coal	-	-	-
Oil	0.77	5.48	1.79
Electricity	0.35	2.49	0.81
Total commercial	1.12	7.97	2.60
Biomass	-	-	-
Human labour	5.88	41.88	13.67
Animal power	13.44	95.73	31.25
Total traditional	19.32	137.61	44.92
Total all sources	20.44	145.58	47.52

Note: Rural population in 1970-1971 = 430 million. Net area cultivated in 1970-1971 = 140.398 million ha.

Source: Revelle, Roger, 1979, "Notes on Energy Probe and Issues in Asia" in Asia Bureau Conference on Energy, Environment Forecasting, Manila.

We can conclude from this analysis that the present pattern of energy use in subsistence farms is not very different from the rest of the agricultural sector. New technologies in the agricultural sector can be broadly classified into two categories: mechanical technologies, which are mainly labour-saving and time-saving; and biological and chemical technologies, which are mainly land-saving, and often absorb higher quantities of labour. It appears that the subsistence farmer has been mainly trying to adopt the biological and chemical technologies so as to maximise the yield from the land, without reducing the input of labour, which is available in adequate or in surplus quantities in the household. It is also clear that the consumption of oil for mechanical equipment such as tractors, in the subsistence sector, is lower than the average for the entire agricultural sector.

The energy used in subsistence sector farming is difficult to isolate, but one can calculate the total use of energy in Indian agriculture and take per capita utilisation as a fair indication of the level of energy use in subsistence agriculture. Table 5 gives the total energy use in agriculture in India, with an attempted estimation of per capita consumption.

ENERGY FOR RURAL INDUSTRIES, ANIMAL HUSBANDRY, AND TRANSPORT

The subsistence economy of rural India also includes some industries. These are normally based on locally available raw materials. Except for some food-processing, metal-based, and clay-based industries which use high temperature heat, these rural industries require only mechanical energy, usually supplied in the form of human labour and animal power. The amount of heat required is generally small. In a village of 500 people living in 100 houses, the requirements for two new houses annually and repairs to old houses may call for about 20 000 bricks. The per capita consumption of energy would be 7 kgoe*. If pottery-making and metal industry energy needs are added, about 10 kgoe of high temperature heat energy would be required per person for industrial use.

Tillage and transport in the rural subsistence sector depend largely on the use of animal power. Bovine animals and some birds are also kept to supply milk, eggs, and meat. Most of these , except the milk-yielding ones and work animals during seasons of heavy work, are left to forage for themselves. The feed requirements for animal husbandry thus create a negligible additional demand for energy.

In the subsistence economy, head-loads, bullock carts, wheelbarrows, tractors, and trucks are all used, depending upon the distance, between the village and the market place. Studies (1,2) show that different modes are the most cost-effective for different distance ranges. It has been calculated, for a particular village in India, that the cheapest modes for transporting materials are the wheelbarrow for distances up to 0.33 km, the bullock cart for distances between 0.33-2.5 km,

---

*Computed on the assumption that the production of each brick would require 1 700 kcal.

tractors between 2.5-8.0 km, and trucks above 8 km.

In the absence of other data, one can compute the energy requirements of transport in the subsistence farm, by assuming that about one trip a week will be made to a market place or another farm perhaps 4 km away. Taking 0.7 hp capacity of a bullock, this would amount to about 25 kgoe of animal power per year. Assuming that about 50 km are travelled by a tractor or truck once in a year, and about 100 passenger km of travel is undertaken, total oil needs would be 5 kgoe per farm. Per capita, the entire transport requirements of subsistence agriculture would therefore amount to 5 kgoe of animal power and 1 kgoe in the form of oil.

DOMESTIC ENERGY CONSUMPTION

Rural households meet their energy needs mostly from firewood, agricultural residue, and animal waste. Some kerosene and electricity are also used for lighting, while in some parts of the country where coal and coke are available, these are also used for cooking. In spite of their limitations, estimates of per capita household consumption from the National Sample Survey appear to be more reliable than others, since they are based on large samples and on a survey conducted by enumerators who have had a number of years of experience of such surveys.

The sample survey has indicated that there is a significant increase in energy consumption with increase in household expenditure, both in the rural and urban areas, but that the elasticity is lower in the rural areas. The National Sample Survey data can be interpreted as follows:

Table 6. Index of energy consumption by expenditure class in the household sector

Expenditure class (Rs/month per capita)	Index of total per capita energy consumption (average for all expenditure classes together = 100)	
	Rural	Urban
0-21	66	48
21-28	80	61
28-43	90	82
43-75	101	96
Above 75	138	125

The lowest income groups consume hardly half that of the highest income groups. The distribution of rural household energy consumption is, however, less skewed than the urban, perhaps because of the easier and more abundant availability of zero-private-cost fuels in rural areas. Whatever the reasons, the subsistence farmer's consumption is lower than the national average. It would be reasonable to take 80 percent of the per capita consumption shown in Table 7 as the per capita consumption of subsistence households. Much of this is firewood which is not obtained from market places but is collected by the rural people themselves. The percentage shares of purchased, collected, and home-grown fuel sources are shown in Table 7.

Table 7. Energy consumption in rural households: shares of fuels and sources of supply

| | Rural per capita energy consumption (% shares) | | |
	Purchased	Collected	Home-grown
Electricity	100.0	0.0	0.0
Oil products	100.0	0.0	0.0
Coal products	65.1	34.9	0.0
Firewood	12.7	64.2	23.1
Animal dung	5.1	26.2	68.7
Others	8.9	61.0	30.1

Source: CSO - National Sample Survey, 1973-1974.

As the expenditure of animal power and human labour is included in the computations in this study, the amount used in the collection of household fuel should also be taken into account here. Revelle's 1970 estimate of animate energy used for household purposes was 7.3 kgoe of human labour and 2.2 kgoe of animal power, or 10 kgoe total.

The energy needs of households, and production in the agricultural and transport sectors can now be aggregated to get a broad picture of the per capita energy needs of the subsistence sector. It is a debatable issue whether human labour should be included. However extensive the use of machinery in agriculture, transport or industry, a certain amount of human labour is also used which is irreplaceable by inert fuel, and this is difficult to isolate. On the other hand, there is a certain amount of human labour which could be replaced by machines using commercial fuel. Since, however, human labour is normally assumed to be in surplus in the subsistence sector, no special insight is gained from including it in these calculations. In the following table which sums up the total energy needs of the subsistence sector, human labour is, therefore, omitted.

The total household energy consumption for sub-sistence rural households can be summarised as follows:

Table 8. Energy consumption in subsistence households (per capita) 1973-1974

(kgoe/capita)

Fuel source	Quantity
Animal labour	2.20
Firewood)	
Agricultural waste)	217.36
Animal waste)	
Other non-commercial fuels	4.72
Oil products	8.72
Coal/coke	6.96
Electricity	0.32
All sources	240.28

As seen from Table 9, the per capita needs in the subsistence agriculture sector are about 290 kgoe. Of this, 240 kgoe or nearly 83 percent is accounted for in the household sector. Agricultural activity accounts for only 11.7 percent. Industry and transport, put together, account for only 5 percent.

Non-commercial energy forms supply about 80 percent of needs, while oil accounts for just 4 percent. It is important to recognise, nevertheless, that this 4 per-cent is one of the critical inputs which cannot be easily reduced, and that the demand for oil would in-crease with any attempt to reduce human drudgery or to increase productivity in subsistence agriculture. There are, of course, new technologies by which it could be substituted, and these are discussed below.

In these computations the energy used in the form of fertiliser and pesticide has not been included. An estimate of this is possible from the tables set out earlier. As indicated in Tables 3 and 4, and taking the

average for all India, about 40 percent of the small
farmers with a holding of less than 2 ha use chemical
fertiliser, at a rate of almost 90 kg per hectare.
Assuming that about 1/6 of this is phosphate and 5/6
nitrogenous fertiliser, the energy use is 57.38 kgoe/
ha (3). For a family of five, the per capita energy use
in the form of fertiliser can be taken as 11.5 kgoe for
a land-holding of 1 ha or 23 kgoe for 2 ha. In addition,
the use of HYV seeds and pesticides may add another 50
percent of the above to total energy consumption. It is
reasonable to estimate the per capita consumption of
fertiliser, pesticide, and HYV seeds to be 16-32 kgoe.

Table 9. Total energy needs of subsistence sector

(kgoe/capita)

Fuel form	Sectors				
	Agricul-ture	Indus-try	Trans-port	House-hold	Total
Animal labour	31.25		5.0	2.20	38.45
Firewood	–)				
Agricultural waste	–)	10.0		217.36	227.36
Animal waste	–)				
Other non-commercial fuels	–			4.72	4.72
Total non-commercial fuels		10.0		228.08	232.08
Kerosene)					
Diesel)	1.79*		1.0	8.72	11.51
Gas)					
Coal/coke	–			6.96	6.96
Electricity	0.81			0.32	1.13
Total commercial fuels	2.60		1.0	16.00	19.60
All fuels	33.85	10.0	6.0	240.28	290.13

Note: * Excludes the use of fertiliser and pesticide.

These figures highlight the fact that in subsistence agriculture the oil requirements for mechanical
energy are a small fraction of even the meagre amounts
used for household purposes, normally lighting. The oil
needs of the subsistence farmers who adopt the modern
technology of HYV seeds, fertilisers and pesticides,
however, are very large compared to their other energy
requirements. Wider adoption of Green Revolution techniques will therefore steeply increase oil dependence.
Such an increase would not be simply a few percent but
would mean a sudden jump to a several-fold greater
reliance on oil.

ENERGY SUPPLY

The pattern of fuel forms used to meet specific
energy needs is a function of the relative availability
of those fuels, their prices, and interchangeability.
Energy in the form of heat is obtained mostly from
local resources, such as fuelwood, or agricultural and
animal wastes. These are bulky fuels with a high ratio
of weight to heat, and can only be collected when they
are available at distances that can be covered conven-
iently by human beings or bullocks - about 3 km for
head-loads and 10 km for bullock carts. Any realistic
estimate of fuelwood availability should consider per
capita forest area and the tree growth in non-forest
areas within a radius of 10 km of the human settlement.
The abstract existence of fuelwood on a national basis
has no meaning to subsistence farmers who personally
gather 90 percent of their firewood (Table 7). In most
villages, in fact, the nearby land is being denuded of
forests or trees, and people have to traverse longer
distances for wood. This is reflected in the steadily
increasing price of firewood relative to food (Table
10).

Table 10. Index of food and fuelwood prices

	1975	1976	1977
Food	100	85	95
Fuel	100	104	108

Source: Von Oppen, M., 1979, "A Note on Recent Developments in the Price of Fuel for Domestic Use in
India", ASCI Seminar.

The other sources of non-commercial energy are agricultural residues whose availability depends on the type of crop grown and the productivity of the land. They are rarely traded. Some, such as paddy straw, have a variety of uses for which they are the preferred material. They are used first as fodder, as thatch for the huts, and as bedding for cattle; only if there is a remainder is it used as fuel.

Studies in India and Bangladesh indicate that when firewood becomes scarce, the subsistence farmer tends to use more agricultural wastes. But, now, the high-yielding varieties of paddy and wheat are producing less residue than the traditional varieties and the gross availability of agricultural residue is declining with the steady increase in the adoption of these crops.

The use of animal waste is also a function of its availability on the farm and the demands on it for other uses such as composting, and plastering walls and floors. Since subsistence farmers generally allow their cattle to graze in the forest and open grazing lands, a part of the animal waste is lost. The efficiency of dung use can be increased by means of a biogas plant, which allows it to be used both as a source of fuel and a source of plant nutrient, but few subsistence farmers have the four head of cattle needed. The number of biogas plants operated by subsistence households is negligible.

The available animal power depends on the animal-to-person and animal-to-cultivated-area ratios. On a national scale the number of bullocks per unit of gross cropped area has remained almost constant while the numbers of tractors, electric motors, and diesel engines have been growing (Table 11).

The increasing power needs of farming have thus been met by the use of additional tractors and engines, but this has been mainly restricted to the larger farms. Subsistence farmers have adopted some improved implements but continue to use bullocks for draught power. There is evidence, however, that a growing number of small farmers are using electric or diesel engines for water-lifting wherever necessary.

FUEL SUBSTITUTION IN SUBSISTENCE FARMING

Energy in the form of heat is supplied in rural areas by coal, firewood, and agricultural and animal waste. The mix of these varies with the season and the year. Kerosene has not been substituted for firewood in cooking to any great extent. Electricity was preferred to oil for supplying stationary mechanical power even before the oil crisis, due partly to the convenience of use and partly to relative price. Mechanical motive power equipment is fuelled by oil products, animal

Table 11. Pattern of energy use in agriculture, 1951–1978

	1951	1961	1966	70-71	75-76	78-79
Total number						
Work animals (millions)	67.4	78.0	78.5	80.1	81.0	81.0
Tractors (thousands)	8.6	31.0	54.0	141.0	208.0	305.0
Electric motors (thousands)	26.0	160.0	390.0	1 417	2 792	3 600
Diesel engines (thousands)	82.0	230.0	449.0	1 377	2 178	2 704
Gross cropped area('000 ha)	131.9	152.8	155.3	165.8	171.16	172.0
No./1000 ha of gross cropped area						
Bullocks	511	511	505	483	473	470
Tractors	0.06	0.20	0.35	0.85	1.22	1.77
Electric motors	0.2	1.0	2.5	8.6	16.3	20.9
Diesel engines	0.6	1.5	2.9	8.3	12.7	15.7

Source: Compiled from Statistical Abstract India 1975, 1978, CSO, Delhi.

power, or human labour.

Certain new technologies can increase the possibilities for oil substitution. Biogas can supply heat or light, or operate either stationary or mobile mechanical equipment. Another option is to produce liquid fuels from biomass, adopting any one of the known methods. But since liquid fuel production from biomass has high economies of scale and local small-scale production would not be competitive with petroleum products, this option is not economic for small rural communities. Another possibility is to make charcoal with fuelwood and then producer gas from the charcoal. Producer gas can be used to drive tractors or trucks. The methods of harnessing solar energy either to provide heat or electricity, and wind energy to give mechanical energy or electricity are well-known. Micro hydroelectric poten-

tial, wherever available, can be harnessed to produce
electricity.

STRATEGIES FOR IMPROVING ENERGY SUPPLIES

The various new proposals for augmenting supplies
of fuels or improving their efficiency of utilisation,
which are currently under discussion, can be summarised
in the following matrix.

	Augmenting supply	Improving efficiency
Solid fuels		
Firewood	Social forestry	Improved cooking appliances Charcoal-making
Agricultural waste		Biogas digesters Improved cooking appliances using agricultural wastes
Animal waste	Better collection systems	Biogas digesters
Liquid fuels	Compressed biogas cylinders Ethanol/methanol from biomass	
Electricity	Micro hydroelectricity Solar electricity Wind electricity Biogas	
Plant nutrient	Compost, green manure	Biogas digesters

It is obvious that many of these are interrelated.
Recent studies of village energy flows indicate a need
to look at energy availability and utilisation in a
comprehensive manner and as a unified system. Interventions to alter the supplies of one form of energy have

to take into account their repercussions on the production and use of other sources in the system. There has been little success, however, in the attempts to design such a comprehensive alternative system for a rural community. The best attempt so far is the one at Pura village in South India, designed and implemented by a group of scientists (ASTRA) of the Indian Institute of Science. After considering various possibilities they felt that the most appropriate arrangement for improving the village energy supply would be a community biogas plant. Managerial expenditure would be financed by commercially marketing part of the biogas to a small industrial plant to be run by the energy group itself; this would enable the rest of the gas to be supplied at near-zero price to the poorest villagers. A similar scheme with government-subsidised management arrangements has been functioning in Uttar Pradesh for a few months now. Preliminary indications are that the advantages of this plant have been largely cornered by the more affluent villagers. Apart from these, there are numerous attempts to augment the supply of one or the other of the essential fuels in the village system. The most prominent of these are the social forestry schemes under implementation in various states of India.

The most successful is the Gujarat social forestry scheme which aims to meet the most urgent requirements for various products in the shortest time possible; to induce villages to participate actively in the plantation programme through appropriate extension and sharing of profits; and to provide additional employment opportunities to landless agricultural labourers. The unique feature of this project is its emphasis on village community participation. The project is designed to take advantage of all available vacant land - such as roadsides, canal and railway verges, community lands, degraded forests, marginal lands and the edges of farmlands and village forests - and to plant fast-growing woodspecies there which have been tested for local adoption. Over a period of five years the project should result in over 100 000 ha of land being identified and planted, at a cost of about $68 million. The cost of raising trees on one hectare of roadside lands comes to about $430-580, around $600-650 for irrigated village forest plantation and $300-350 for unirrigated. The resulting production cost of fuelwood comes to $13-14/tonne, assuming a yield of 5 tonne/ha/year over a 30 year period. The widely recognised problems of "managing" such dispersed woodlots are to be resolved by 'social security' arrangements. For example, private farms would be allowed to settle and look after an area of forest land allotted to them. From roadside and canal side afforestation, the village governing body (Panchayat) would be given 50 percent of net profits.

Other than such social security arrangements the rest of
the work of raising the trees would be attended to by
the Government Forestry Department.

Recent evaluation indicates that although the physical targets are being achieved as planned, the extent
of participation by the people in the project and their
identification of their interests with those of the
project has not materialised to the level expected. But
there is a growing awareness among the participating
rural population of the potential for improving their
living conditions. Organisational ability to harness
this slowly emerging enthusiasm is still lacking.

In these attempts to increase the supply of energy
for consumption and production purposes in rural areas
there has been no component to increase the availability
of plant nutrients. Some integrated rural energy projects have discussed the use of water, algae, and solar
energy to produce not only energy for the village community but also food for the people, plants, and animals.
The problems of managing such integrated systems have
made action difficult but discussion on such a possibility persists.

NEED FOR REORIENTING NEW VILLAGE ENERGY PROGRAMMES

The analysis in this paper reveals that the energy
needs of subsistence farming are supplied not only by
non-commercial fuels, animal power, and human labour but
also by small and critical quantities of oil products
for household use, for running stationary and mobile
engines, and for supplying chemical fertilisers. The
replacement of chemical by organic fertilisers will not
be easy. However, opinion surveys indicate that many
farmers would prefer organic manure to chemical fertilisers if sufficient quantities were available. New energy systems should therefore augment plant nutrients
while improving the supply of fuel.

The most promising systems appear to be those based
on biogas. But in many locations animal populations may
not be adequate to supply biogas for all needs. The
production of fuelwood for direct use and for charcoal
production and producer gas generation would be necessary in many places. A minimum programme which could
meet, in a large measure, the current and emerging needs
of the subsistence sector would have to include fuelwood
plantations, charcoal-making, producer gas and biogas
utilisation on a large scale.

Modifications are also possible in the use of energy in small farms to reduce the dependency on chemical
fertilisers. But such experiments are normally outside
the scope of energy studies and pursued by agricultural
scientists. There is, therefore, a need to bring about
greater collaboration between energy specialists and

agricultural scientists in order to develop farming systems appropriate to local circumstance which optimise the use of all energy resources, including chemical, create employment, and maintain the ecological balance.

REFERENCES

1. Jagdish, K.S., Energy and Rural Building in India (forthcoming).
2. Reddy, Professor A.K.N., 1979, Alternative and Traditional Energy Sources for the Rural Areas of the Third World, The Royal Institution.
3. Conversions used here were adapted from Pimental, et al., 1973, Science, 182, November:
   1 kg nitrogenous fertiliser = 1.848 kgoe
   1 kg phosphetic fertiliser = 0.323 kgoe
   1 kg pesticide = 2.31 kgoe
   1 kg HYV seeds = 0.347

11
Review

Marcela Serrato

The discussions held during the Symposium brought out the enormous difficulty that still exists in finding a common basis for analysis and prescription in this area. A set of definitions which would provide a framework for first examining the issues under discussion, and then designing and implementing programmes of action based upon the resources now available, remains to be agreed.

This review is, therefore, not attempting a consensus; it endeavours, rather, to reflect the variegated pattern of individual ideas expressed during the Symposium. It presents them as they emerged, in their multiplicity and contradictions. Nor does it attempt to deal with the details of the individual case-studies covered in the previous eight chapters, except where they contribute to points of general significance. The aim is simply to highlight some of the more important issues on which further analysis and discussion are required before practical energy programmes for subsistence agriculture can be formulated and implemented on a worldwide basis.

Energy is a basic necessity of subsistence and development, as important as water and land have always been. The present new dimensions of the world's rural energy problems lie in the increased pressure of population upon traditional energy resources, the need to develop new agricultural lands to meet food requirements, and the environmental shock caused by the widespread destruction of forests. To these must be added the relatively worsening poverty in which many subsistence dwellers now find themselves. The rural energy crisis cannot be separated from the inaccessibility and vulnerability of the poor throughout the developing world.

The most fundamental need is to prevent further deterioration in subsistence agriculture. Once this has been assured, and assuming that it can be, the next step is to devise the means by which the economic level of subsistence can be raised to that of the local market economy. This requires the creation and retention of agricultural surpluses so that they can be deployed to finance an increase in productivity and a raising of living standards.

Fuel, however, is not the only critical factor. Simply assigning greater quantities of energy to subsistence agriculture will not in itself bring about significant change. The deep-rooted questions of population growth and malnutrition may push energy problems into a secondary position, because there is no way they can be solved while the lack of an adequate food supply is the dominant issue in people's lives. Rural development requires a set of programmes which includes providing potable water, improving agricultural techniques, safeguarding resources in the environment, introducing basic means of transport, and furnishing access to finance for capital investment. Rural energy initiatives need to be integral parts of such programmes and aimed at a greater degree of social participation and increased rural self-sufficiency.

Respect must also be paid to the potential of the subsistence sector. This should not be seen as a marginal element acting as a burden on the economy, but as a vitally contributing and productive sector in its own right. As well as providing the bulk of food for the rural population and supplying a portion of the urban market, it also furnishes a cheap labour force for agro-industry and export crop production. The technical possibilities that would permit small farms to increase their productivity need to be analysed, and the aim should be to ensure that the subsistence sector at least has the technical means for meeting its own staple food requirements.

The stage has not yet been reached where comprehensive and effective energy strategies for subsistence agriculture can be devised. The questions are still too complex. There is a constant interaction between social and economic forces; there is also a disparity in the rates of change in response to these forces. Because economic change is much more rapid than evolution in social patterns, new technology can be difficult to introduce into areas where traditional ways of life are dominant. The case of Mexico illustrates the way in which a new technology, in this case the Green Revolution, created divisions in the agricultural sector. The innovations resulted in the establishment of an agricultural export sector with access to energy and further technical inputs, and did so in a way which acted to the detriment of the subsistence sector.

The most that has so far been achieved at this level of analysis is that a relation has been established between certain conditions in subsistence agriculture and some possible policies. There are serious problems in effectively organising energy use, technology, and subsistence production in a coherent manner and some of these basic problems would remain even if present forms of social organisation were modified. There is therefore a continuing need for discussion of different mixtures of technical inputs and output goals.

Another central problem is that of governmental attitudes to rural energy problems. There is still a concentration on large-scale and advanced technical developments instead of small-scale and specific efforts to meet the needs of the poorest people. Thus, hydropower and solar energy, or the advanced crop varieties of the Green Revolution receive attention while the small communities of subsistence farming which cannot benefit from these continue to be neglected. The task here is to raise the public's awareness of this sector which has little or no political voice. In most developing countries there is, in fact, no energy policy directed towards the needs of subsistence agriculture.

Nevertheless, and in spite of the remaining questions, certain things are already clear. Traditional sources are not sufficient to cover the increasing energy needs of the poorest rural sectors. In the form of fuelwood they presently meet most of the energy needs of rural dwellers in many countries. In Guatemala, for example, wood is the sole cooking fuel of 80 percent of the rural population.

It is in the supply of wood that some of the most serious problems are emerging. Around 100 million people now live in conditions of acute fuel scarcity in the rural areas of the developing world, and another 700 million are consuming their wood resources faster than they are being replenished. If present trends continue, by the year 2000 there will be around 2.4 billion people without sufficient wood to meet their daily needs and for whom alternative fuels will have to be found. One of the crucial tasks of the moment is to draw the attention of policy-makers to the present position and the speed with which it is worsening. There is a truly urgent need for the countries most affected to recognise the full dimensions of their problem and begin to implement action programmes as quickly as possible.

There is thus an evident need to increase energy supplies and improve the efficiency of energy use in order to relieve the pressure on traditional fuels, and in particular on fuelwood. At present, this mainly concerns the domestic sector where the major proportion of energy consumption occurs. Beyond that, and in view of the fact that apart from some favoured areas there can be no major expansion of arable land in the near future, increased agricultural output will have to be achieved by increasing the effective energy inputs to agriculture.

Studies have been done on the relation between capital, labour, and energy in US industry; but what the corresponding relationships are for agriculture in developing countries remains to be established. Empirical data are required which will enable these to be understood. In the case of Brazil, for example, there are indications that the energy and capital needs of subsistence agriculture are relatively heavier than in large-scale farming. It would be useful to determine which kinds of energy are more efficient from the point of view of increasing productivity. The key factor is not simply meeting the energy needs of daily consumption, but securing the energy inputs which will increase the productivity of the land.

The question of a lack of effective energy demand in the subsistence sector must also be considered. This is well illustrated by the case of Mexico. The country does not face an energy crisis; it has a huge exportable surplus of petroleum. Yet it has a subsistence sector virtually devoid of commercial energy. The striking similarities between the subsistence sectors of Senegal and Nigeria reinforce the point. Despite the existence of a national energy surplus in one and an energy deficit in the other, the energy position of their subsistence agricultural sectors is very similar.

The definition of subsistence agriculture is important but it must be flexible because of the wide variety of conditions found in different parts of the world. Size of landholding as a criterion depends on the viewpoint from which it is seen; from an Asian perspective, for example, Brazil would not appear to have any significant subsistence agricultural sector. Nor can subsistence be defined by the technology used or by the relative proportions of the production inputs. A more important determinant may be the economic and social structure in which the subsistence sector evolves; often this is such that it does not offer incentives or opportunities for development and economic progress. Each area needs to be considered in the light of its own special local characteristics and any solutions must take these into account.

There is a pressing need for local data. The way in which subsistence agricultural energy-use is treated in national energy statistics reveals the minor status the whole sector tends to have in national planning. The consumption of wood and charcoal should be included in national energy balances. At the least, this would draw national attention to the importance of these fuels and the number of people who depend on them. Data collection should also be carried out on a seasonal basis. The changes which occur throughout the year should be monitored. These can have extremely severe effects, depriving farmers of both fuel and food, and causing many families to fall below subsistence standards at certain times of the year.

Such data collection will help to create a political willingness to improve conditions in the subsistence sector, increase the political influence of those belonging to it, and improve their capacity to absorb the different technologies available. In some countries, Guatemala for example, there is a strong competition for energy between the urban and rural sectors. Reliable data would aid in the elaboration of policies specifically designed to help the rural sector. This would also allow typologies of circumstances to be devised, both qualitatively and quantitatively, which would permit an easier replication and diffusion of successful initiatives. It is often difficult, however, for those who wish to collect such data to obtain the support of their governments and local institutions. Foreign agencies could render an important service by making this kind of data collection a specific target for funding.

When fossil fuel resources are restricted it is of the utmost importance to analyse the possibilities of substituting one fuel for another, and the incentives required to promote such substitutions. When new energy sources are considered for this they should not be treated as isolated technical initiatives; they must be seen as part of a total package which is designed to meet the full spectrum of local energy needs, and which leaves the way open to future development and expansion of energy use. Cost benefit studies should be used to ensure that the best choice is made between conventional and non-conventional alternatives in any particular application.

Renewable energies are not necessarily new; they have never ceased to play a dominant role in the supply of energy in the rural areas of the developing countries. Now, however, as the natural endowment of renewable energies in the form of fuelwood diminishes, most replacements are inaccessible to the small farmer because of cost. Moreover, even when they are available at an acceptable cost, there are considerable problems of diffusion and the rate of their dissemination usually bears no relation to the speed at which conditions are deteriorating in the subsistence sector.

It is therefore necessary to exercise care in the promotion of these technologies. If renewable resources are really too costly, or unreliable, other courses of action should be considered, in particular, the possibility of increasing the efficiency of use of conventional fuels.

One approach, in the short term, could be the

establishment of ways of financing the supply of conventional energy sources to the rural areas while embarking, at the same time, on programmes of energy saving and forest plantation. Guatemala's experience with kerosene subsidies, however, reveals that unless based upon a clear understanding of the sector of the population which relies on forest resources, the conditions under which commercialisation of fuelwood occurs, and the mechanisms by which kerosene is actually adopted as a substitute fuel, subsidies will not yield the expected results.

FUTURE POLICY DIRECTIONS

Most of the above issues can be seen as disaggregated aspects of a fundamental general problem. This is how energy demand should evolve in the developing countries, given that the dominant direction of technical progress, and hence the supply of technology, neither evokes or meets energy demands which correspond to the most pressing social needs. In the commercial market those energy sources most applicable in the industrialised countries command the brightest prospects and hence have the highest commercial priority; those with a specific applicability in meeting the energy needs of the very poor in the developing countries have not received the same attention. The evolution of energy demand in the developing countries will have to be modified if it is to be related to the most likely direction of progress in technical knowledge and hardware.

Energy strategies will have to be designed with the interest of the poorest sectors clearly in mind. New and renewable energy technologies have the advantgage that they can reduce the dependence of farming communities on external sources of energy supply. But it is also essential that the level of access to fossil fuels is raised, as these remain the basis for increased agricultural production when used directly as fuels for pumping and draught power, or indirectly as fertilisers and pesticides.

Fuelwood is particularly important. At present there is no practicable substitute for wood for rural cooking needs. In addition, deforestation brings many other problems; they include land erosion, desertification, and even climate modification. By no means all forest depletion is to be attributed to fuelwood collection. Other important influences are the expansion of land use for agriculture, and the industrial exploitation of timber. Yet in spite of the problems, and the crucial role of wood as a fuel, reforestation is still a matter of low priority for most governments. The long time horizon before any commercial return is undoubtedly

a major reason for this. Practical policies will therefore have to place an emphasis on encouraging farmers
to grow, manage, and use in the most efficient manner
their own resources of fuelwood.

Although large-scale energy planning will undoubtedly be required, possibly even at a regional level, it
must not be allowed to get in the way of the study of
specific local needs. New systems and combinations of
energy technologies will be needed which are appropriate
to the particular requirements of subsistence in each
different location. There are certainly no easy or
readily available solutions and the development of
effective measures will be a prolonged process. This is
partly because of the present state of most alternative
energy technologies, but also because of the poor knowledge of the factors involved in the diffusion of new
energy systems under widely different circumstances in
different parts of the world. The immediate objectives
must therefore be to relieve the pressure on traditional
resources for sufficient time to allow technologies
acceptable to rural communities to be devised and disseminated, and for an energy transition based on them to
take place; at the same time the risks inherent in any
change in existing systems of energy use must be kept to
a minimum.

Jamaica illustrates the extreme case of a country
in which no comprehensive short-run solutions to energy
problems are available. This raises the question of
global responsibility for those large areas of subsistence in many countries which must receive external
aid at least until they have secured sufficient of their
own resources to ensure their survival.

Some of the changes required for the successful
implementation of new energy strategies can be of a
fundamental nature. Land reform may be an essential
condition without which rural development cannot occur.
Equally important may be a continuity of policy in view
of the long maturing period for many rural energy programmes. This is illustrated by the case of Korea,
where the country's success in dealing with its rural
energy problems is in part due to the long period of
political stability which has permitted a continuity of
policies.

There is a need to strengthen institutional capabilities. Extension agencies for technical training are
required on the government side; and on the side of the
farmers there is a need for organised groupings capable
of mobilising widespread action. These have a special
relevance because of the inaccessability and dispersed
nature of the subsistence agricultural population. At
present the institutional position in these respects is
extremely weak. There are few institutions with specific responsibility for the subsistence agricultural

sector and few effective groupings within it. This means that the compilation of reliable information is greatly hindered, and that the recycling of experience is rare.

International agencies can play a major role provided the different interests of both donors and receivers is recognised on both sides. Donor agencies can exert a powerful influence by the manner in which they give or withhold aid in particular instances. If they are to increase their effectiveness in dealing with rural energy problems they must be prepared to be flexible in both their methods of action and in their aid-granting criteria so as to ensure that assistance reaches the people in greatest need. Technical assistance should provide long-run support for political action. This implies that aid should be channelled in such a way that it reaches the effectively organised rural groups. Moreover, such aid should not concentrate solely on supply measures; it is equally important to ensure that measures are taken to raise the level of effective demand.

In general the contributions of aid agencies tend to be directed towards projects with long periods before they reach maturity and begin to show large-scale benefits. It is also necessary to allow for contributions which help solve the immediate problems of subsistence farmers. Flexibility is required in view of the uncertainties about long-term technical possibilities and the future evolution of energy demand patterns.

Energy is a multisectoral problem and must be treated accordingly; isolated solutions will not be achieved as long as the basic problem of poverty remains. Energy should therefore play a promoting role in development out of rural poverty. It should be part of a strategy which encourages the use of local materials, and is compatible with local requirements, available resources, and social patterns. It should also keep open the possibility of access to new developments in technology and the biological sciences. This will permit a future evolution which takes full advantage of traditional knowledge and experience and combines it with a careful management of resources in the raising of rural standards of living.

In the end, the best solutions will be those which create the conditions in which development can occur and thereby lead to the transcendence and elimination of subsistence agriculture as a way of life.

Appendix:
Participants at Final Symposium

Afolabi-Ojo, G.J.
Project Coordinator, Ife-UNU Rural Energy
  Research Project
Department of Geography
University of Ife
NIGERIA

Aguinaga Diaz, Jorge
Director, Proyecto Nacional de Energia
Ministerio de Energia y Minas
PERU

Espinal Oliva, Andronico
Instituto Hondureno de Desarrollo Rural (IHDER)
HONDURAS

Arias Chavez, Jesus
Director, Grupo de Ecodesarrollo Xochicalli
MEXICO

Biermann, Eberhard R.K.
German Appropriate Technology Exchange (GATE)
Gesellschaft fur Technische Zusammenarbeit (GTZ)
FEDERAL REPUBLIC OF GERMANY

Bravo, Victor
Instituto de Economia Energetica (IDEE)
Fundacion Bariloche
ARGENTINA

Caceres Estrada, Roberto
Director Ejecutivo
Centro Mesoamericano de Estudios sobre Tecnologia
  Apropiada (CEMAT)
GUATEMALA

de Montalembert, Marc
Head, Policy Planning Section
Forestry Department
Food and Agriculture Organisation of the United
  Nations (FAO)
ITALY

de Oliveira, Adilson
COPPE
Universidad Federal de Rio de Janeiro
BRAZIL

Eckhaus, Richard
Department of Economics
Massachusetts Institute of Technology (MIT)
USA

Floor, Willem
Policy Planning Section
Ministry of Foreign Affairs
THE NETHERLANDS

Foley, Gerald
Senior Fellow
International Institute for Environment
  and Development (IIED)
UNITED KINGDOM

Gewald, Nico
Director, Proyecto Lena, Programa Recursos Naturales
Centro Agronomico Tropical de Investigacion
  y Ensenanza (CATIE)
COSTA RICA

Giesecke, Ricardo
Departamento de Cooperacion Tecnica
Programa de Naciones Unidas para el Desarrollo
NICARAGUA

Granados Vazquez, Rafael
Comision Ejecutiva del Rio Lempa (CEL)
Superintendencia de Energia
EL SALVADOR

Kim, Yoon Hyung
UN Asian & Pacific Development Center
MALAYSIA

Guzman, Oscar
Programa de Energeticos
El Colegio de Mexico
MEXICO

Martin, Jean-Marie
Institut Economique et Juridique de l'Energie
FRANCE

Islam, Mohammad Nurul
Chemical Engineering Department
Bangladesh University of Engineering
  and Technology (BUET)
BANGLADESH

Rodriguez Elizarraras, Gustavo
Secretario Ejecutivo
Organizacion Latinoamericano de Energia (OLADE)
ECUADOR

Saravia Tellez, Danilo
Director, Centro de Investigacion de Tecnologia
  Apropiada (CITA-INRA)
Instituto Nicaraguense de Reforma Agraria
MIDINRA
NICARAGUA

Sankar, T.L.
Director, Institute of Public Enterprise
INDIA

Tjondronegoro, Sediono M.P.
Social Economic Department
Institut Pertanian Bogor
INDONESIA

Sene, El Hadji
Director, Direction des Eaux et Forets
SENEGAL

Serrato, Marcela
Programa de Energeticos
El Colegio de Mexico
MEXICO

Stassen, H.E.M.
Director, Gasifier Project
Twente University of Technology
THE NETHERLANDS

Thomson, Brian
Department of Regional Development
Energy and Natural Resources
Organization of American States
USA

Ulbricht, Peter
PLE/BMFT
Embassy in Mexico
FEDERAL REPUBLIC OF GERMANY

Urquidi, Victor
President, El Colegio de Mexico
MEXICO

van Buren, E. Ariane
Senior Research Associate
International Institute for Environment
  and Development (IIED)
UNITED KINGDOM

van der Pluijm, Theodore
Latin America Division
Economic Planning Department
International Fund for Agricultural Development (IFAD)
ITALY

Vasquez, Mario
Instituto Nicaraguense de Energia (INE)
NICARAGUA

Ventura, Arnoldo K.
Executive Director, Scientific Research
  Council
JAMAICA

Wionczek, Miguel S.
Director, Programa de Energeticos
El Colegio de Mexico
MEXICO